MEETING BASIC LEARNING NEEDS IN THE INFORMAL SECTOR

UNESCO-UNEVOC Book Series
Technical and Vocational Education and Training:
Issues, Concerns and Prospects

Volume 2 2

Meeting Basic Learning Needs in the Informal Sector

Integrating Education and Training for Decent Work, Empowerment and Citizenship

Edited by

MADHU SINGH
UNESCO, Institute for Education, Hamburg, Germany

Springer

A C.I.P. Catalogue record for this book is available from the Library of Congress.

ISBN-13 978-90-481-6862-0 (PB)
ISBN-13 978-1-4020-3427-5 (e-book)

Published by Springer,
P.O. Box 17, 3300 AA Dordrecht, The Netherlands.
www.springeronline.com

Printed on acid-free paper

The choice and the presentation of the facts contained in this book and the opinions expressed herein are not necessarily those of UNESCO and represent no commitment on the part of the Organization. The designations employed and the presentation of material throughout this publication do not imply the expression of any opinion whatsoever on the part of UNESCO concerning the legal status of any country, territory, city or area or of its authorities, or the delimitation of its frontiers or boundaries.

CONTENTS

BOOK SERIES SCOPE

The purpose of this Book Series is to meet the needs of those interested in an in-depth analysis of current developments concerning various aspects of education for the world of work with particular reference to technical and vocational education and training. The Series examines areas that are at the 'cutting edge' of the field and are innovative in nature. It presents best and innovative practice, explore controversial topics and use case studies as examples.

The audience for the Book Series includes policy-makers, practitioners, administrators, planners, researchers, teachers, teacher-educators, students and colleagues in other fields interested in learning about TVET, in both developed and developing countries, countries in transition and countries in a post-conflict situation.

The Series complements the International Handbook of Technical and Vocational Education and Training, with the elaboration of specific topics, themes and case studies in greater breadth and depth than is possible in the Handbook. The Book Series also augments the various other publications in the International Encyclopaedia of Technical and Vocational Education.

Topics to be covered in the Series include: training for the informal economy in developing countries; education of adolescents and youth for academic and vocational work; financing education for work; lifelong learning in the workplace; women and girls in technical and vocational education and training; effectively harnessing ICT's in support of TVET; planning of education systems to promote education for the world of work; recognition, evaluation and assessment; education and training of demobilized soldiers in post-conflict situations; TVET research; and school-to-work transition.

The Book Series Technical and Vocational Education and Training: Issues, Concerns and Prospects, and other publications in the International Encyclopaedia of Technical and Vocational Education and Training, are publications of the UNESCO UNEVOC International Centre for Technical and Vocational Education and Training (UNESCO-UNEVOC) in Bonn, Germany.

Those interested in obtaining more information about the Book Series, or who wish to explore the possibility of contributing a manuscript, should (in the first instance) contact the publishers.

INTRODUCTION BY THE SERIES EDITORS

Work is a major feature in most people's lives. Not only does it provide them with the means of survival in terms of food, clothing and shelter, but also the type of work undertaken by individuals and groups has a major impact on their self-identity, social status and standard of living. Improving education for the world of work can help increase the real incomes of workers in both the formal and informal sectors of the labour market, provide citizens with more choices in their working lives, help alleviate poverty, and empower individuals who would otherwise be marginalised.

As an important part of education for the world of work, technical and vocational education and training (TVET) has been identified by UNESCO Member States as a priority area within UNESCO's range of programme activities. This is to be expected since there is overwhelming evidence demonstrating that TVET can play an essential role in promoting sustainable development and economic growth, with clear benefits for individuals, their families, local communities and societies in general.

However, TVET is currently faced with several important challenges. Some are posed by the displacement of the traditionally strong focus upon manual work in favour of mental work, or at least the changing mixture of competencies required in the workplace. The boundaries between manual and mental work are fading away, as many traditional forms of work and the respective preparation processes for learning to work undergo changes. In addition, the shift from the Industrial Age to the emerging Information Age, and from localisation towards globalisation, has considerable implications for education and training for the world of work and TVET, as do moves to effectively harness information and communication technologies (ICTs) to improve the reach and quality of delivery of TVET programmes.

A major area of debate at the current time concerns the place and role of TVET in the development of individuals and communities living and working in the informal sector. Traditionally, the Technical and Vocational Training and Education sector has played a limited role in the informal labour market. However, the pressures in favour a greater role for a global market, stress on globalisation and technological change, the size, diversity, and the strength and sheer tenacity of workers and owners in the informal sector have combined to bring about a reappraisal of the links. Governments in developing countries have had to acknowledge that public service and formal sector jobs can no longer be a nation's main source of employment. The formal sector of the economy is shrinking. It is therefore not difficult to explain the re-emergence of the informal sector agenda. The policy constituency in developing countries is looking at different education and training perspectives for supporting communities and individuals in self-employment and micro-enterprise.

This publication presents case studies that integrate education and training with the achievement of societal goals of greater democratisation, participatory citizenship and decent work economy. Drawing from the International Labour Organisation's Decent Work Agenda, this book aims at a shift away from the narrow mechanical connotation of skills development and employment towards a rights-based approach in which the meeting of basic learning needs and the right to basic education are singled out as pivotal. It takes the stance that promoting the right to basic education is crucial for overcoming oppression and indecent working conditions. Education is indispensable for protecting other human rights – health, liberty, economic well-being and participation in the cultural and political life of the community as well as work-related issues such as representation, dialogue and security.

The present volume looks at the interlinkages between EFA and work. Basic education in its current state is not imparting the necessary skills for entry to the labour market. In view of this gap, the case studies pose the crucial questions of what essential skills and which basic learning needs have to be addressed for productive and decent work. The case studies stress the need to build education for all on a firm foundation of literacy, numeracy, science and technology, and values of citizenship; they call for a better balance between vocational and general education; they question the often narrow vocationalist tendencies in non-formal education and instead propagate its linkages with formal learning and its enhancement through inter-sectoral linkages with health, culture, environment, infrastructure, and basic needs such as provision of housing, water and sanitation.

The case studies do not emphasise one kind of education rather than another. They highlight different modalities in different settings – basic education, vocational training centres, in enterprises, in non-formal education – from a systemic and integrated perspective.

The publication of this volume launches the UNESCO-UNEVOC International Encyclopaedia of Technical and Vocational Education and Training, and the Book Series Technical and Vocational Education and Training: Issues, Concerns and Prospects. The following contributions seek to demonstrate the action that national governments, NGOs, donors, business and community-based organisations are taking through a whole range of learning programmes, in education and training systems, and in the world of work itself, in order to make an impact on attitudes and capacities relevant to the informal sector. Although this book mainly provides case studies of learning programmes for the informal economy in countries in South Asia, Latin America and Egypt, the lessons learnt have much to offer to researchers, policy-makers and practitioners working in other parts of the world.

Rupert Maclean
Director, UNESCO-UNEVOC International Centre
David N. Wilson
Professor at OISE, University of Toronto,
and Principal Research Fellow, UNESCO-UNEVOC International Centre

PREFACE

In advancing the vision of adult learning articulated at the International Conference on Adult Education (CONFINTEA V) held in Hamburg in 1997, the UNESCO Institute for Education has been conducting studies on the different areas and dimensions of 'Adult Learning and the Changing World of Work'. One question that has been central to this area is: What constitutes adult learning for those who traditionally secure their survival in the informal economy, as well as for those school leavers and dropouts who are forced to work in this sector?

In answering this question, the informal sector or popular economy may be defined in various ways, but there is an increasing recognition that it is a phenomenon that has come to stay and that government policies aimed at economic and social development, including national education and training policies and programmes, should target those who work in this sector. In particular, basic education and continuing education and training are being seen as key to empowering people and as crucial to strategies for reducing poverty. Moreover, there is a growing awareness that education is a human right of fundamental siginificance to promoting decent work and humane living conditions.

It is in view of such considerations that UIE and the ILO planned to conduct studies in South Asia (Nepal, Bangladesh, India) to develop an understanding of the quality provision of education and skills development in and for the informal sector. But while the present volume had its start in these South-Asian country studies, they have been expanded upon by including case studies from other countries. The two-fold aim in doing so was to provide an inter-regional perspective and to incorporate cross-cutting issues widening the conceptual and analytical understanding of the complex educational processes in this sector.

This anthology has two main aims. The first is simply to bring together the facts about the basic learning needs and skills of people working and living in the informal economy and to present case studies from different countries examining the rich variety of educational and training strategies for meeting these learning needs. The second aim is to present an understanding of knowledge and skills acquisition in the informal sector from both a systemic and an integrative perspective. The chapters presented below portray the grave problems facing educational and training systems vis-à-vis informal sector workers, even as they look at holistic solutions to these problems, that is, solutions that take into account principles of lifelong learning and innovations in informal, non-formal and formal adult learning. The systemic and integrative perspective offered here goes beyond the educational and training domain in order to understand the role of social partners and the interfaces between the educational system, the broader institutional environment, and links to social and economic policies.

Both aims call for a wider, more encompassing vision than is ordinarily in evidence concerning the informal economy, which has largely remained outside the purview of educational analysis. Such a broad frame of vision is also called for because the informal world of work is quickly becoming more global and interlinked, as well as a sphere in which both survival and growth call for the use of comprehensive educational and training strategies tied to issues of equity, cost-sharing, outreach, scale, rights and entitlements, economic and social empowerment and civil society participation. The dearth of livelihood opportunities and profound inequalities in societies and economies around the world have of necessity brought these concepts into sharper focus in relation to national educational goals and policies.

It is our hope that this publication will contribute to a greater educational and policy dialogue about how best to deal with segments of the population which lie outside the system of formal work and education. We also trust that it will facilitate the identification of concrete actions promising constructive changes in educational and training systems for improving living and working conditions in the informal economy.

Adama Ouane
Director, UNESCO Institute for Education
April 2005

ACKNOWLEDGEMENTS

I should like to express my gratitude and thanks to the following persons:

Josiane Capt, from the International Labour Organisation, for collaborating with the UNESCO Institute for Education in conceiving the country studies and jointly formulating the terms of reference for the country studies from Nepal, Bangladesh and India, as well as for granting permission to Sara Silveira and Anaclara Matosas to revise and update information presented in the ILO's *In Focus Program on Skills, Knowledge and Employability* (IFP/SKILLS). Their revised article is an expression of the co-operation and joint work between IFP/SKILLS, Cinterfor/ILO and UIE.

Sandra Rothböck, formerly at the International Labour Organisation, New Delhi, India, for facilitating and collaborating on the case studies from Northern and Southern India.

Rashed Al Mahmud Titumir, Amit Mitra, V. V. Krishna and Poorna Adhikary for conducting detailed and extensive country studies on this important sector.

Peter Gerasch, Arturo Durán, Bernd Overwien, Enrique Pieck, Laila Iskandar, Sara Silveira, Anaclara Matosas and Christine Nathan for their generous responses to my short call for contributing papers to this publication in order to enlarge South-South exchange of experience and for adding an international dimension to the country studies already commissioned for South Asia.

Kluwer Academic Publishers for granting permission to reproduce Bernd Overwien's article "Informal Learning and the Role of Social Movements", which appeared in the special issue of the *International Review of Education* on researching work and learning, an issue for which I was guest editor.

Marcus Brainard for his valuable comments on the manuscript and painstaking editorial assistance in preparing it for publication, and also Inke Rosebrock for contributing to the index of this book.

Finally Anja, my daughter, who inspires me and who continues to believe that my work is valuable and worth the effort and sacrifices.

Madhu Singh
UNESCO Institute for Education
April 2005

ACRONYMS

APE	Association for the Protection of the Environment
AGCCD	Association of Garbage Collectors for Community Development
AMM	Annapurna Mahila Mandal
ASCE	American Society of Civil Engineers
ASTRA	Application of Science and Technology to Rural Areas
BBS	Bangladesh Bureau of Statistics
BIMT	Bangladesh Institute of Marine Technology
BMET	Bureau of Manpower, Employment and Training
BSE	Barefoot Solar Engineers
BTEB	Bangladesh Technical Education Board
CID	Community and Institutional Development, Cairo
CAPART	Council for Advancement of Peoples Action and Rural Technology
CEI	Integral Education Centre
CESDER	Centro de Estudios para el Desarrollo Rural
CIMO	Calidad Integral y Modernización
Cinterfor/ILO	Centro Interamericano de Investigación y Documentación sobre Formación Profesional/International Labour Organisation
CONAFE	Consejo Nacional de Fomento Educativo (Mexico)
CONFINTEA	Conférence Internationale sur l'Education des Adultes
CSIR	Council of Scientific and Industrial Research
CTD	Centre for Technology Development
CTD/STD	Centre for Technology and Society for Technology and Development
CTEVT	Council for Technical Education and Vocational Training
DANIDA	Danish Agency for Development Assistance
DCSSI	Development Commissioner of Small Scale Industries
DDC	District Development Committee
DFL	Disease-Free Laying (of Tasar moth eggs)
DHAN	Development for Humane Action
DHRDC	District Human Resource Development Committees
DOEACC	Department of Electronics Accreditation of Computer Courses
DST	Department of Science and Technology
DTE	Directorate of Technical Education
DWCRA	Development of Women and Children in Rural Areas
ECLAC	Economic Commission for Latin America and the Caribbean
ENRED	Foro de Redes de América Latina y el Caribe
EPC	Employment Promotion Committee
FORMUJER	Regional Programme to Strengthen the Vocational and Technical Training of Low-Income Women
FPO	Fruit Products Order
GDP	Gross Domestic Product
GIAN	Gujrat Grassroots Innovation Augmentation Network
GOI	Government of India

GTZ	German Agency for Technical Assistance
HSC	High School Certificate
HSEB	Higher Secondary Education Board
HSTP	Hoshangabad Science Teaching Programme
IAMR	Institute of Applied Manpower Research
IADB	Inter-American Development Bank
IDRC	Internation Development Research Centre
IGNOU	Indira Gandhi National Open University
ILO	International Labour Organisation
INA	Instituto Nacional de Aprendizaje (National Training Institute)
INATEC	Instituto Nacional de Tecnología
INFOCAL	Instituto Nacional para la Formación y Capacitación Laboral/National Institute for Labour Training
INPRHU	Instituto de Promoción Humana
INVUR	Instituto de la Vivienda Urbana y Rural
ITI	Industrial Training Institute
KSSP	Kerala Shastra Sahitya Parishad
KVIC	Khadi and Village Industries Commission
MAWTS	Mirpur Agricultural Workshop and Training Programs
MAYA	Movement for Alternatives and Youth Awareness
MEADOW	Management Enterprise and Development of Women
MOE	Ministry of Education
MOLE	Ministry of Labour and Employment
NATRAS	Niños y Adolescentes Trabajadores
NCERT	National Council of Educational Research and Training
NCTB	National Curriculum and Textbook Board
NCVT	National Council for Vocational Training
NIF	National Innovation Foundation
NGO	Non-Governmental Organisation
NORAD	Norwegian Agency for Development Co-operation
NOS	National Open School
NPC	National Planning Commission
NSS	National Skill Standard
NVTC	National Vocational Training Centre
OECD	Organization for Economic Cooperation and Development
OEP	Organizaciones Economómicas Populares
ORGANIC	Organisation of Self-Help Collective
PET	Programa de Economia del Trabajo
POCET	Programa de Educación para el Trabajo
PRADAN	Professional Assistance for Development Action
PROIMUJER	Programme for the Promotion of Equal Opportunities for Women in Employment and Vocational Training
SENA	Servicio Nacional de Aprendizaje
SETU	Social, Educational and Training Unit of the Church in Delhi
SEWA	The Self-Employed Women's Association
SHG	Self-Help Group
SIDA	Swedish Agency for International Development
SKIP	Skills for Progress
SPMS	Sri Padmavathy Mahila Abyudaya Sangam

SSC	Secondary School Certificate
SSD	Science and Society Division
STD	Society for Technology Development
STEP	Support to Training and Employment Programme
SWRC	Social Work Research Centre, Tilonia Rajasthan
TEVT	Technical Education and Vocational Training
TRC	Technology Resource Centres
TRDEP	*Thana* Resource Development and Employment Programme
TRYSEM	Training of Rural Youth for Self-Employment
TTC	Technical Training Centres
TTTC	Technical Teacher Training College
TVET	Technical and Vocational Education and Training
UCEP	Underprivileged Children's Educational Programme
UIE	UNESCO Institute for Education
UNCHS	United Nations Committee on Human Settlements
UN-HABITAT	United Nations Human Settlements Programme
UNDP	United Nations Development Programme
UNEP	United Nations Environment Programme
UNESCO	United Nations Educational, Scientific and Cultural Organization
UNICEF	United Nations Children's Fund
UNIDO	United Nation Industrial Development Organisation
VDC	Village Development Committee
VEC	Village Education Committee
VET	Vocational Education and Training
VTCDs	Vocational Training and Community Development
VTI	Vocational Training Institutes
VTTI	Vocational Teacher Training Institute

INTRODUCTION

Madhu Singh

The informal sector is an important segment of the economies and societies in developing countries. In recent years a number of governments, in addition to a wide range of non-governmental education and training providers, have taken steps to develop and deliver learning and training programmes for young people and adults in the informal economy, in which about 500 million people around the world are working and living. Building knowledge and skills for the masses in this sector is central to alleviating poverty. It is increasingly acknowledged that, especially for disadvantaged young people and adults, education and training need to be comprehensive in order to develop wider aspects of citizenship, decent work and empowerment, since most of the disadvantaged are confronted with problems that are largely rooted in broader social, political, environmental and economic contexts.

The aim of this volume is to provide accounts of learning and training programmes in the informal sector that range over the vast territory of educational activity and give young people and adults an opportunity to gain the knowledge and develop the values, attitudes and skills which will enable them to improve their capacities to work, participate fully in their societies, take control of their own lives and continue learning. The programmes are significant in that they attempt to integrate education and training. Special emphasis is placed on the participation of all stakeholders, especially civil society organisations and social movements.

Until recently there has been limited information on educational processes and suitable learning environments for youth and adults in the informal economy. The determination to achieve Dakar Goal 3—'ensuring that the learning needs of all young people and adults are met through equitable access to appropriate learning and life skills programmes'—makes it all the more necessary that renewed attention be given to the informal economy with respect to learning needs and basic skills. Among the six goals set in the Dakar World Education Forum (UNESCO, 2000), it is especially Goal 3 that addresses the informal sector. At present, basic educational abilities in this sector are generally deficient. While there are other cross-cutting goals—literacy (Goal 4), eliminating gender disparities (Goal 5) and ensuring educational quality (Goal 6)—which are equally relevant to ensuring that the basic learning needs of youth and adults in the informal sector are met, it is Goal 3 that is pivotal.

CONCEPTUAL FRAMEWORK: INTEGRATING EDUCATION AND TRAINING AND CONSTRUCTING A NEW CITIZENSHIP

Historically vocational training and adult learning have been viewed as two distinct and discrete traditions, unconnected and even antithetical to one another. Vocational training

Madhu Singh, (ed.), Meeting Basic Learning Needs in the informal Sector, 1-21.

seeks as a rule to develop the occupational skills of the workforce in order to make it more productive and efficient, and it is generally criticised for its narrow instrumental approach, focused as it is on learners as workers. By contrast, adult learning has tended to concentrate on learner-centred approaches to learner participation in wider environments, approaches which understand the world, personal autonomy and responsibility as components of people's collective destiny. These educational approaches are underpinned by strongly humanistic values, which are given expression in the general concern to promote social justice and which may be seen as the core of the common culture of adult non-formal education (Bagnall, 2003). Thus, while vocational training is seen as the province of work-specific skills and technical aptitudes, adult learning and education are seen as the province of human values, understanding and complex capabilities. Competency-based approaches to vocational education and training have further contributed to sharpening this distinction.

Although, in view of the poverty of a large segment of those living and working in the informal economy, the focus of education and training doubtless needs to be on enhancing opportunities for disadvantaged persons to engage productively in work and thereby enhance their economic potential, it is increasingly acknowledged—and is reflected in the case studies in this volume—that programmes need to transcend the traditional paradigms of training and adult learning, for poverty means not only having less capital but also less knowledge, less in both quantity and quality.

Acknowledging the specificity of work in the informal sector necessitates an integrated approach to education and training which goes beyond training for the formal labour market. Enrique Pieck argues that training strategy for poor people 'makes necessary a reformulation of the notions of work, employment, employability and productivity. These terms do not necessarily follow the logic of the formal labour market, nor do they imply that the skills being promoted are necessarily linked to the technologically oriented sectors.' In the context of a bilateral training programme, Peter Gerasch and Arturo Durán argue that the criterion for setting up an educational and training programme in Nicaragua in which trainees constructed their own housing was primarily to find a solution for low-income families to the problem of housing shortage and congestion there and less to integrate trainees into the local labour market—though the authors admit that the latter is equally important, especially after the educational and training project has ended. Here the perennial problem of the conflict between vocational training for the labour market and informal training for self-employment becomes visible. The authors argue that it is necessary to formulate a policy to facilitate the link between education *for living* and education *for making a living*.

This holistic view of education is authoritatively reflected in the Delors Commission's Report to UNESCO of the International Commission on Education for the Twenty-first Century, *Learning: The Treasure Within* (1996). It integrates the notions of education and training by identifying the four pillars of learning as 'learning to know', 'learning to do', 'learning to live together' and 'learning to be'. This view of education transcends the apparent opposition between vocational training and general education. The Delors Commission Report is an important statement inasmuch as it provides guidance for the long-term development of an integrated educational and training system. Historically there has been a fairly sharp distinction between what people were thought to be learning in various learning environments. Some skills were thought to be acquired in vocational education and work-based learning, while others were thought to be acquired in general education.

As we develop our educational and training systems for lifelong learning, the distinction between education and training becomes increasingly blurred. Whereas some skills are learned at school, others may be acquired in non-formal adult learning programmes, at work or in the local community. Informal learning activities are also gaining in importance. Bernd Overwien presents this enlarged view of learning, which emphasises the informal acquisition of skills on the job and in social movements of popular education. All this is relevant from the point of view of developing flexible lifelong learning policies for informal economies, in which many young people and adults have not received good initial schooling.

Changes in the world of work have caused the focus of training for employment to shift to generic rather than job-specific skills, while general education increasingly prepares one for survival and self-realisation in a highly technological world of work. For the lifelong learner, it is not important whether the learning situation is classified as education or training or whether training should be added to education, or vice versa. What matters for such a learner is instead the education of the whole worker—not because it is required for production alone, but because it affects him or her as a critical being with a social and cultural understanding of the world.

Alongside this integrative perspective on education and training, new notions of citizenship can be seen to be emerging. The result is that civil society organisations are increasingly coming to view the fulfilment of the basic learning needs of young people and adults who work and live in the informal sector as a serious responsibility of society as a whole and not only of the state. To promote citizenship and democracy, as well as to rebuild civil society, it is necessary to create spaces and opportunities within society so that citizens may actively participate in it. NGOs, social movements, community development associations and trade unions are taking charge of these spaces and demanding that others be created. Overwien argues that we can learn much from popular educational movements in Latin America, some of which have established successful collaboration with the business world. These concrete experiences then take the form of a wider emphasis on the construction of democratic processes.

In the organisation of the work of civil society organisations, the struggle for rights and entitlements (equality, right to decent work and basic education) constitutes the foundation for the emergence of a new notion of citizenship. It is also increasingly acknowledged that decent work and this new understanding of citizenship are possible only when the very notions of skill development, capacity enhancement and training are reformulated in terms of a rights-based approach. As Amit Mitra argues, 'It is important to re-conceptualise and move away from its narrow mechanical and mere employment connotations.' In addition to work and employment itself, decent work includes rights at work, security, representation and dialogue. This makes it necessary to create an enabling environment by building up the self-image and social and negotiating skills of informal sector workers. The pedagogy of empowerment envisions trainers as facilitators who enable the community to learn on its own, engage in teamwork and improve its collective lot. The least common denominat or of any training package should be the right to decent work, to the basic security of income and other social security and to choose work that is not dehumanising and degrading. The rights framework would also stress labour market mobility (irrespective of case, gender and ethnicity), occupational safety and health, equal work for men and women and fair wages for adults so that they are not forced to take their children out of school and put them to work.

From a gender perspective, removing the decent work deficit is the most urgent challenge, for doing so makes it possible to overcome the exclusion and marginalisation of women. Work is a fundamental component of life, self-affirmation and social esteem for both men and women. But for women it involves the fundamental move away from the assigned model of a life dedicated exclusively to reproductive and unpaid work, a model which represents an additional impediment to overcoming social barriers and prejudices regarding their rights and capabilities, and thus inhibits their equal participation in decent employment. According to Sara Silviera and Anaclara Matosos, the new notion of training is one in which an individual's abilities and values are strengthened, in addition to his or her occupational competencies, and in which there is greater balance between requirements of education and training, the production system and gender .

In the case studies presented here, practitioners have a strong commitment to increase social equity. The approaches to adult learning address issues include educational, social and economic disadvantages, the exploitation of women, indigenous peoples and ethnic minorities, and the marginalisation of groups. By emphasising education and training for all, a society in fact lays the foundation for active citizenship and social stability, thereby preventing social exclusion and contributing to the strengthening of democratic social structures. It is these results that make it clear that integrated systems of education and training must provide education to all people so as to give them the tools they need for autonomous action. Such systems must create a balance between human and social capital—where human capital is the learning that allows people to fulfil their individual potential and social capital is the network of relationships that allows a community to be cohesive and purposeful. Clearly, education given to adults and young people in the informal sector must develop both kinds of capital by bringing out the learners' individual talents and preparing them to contribute to their communities. The implementation of broad-based, continuing education and training programmes makes it more likely that youth and adults will become involved in the life of the community, contribute to a more cohesive society and engage with the cultural, political and social issues around them. That provides the basis for a better society.

When dealing with disadvantaged groups, it is necessary to emphasise both their right to basic education and its role in overcoming oppression and indecent working conditions. While the intrinsic value of education forms the core of its status as a human right, education is also an indispensable means for unlocking and protecting other human rights. It provides some of the scaffolding necessary to secure the rights to good health, liberty, security, economic well-being and participation in the cultural and political life of the community: 'Where the right to education is guaranteed, people's access to and enjoyment of other rights is enhanced and the imbalances in life chances are lessened' (UNESCO, 2002).

Thus it is the worker as learner and the importance of learning processes that are crucial. As Overwien points out, what is needed as a rule are learner-centred strategies which also strengthen the subject, especially within macro-contexts in which economic and employment possibilities are limited. In a different context, Gerasch and Durán point out that in construction projects in which, for example, the administration of the project and meeting evaluation deadlines is central to the programme, in addition to its training and educational components, it is not uncommon for construction tasks to take precedence over learning and educational processes, with the consequence that workers become hesitant to identify themselves as learners. This situation needs to be corrected especially in a country like Nicaragua, where half the population is below 18 years of age and the average length of education of the population aged 25 is only 5.8 years. Thus mere survival strategies employed by many adult learning agencies are an insufficient response to the complexities, dangers and opportunities ahead.

EDUCATIONAL PROCESSES AND BASIC LEARNING NEEDS IN THE INFORMAL SECTOR

Although education and training are identified as key determinants of informal sector growth and development, as well as of poverty eradication, few educationists have actually provided a comprehensive picture of the educational process in working life. In fact it is only recently—in the early 1990s—that a series of empirical studies were undertaken to determine adult educational needs in the informal economy (Institute for Scientific Co-operation, 1997).

This research has attended to the different processes of learning and acquiring competencies which are seen as fundamental for workers in the informal sector. Learning is understood, on the one hand, as the acquisition of technical skills and abilities on the level of enterprise and related in varying ways to the production process in an enterprise and, on the other hand, as the acquisition of organisational skills and small entrepreneurial and social competencies external to the production process. Social competencies include those directed inward (towards the individual personality) and outward (towards others). The former include self-awareness, the ability to learn, motivation, creativity, intellectual agility and the capacity for planning ahead; the latter include the ability to communicate with others, the ability to co-operate, to develop mutual trust, tolerance and flexibility (Burckhardt, 1997). A certain number of cognitive skills—knowledge base, numeracy, literacy and communication skills, as well as knowledge of languages (local, national and foreign)—are decisive for the acquisition of work-related, vocationally specialised competencies in the informal sector. Literacy skills are used to decode words, make measurements, read catalogues and instructions. But they are also used to develop communication skills, such as giving advice, negotiating, convincing, transmitting knowledge and promoting products. Generally speaking, literacy and other cognitive skills facilitate the organisation of economic activities and qualify persons for urban life.

The Jomtien Declaration on Education for All (1990) introduced the concept of 'basic learning needs', which bears on the basic needs of individuals, groups and societies. It identified seven areas of basic learning needs common to children, youth and adults:

surviving, developing one's full capacities, living and working in dignity, participating fully in development, improving quality of life, making informed decisions; continuing to learn. The Dakar World Education Forum (2000) alluded to Delors Commission's four pillars of learning—learning to be, learning to do, learning to know and learning to live together—and in addition reaffirmed that education should be geared to tapping each person's talents and potential, as well as developing learners' personalities, so that they can improve their lives and transform their societies. The UNDP's notion of basic learning needs (UNDP, 2001) is related to human development goals. According to it, 'The most basic capabilities for human development are to lead long and healthy lives, to be knowledgeable, to have access to the resources needed for a decent stand of living, and to be ale to participate in the life of the community' (p. 9). The Memorandum on Lifelong Learning of the European Commission states (2000, p. 5): 'The knowledge, skills and understanding that we learn as children and as young people in the family, at school, during training and at college or university will not last a lifetime'. Further central points are high quality basic education for all as an essential foundation, learning to learn skills and a positive attitude towards learning. According to CONFINTEA V, The Fifth International Conference on Adult Education (UIE, 1997, p. 2), 'The objectives of youth and adult education, viewed as a lifelong process, are to develop the autonomy and the sense of responsibility of people and communities, to reinforce the capacity to deal with the transformations taking place in the economy, in culture and in society as a whole, and to promote coexistence, tolerance and the informed and creative participation of citizens in their communities, in short to enable people and communities to take control of their destiny and society in order to face the challenges ahead. It is essential that the approach to adult learning be based on people's own heritage, culture, values and prior experiences and that the diverse ways in which these approaches are implemented enable and encourage every citizen to be actively involved and to have a voice.'

Literacy is a foundation and remains the heart of most basic and most sophisticated competencies. But the concept and scope of literacy have changed over the past decades. The renewed vision of literacy emphasises it as a social responsibility and that it is acquired in broader socio-economic interventions: Literacy goals include literacy acquisition, development and effective use, and literacy can only be made sustainable by creating literate environments and literate societies.

The international community no longer sees these basic learning needs as compartmentalised but as part of the broader aim of learning and the lifelong learning process, where basic learning is embraced as a social and cultural practice shaped by the context of daily life.

Seen from the perspective of the workers in the informal economy, these basic learning needs are significant, especially when they are viewed in connection with the goal of citizenship and decent work. 'Decent work' is central to people's lives. It implies improved status, self-esteem and dignity. Work is broader than occupation and employment and takes into account the wider environment and the worker's living and working conditions, be it the housing situation (Gerasch & Durán) or the situation of street children (Overwien) or garbage collectors (Iskandar). Work is not static but dynamic and changes according to circumstances. Meeting basic learning needs depends on the acknowledgement of work as a field in which one can realise one's creative potential insofar as forms of work allow one to become aware of one's personal abilities. This kind of learning process should be at the core of non-formal education and training programmes for youth and adults. Such programmes should be geared towards the development of an individual's personal abilities.

THE SOCIO-POLITICAL AND ECONOMIC CONTEXT AND BASIC NEEDS IN THE INFORMAL ECONOMY

Basic learning needs in the informal economy are inextricably linked to the basic needs of individuals and groups, and these basic needs are influenced by the socio-economic and political conditions in the informal economy. The informal sector is highly heterogeneous, including as it does production units with different features and in a wide range of economic activities. Typically, three categories are distinguished in the informal sector (ILO, 1998, p. 167): the small or micro-enterprise sector is the strongest and most dynamic sub-sector; the household-based sub-sector, where most of the activities are carried out by family members; and the service sector, which comprises domestic helpers, street-vendors, etc.

Basic learning needs of individuals and communities differ according to their perceptions of these needs. Often the very poor and illiterate communities in the informal economy are excluded from information and knowledge since their learning needs are assumed to be limited in scope. Participants in the informal sector in developing countries are more likely to be poor and have low literacy rates and skill levels. While some levels of education (a minimum of primary or secondary education) characterise young people and adults at the 'upper end' of the informal sector, those in the 'lower end' may be said to be characterised by illiteracy to below primary level of education, as V. V. Krishna points out below in his article on education training and skill formation for decent work in Northern India. In the Asian and Arab contexts, the majority of young people and adults acquire the essential skills for performing an informal sector activity outside the school system. This generalisation cannot be made for the Latin American context, however, since there the system offers more than four years of schooling to more than 50 percent of the population (Corvalan, 1997).

Children, youth and adults in the informal sector have unmet basic learning needs. Such needs vary according to age, gender, context and culture. Women need to be singled out as a specific target group in the informal sector, as they are over-represented therein. In Asia and Africa their share in the informal sector is estimated to be typically 60–80 percent. This is an underestimation, however, since unpaid family help and home-based workers are excluded from enumeration, and it is in these categories that women make up the largest percentage. In Latin America, self-employment generates nine of every ten new positions for women, but since they require few qualifications, these positions are also marked by greater instability in employment and a lack of social protection. Silviera and Matosas found that in Latin America 49.7 percent of female employment was informal while for men the figure was 43.8 percent. Domestic work accounts for 22 percent of the new jobs for women generated between 1990 and 1998. Women are underrepresented as employers in the micro-enterprise sector. However, the authors also point out that a number of new fields—such as new technological services, phone sales, consultancies, internet, out-sourced manufacturing, small machine assembly and many other activities that have to do with the transfer to the productive field of many domestic activities—have been added to the traditional tasks of clothing and textile services, and these generate new educational and training requirements.

Women and young people are more likely to be engaged in hazardous work in the informal sector, such as work in the brick-kiln industry or carpet manufacturing. Laila Iskandar highlights this for the garbage collectors of Cairo, who survive on their sorting ability to recover as much as is humanly possible, to process, re-manufacture and trade it. This exposes them to a social environment of untold health hazards and unspeakable human indignity. Christine Nathan points out that women construction workers are subject to miserable working conditions. They are employed on a casual basis and have neither security of service nor any bargaining power for demanding a minimum living wage or standard of living. They face a great deal of discrimination when it comes to hiring or promotion, and their work is generally undervalued in the job market. Construction workers report a variety of health problems, which they ascribe to their work. Women also have more precarious jobs, and they have to work longer hours to compensate for their low wages: Often women are compelled to take up such physically arduous tasks because they feel they are responsible for the survival of their families and the mitigation of their poor circumstances.

The informal sector is also the predominant employer of child labour in developing countries. Conservative estimates suggest that 20–30 million children work in South Asia alone. In the Egyptian case study, Iskandar highlights economic factors that instigate child labour. Female-headed households are often among the most vulnerable and rely largely on child labour as a source of income.

The informal sector also tends to be exposed to a high degree of risk, although there is little or no availability of formal insurance mechanisms. When layoffs occur in the formal sector in urban areas, the poor who are likely to lose their jobs first swell the ranks of the urban poor in the informal sector. The growing number of dropouts from the school system make up the pool of cheap labour; they are absorbed in the informal and domestic sectors, where the terms and conditions of work are extremely poor (Adhikary). By their very nature, informal enterprises are especially vulnerable to dynamic changes in the economy, such as technological changes that result in redundancy.

Given the absence of formal safety net mechanisms, informal sector households must find ways to reduce vulnerability by tapping informal group-based networks that have been developed over the years. Overwien argues that there is a close connection between these social networks and the existence of social movements and learning processes which can support productive potential through co-operative economic activities. He says that the learning processes linked with such social networks have been neglected in earlier investigations. However, in recent studies researchers have begun to trace the close links between educational approaches critical of political rule and a practical approach based on people's need to survive.

In general, the literature has tended to view the informal sector in developing countries as a fallback option for the livelihood of those who cannot participate in the formal sector. While such a view has some basis, it ignores the growing evidence that certain people prefer to work in the informal sector. On the one hand, informal sector jobs can offer flexibility in participation. On the other, for many it offers the promise of higher returns because in most developing countries certain markets are inadequately serviced by formal enterprises, such as small repair services for all kinds of mechanical and electrical devices from watches to cars. While it is important to bear in mind this dual picture of the informal sector, the fact remains that an overwhelming proportion of the poor is found to be concentrated in this sector. Their work in the informal sector by no means enables them to recover from poverty (Silviera & Matosas).

INFORMAL PROCESSES OF INSTITUTIONALISATION

Education is only one problem in the informal sector. The other is the lack of institutional support. Professional training institutions and their study programmes have been geared mainly towards the formal labour market rather than the informal economy.

Regarding formal training in Bangladesh, Titumir points to the absence of institutional structure for dialogue with local enterprises and industries. The private sector has made little effort to institutionalise initiatives for the informal sector and has invested little in this sector. The situation is not any different, therefore, from over 30 years ago when Philip H. Coombs (1968) wrote in the *World Educational Crisis* that 'Educational systems are falling far short of turning out the right combinations of manpower needed for optimum development' (p. 74). A particularly troublesome sector is TVET at the secondary or post-secondary level. Yet 'they are nonetheless exported and imported at great expense into less developed countries, side-by-side with shorter and more flexible non-formal training schemes, delivered by a different breed of advisers' (p. 76).

Even where the state and actors and agencies in the private sector have created some institutional support structures, the relevance of their educational and training programmes remains limited to the 'upper end' of the informal sector, at the cost of the most disadvantaged and those most in need of education.

Informal Institutional Modes of Learning

Although institutional contexts can support the learner in his or her learning activities, these organisational contexts need not take the form of school. Learning also takes place within social movements as learning environments and through informal apprenticeships. For millions of people, these informal institutional modes of learning are still the only ones available. Considerably more young people acquire occupational competencies through an informal apprenticeship than would be possible in the framework of state projects and programmes.

Self-regulatory mechanisms, such as trade and other associations, can play a key role in basic and further education. Informal trade associations are important for the future development of trades, the propagation of new ideas and the development and maintenance of collective trade standards. Such aspects of social organisation should be acknowledged as important for human and social capital in the informal sector. To be effective in self-help organisations, participants must have the necessary communication skills and knowledge of rules and possibilities of action. These skills would allow them to demand that local institutions become responsive to their real needs. Informal associations and co-operatives must make decisions about what their workers should learn, how they should learn and with what degree of mastery. A fundamental training question is what factors can be harnessed for growth and which constraints removed. Some of these have to do with access to credit, rural production technologies, and markets.

Interfacing Education with Institutional Environments: The Role of Civil Society Organisations

In the absence of formal institutional support structures, it is civil society organisations that are creating spaces and opportunities for interfacing education with economic and institutional environments and thus promoting a new dimension of citizenship. Krishna shows that NGOs play an important role in providing 'consultancy for technology diffusion to the informal sector' and in bridging the 'communication and structural gaps' between formal and informal sectors.

The rapid expansion of NGOs and bilateral and multilateral agencies working in community development programmes in Nepal and Nicaragua has been due to the fact that they act as a catalyst for communication between governments and communities. Community development programmes which are social welfare and public service projects provide entry points for training and education for young people and adults. They also offer an avenue for the combination of entrepreneurial ideas and spirit with social commitment (Faltin, 1999) because they extend beyond training and production to participation in community affairs and local economic development. In this way, providers of education and training programmes are made accountable to the community. Gerasch and Durán highlight how community links can be forged through need-based courses and services in water, health, sanitation and housing.

The success of NGOs working with youth and adults in the informal sector has increased their credibility with the local communities. Iskandar shows that community development associations working with rag-pickers are highly successful because these associations are deeply rooted in the life of the community of rag-pickers. In Overwien's case study, NGOs such as INPRHU work with local structures and seek training opportunities in existing workshops. Thus NGOs can be said to have an edge over other formal institutions. Especially those NGOs which adopt the participatory approach to research are in a better position to understand individual actors and communities and to design training programmes for skills development and support services. Seen from the perspective of decent work, empowerment and citizenship, and based on the evidence from the case studies in this volume, it can even be argued that NGOs tend to give a fuller organisational substance to democratic, participatory and humane values.

However, studies have also expressed a cautionary note about the role of NGOs. More often than not, their role in the informal sector is temporary or intermediary to long-term strategies. Krishna notes that, while many NGOs (particularly those which deal with micro-finance and micro-enterprise projects) do impact on the lives of the poor, their impact is only minimal because they often tend to stabilise people at low socio-economic levels. Furthermore, given that NGOs are becoming increasingly dependent on public and private funds, they have a tendency to compromise on what they consider to be the 'right approach' and to carry out the projects favoured by their donors. Furthermore, NGOs frequently develop dynamics of their own which can endanger many of the principles of education. For instance, Overwien notes that the interest in guaranteeing stable jobs with corresponding influence sometimes conflicts with the need for democratic structures. In an evaluative study of training programmes in four Latin American countries, it has been shown that while most NGOs focus on a community's basic needs, they do not promote an educational curriculum that would give youth and adults a 'second chance' to enter the educational system and continue learning. Moreover, NGOs are usually more interested in social action than in training tailored to specific trades (Gallart, 2001).

Role of Trade Unions

Only some trade unions in the past have taken up the struggle for the improvement of the working and living conditions of youth and adults in the informal economy, especially with regard to the equal treatment of women or access to basic education. Furthermore, trade union work has tended to be concentrated mostly in urban areas. Trade unions have paid insufficient attention to rural workers and to issues of child labour, especially to the question of whether children should receive training and be allowed to work under the same decent working conditions as youth and adults working and living in the informal sector.

However, this is changing. There seems to be growing interest among trade unions to participate in the debate on training and educational policies and strategies for the informal sector. Trade unions are playing an important role in the debate surrounding the culture of rights and decent work in the informal sector and are increasingly collaborating with governments on concrete programmes.

However, as Nathan points out in her article on adult learning for women construction workers, trade unions believe that they cannot pursue a strong policy for improving the competencies of workers in the informal sector without having programmes at the national level. They also feel that partners in the labour market need to exercise their responsibility by actively addressing the problem and starting to co-operate. She notes that employers still show strong resistance when it comes to educational and training concerns and the upgrading of competencies in the informal sector.

SYSTEM REFORM

A broad consensus emerging from the case studies presented here is that most countries need to overcome considerable inertia in their existing educational and training systems in order to reach youth and adults effectively in the informal sector and enhance their income and living conditions. What has also emerged from these papers is that system reform needs to be guided by at least five objectives which address some of the educational and training concerns of the informal sector. These are: (1) Basic education should be regarded as an essential prerequisite and foundation for access to further training and education and as a basic right for unlocking other rights, such as the right to decent work, employment, cultural and political participation, economic well-being and security. (2) The quality of non-formal education needs to be improved and its link to the formal education and training system strengthened. (3) The existing educational and training system must be reformed. (4) Education and training outcomes and benefits from learning programmes must be improved. (5) Gender issues need to be integrated into policy and training for women in the informal sector.

Articulation of Skills Development with Basic Education

An important starting point for the reform of any system is the recognition that a large number of children either do not participate in formal schooling or are unable to get through even the primary level of education. They are simply pushed out by the school system. The low quality of public education is marked by high wastage, low quality of physical facilities in schools, lack of pedagogical activities, untrained teachers and ineffective supervision. According to Titumir, the educational system does not reach the disadvantaged and consequently reduces their chances to enter the competitive labour markets in the new economic order. According to Poorna K. Adhikary, poorly educated, unemployed youth—particularly those from socially and economically disadvantaged communities—have become a grave problem in developing countries.

Not only is basic education not accessible to many but often the quality of basic education is so poor that even receiving a full basic education is not a guarantee that one will have basic skills. According to Pieck, formal basic education has not been providing the skills and competencies needed to prepare school graduates for their incorporation into the world of work. In this context, the articulation of skills development with basic education becomes crucial.

While schools can play a positive role for working children and adolescents, the traditional school concepts have resulted in their exclusion so far. As a result, several authors in this book raise the question of how young working people acquire competencies and what competencies are crucial for their lives and work. Considerably more young people acquire occupational competencies through an informal apprenticeship than would be possible through government or NGO-run programmes. The Delors Commission Report is also appealed to regarding the necessary shift away from knowledge-dominated learning to a focus on the abilities of the learner.

The present case studies highlight the importance of key competencies which prove particularly important in the context of the informal sector and which need to be promoted through basic education. Krishna points out that it is crucial to promote collective competencies in a sector which shows a stagnation of wage levels despite expansion and improvement in many economies in developing countries. He argues that one cause of this is the lack of bargaining power on the part of the micro-entrepreneurs. An important source of collective competencies is the representation of interests through local organisations and learning by negotiating, particularly within expanding markets. Collective competencies can be promoted by supporting the participation of informal sector workers in informal trade associations, self-help groups, co-operatives and credit societies. Krishna also shows how the objectives of training in *'social' and 'collective' competencies*, including leadership, can be combined with the micro-financing in the informal sector by designing an appropriate methodology of loan disbursement to groups of women. This collective orientation helps to strengthen the individual, especially within a macro-context in which economic and employment possibilities are limited.

'Life skills' is another important notion that has been gaining in importance since the Dakar goals were sett and which has great relevance for developing non-formal basic education for young people and adults in the informal economy. According to Pieck, 'life skills' is a concept that links technical training activities with the notions of human development and quality of life enhancement. It entails both 'generic skills' (such as problem-solving, team work, critical thinking, learning to learn, management and organisational skills) and 'context-dependent skills' (such as computer literacy, media literacy, health literacy, economic literacy and emotional literacy). Literacy is a fundamental skill, a basic tool for acquiring basic competencies in other domains.

The studies gathered here also point up the fact that new skills is particularly important for the informal sector workers. The Training programmes examined by Pieck, such as SENA and CIN, have highlighted the need to incorporate curriculum elements designed to impart new skills and technological literacy that are common to both the formal and the informal markets in order to prevent social exclusion. Persons in the informal sector should be given the opportunity to join the formal labour market. This would take into account the already existing connections and overlaps between the informal and formal economies.

Thus not merely access to basic education but also the quality of basic education, taking into account its articulation with the development of basic skills, can be a means of ensuring mobility and higher income and the advantages of further education and training opportunities.

Role of Non-Formal Education

In developing countries the provision of basic education by means of non-formal education is of greater importance than the formal educational system. But while there are efforts to create a balance between education and training, non-formal education nontheless appears to be increasingly dominated by an emphasis on vocationalism. Pieck refers to today's non-formal programmes as merely responding to temporary occupational needs of young people and adults. According to Adama Ouane, this has been partly fuelled by government policy initiatives:

> ... scratch below the surface of most local, national and international policy documents and a commitment will be found not to learning but to skills development The vocationalist drive and logic help to ensure that the requirements of business, enterprise and other vocationally oriented goals are to be part of teaching and research agendas of all educational institutions. One of the implications of such a shift towards market and wealth generation raises the question of what counts as education and adult learning. Preparation for paid employment seems to be the short answer. The adoration of competencies and competency-based learning with their emphasis on functional skills further narrow the focus of adult learning, especially in the area of work-based learning. (Ouane, 2002, p. 20)

In his recent book Richard G. Bagnall (2003) highlights that the growing emphasis on skills development within non-formal education has resulted in the marginalisation of non-formal education. The field of non-formal education has come into disrepute because of the prevailing focus on the efficient learning of vocational skills. There is a tendency for these skills development programmes to serve labour market interests. The emphasis on competency standards set by industry, vocational education and training instructors or governments is completely contrary to the work of local and community organisations to create spaces for meeting individual and collective learning needs. The result is that the more general educational values tend to be diminished or lost. From Adhikary's case study of Nepal below, one can see that there is a division between those organisations which impart skills and those which adopt a more general approach to training.

Thus, many non-formal skills development programmes are in effect mere training courses without any strategic links to educational systems or development programmes. Training projects which point a way to employment orientations usually focus only on the individual and his or her economic possibilities and ignore the learning process.

Improving the Quality of Non-Formal Education Programmes

It has been suggested that to improve non-formal adult education, it is necessary to tap into the supply of formal education (Gallart, 2001). It has also been recommended that such training programmes be integrated into the programmed activities of NGOs which have a great deal of experience in dealing with poor youth at risk, thus enhancing the possibility of responding to the particular needs of subgroups of young adults.

The present volume shows that quality learning for informal sector workers has to do with making learning participatory and experiential and creating rich learning environments. Participatory learning involves the experience of engaging, and reflecting in the processes of learning, rather than participation rates in themselves. It is a process in which communities effect their own cultural and economic life and in which literacy and basic education is seen as a gateway to this participation.

Because learning is not a commodity but a process of transformation, providers of learning programmes in the informal sector must give clear reasons for instigating and motivating learners to enrol. This has been shown very clearly in the non-formal programmes reported here, and particularly in the Cairo case study on garbage workers in which training and education have been incorporated into traditional economic activities originating from the local cultural and social environment itself. Not only is learning linked to the reality of work but the learning organisation of non-formal education is flexible, community-based and extends to the home and the street; it is social, fluid and involves earning while learning, an experience that values, for instance, the garbage collectors as individuals and is filled with dignity and respect. The teaching methods are participatory, learning is experiential, the school environment is democratic and self-financed, learning schedules are flexible, instructors come from the neighbourhood, assessments are individualised and learning is self-paced. As a consequence of this approach, such non-formal education is able to achieve greater learner involvement, ownership and commitment. It is clear from this example that education and training programmes for very poor youth and adults need to offer very clear, concrete and immediate reasons to justify enrolment and ensure perseverance.

Equally important for participatory learning to take place is that non-formal learning programmes take account of the views of learners and potential learners. Silveira and Matosas have elaborated this in the framework of the FORMUJER programme in Latin America, as well as the importance of the involvement of adults and young people in defining, preparing and managing a feasible employment and training project. The occupational projects include courses of action defined by women and men themselves with the purpose of achieving productive insertion in the workforce or improving their employment. In the process of designing their own projects, adults and young people are able to augment key competencies, develop autonomy, strengthen personal relationships and access the public world.

The *development of rich and dynamic learning environments* is another key element in quality learning because it is critical to the sustainability of the use and retention of basic skills. It emphasises the importance of viewing quality non-formal learning as a complex interaction between: (1) widening social and intersectoral participation, (2) strengthening social institutions and (3) promoting co-operation between formal, non-formal and informal learning. Pieck, for instance, provides examples of non-formal programmes that articulate with various institutions, such as health, early and basic education and nutrition, in order to broaden the scope of these institutions and make them economically relevant to people living in impoverished areas. The real challenge is to make certain that such inter-institutional collaboration is reflected in learning programmes, curricular models, and teacher training initiatives. Among the institutions which Pieck mentions, the Integral Education Centre (CEI) in Brazil has courses that cover a range of possibilities, such as instruction in driving, music, mechanics and physical education. In the Egyptian case study, 'community curriculum' incorporates culture, arts, sports and other extra-curricular activities.

Quality adult learning is both *embedded in a life context*. It recognises that learning is linked to experience, language, cultural practices and interests in settings and environments which are outside organised education and which may include sources such as families and communities, other institutions and the media. Young people, especially out-of-school young adults, feel motivated to learn when their learning is mediated by activities that are related to their daily lives. The ability of adults to learn effectively has much to do with making sense of the varied experiences at work, in school, in community activities and in social movements. By reflecting on their experience, adults have been shown to experience heightened feelings of self-worth. Furthermore, many social and economic problems can be solved through the appropriate transfer of knowledge from informal experience. A major challenge is to include more informal educational activities and the living and working environment in the educational processes and to cease to regard work and education as distinct endeavours.

Benefits from Learning Programmes

The application of skills assessments in countries where large numbers of people are working in the informal sector is a challenging task given the highly contextual nature of most programmes. However, the small amount of evidence gained so far from impact assessments suggests that non-formal learning programmes have helped workers to enhance their social and economic status and to function effectively in their daily lives and social contexts. The non-formal learning projects for working youth from poor and disenfranchised garbage communities in Cairo show that they have been able to improve the nutritional and health situation, to provide youth with the ability to face life crises and to offer lifelong learning opportunities through literacy, primary health care, social activities and recreation.

Although data are not available on the impact of education and training on production, productivity and standards of living, people who have completed education and training courses tend to be more confident and more likely to take initiative in developing their own enterprises and to get involved in the operation of their co-operatives. These women and men tend to feel that they can no longer be easily cheated when they buy inputs or sell produce. These psychosocial aspects should be taken into consideration when designing educational and training policies since they do impinge on the productivity of current livelihoods and on individuals' willingness to seek opportunities to develop new businesses. Krishna and Mitra provide clear examples of how education and training can help people to build community capacity and solidarity and become aware of their rights, as well as to find self-expression and self-esteem. These are all fundamental aspects of greater participation in and ownership of the development process, which a rights-based approach would advocate. Disadvantaged youth, as Pieck shows, were able to prolong their formal education by attending remedial courses in Brazil's SCV. Often the most frequently mentioned gains from learning programmes have to do with feelings and attitudes rather than qualifications and jobs. The true impact of learning may not always be apparent in the short term.

Gerasch and Durán speak of the 'double benefit' from the self-construction training programme: not only does it provides housing but also a 'second chance' education and training to those who have discontinued primary or secondary education. Educators and facilitators have been trained to introduce functional basic education and youth have been trained in various marketable skills, crafts, sanitation, appropriate technologies and housing construction.

Bridging Formal, Non-Formal and Informal Education and Training

Instead of resting satisfied with a patchwork of pilot projects which integrate informal learning into the formal learning process, a country's entire educational and training system should be looked at from a systems perspective .The various subsystems should be integrated into one overarching system in which the various points communicate with each other and offer progressive educational opportunities to all, including special target groups. The main problem, then, is one of defining strategies whereby skills for economic success can be combined with skills for personal development and active social participation (Corvalan, 1997).

How should this dynamic educational system look? Adhikary proposes that the divisions between formal, non-formal and informal education should be bridged by opening co-lateral entry options. Non-formal education could act as a bridge between formal basic education and training and the attainment of life and work goals. The lifelong learner must be able to move in and out of the educational and training system at various stages of his or her life, to obtain and accumulate unit credits towards awards, to move between institutions, to be accredited for skills obtained in different learning settings, including the workplace and the community, and to move horizontally and vertically in an educational and training frame without landing in a cul-de-sac.

Pieck proposes a two-pronged strategy. On the one hand, non-formal strategies such as bridge courses are needed to prepare children for entry into schools and remedial learning centres which provide pedagogic support to heighten school performance. On the other hand, many government programmes highlight the need for multiple ways of delivering schooling and regard educational programmes outside the formal school system as suitable for 'balancing work and education' and thereby for addressing the reality of work in the lives of poor children. In both strategies, however, the stated intention is to address the question of *equivalence with the formal system*—for example, through the creation of National Skill Testing Committees, such as those reported by Adhikary, and the inclusion of modules of basic education in non-formal training programmes, such as those highlighted by Titumir.

Evidence from empirical studies has shown that while people in the informal sector acquire most vocational competencies in the context of their work experience, they usually acquire their verbal, mathematical and general skills in school. Promoting creative attitudes, independent thought and action, risk-taking, initiative, problem-solving and other life skills must therefore be given high priority when seeking to improve the quality of the curriculum in educational institutions attended by people from the informal sector. In the initial education of young people, the goal should be to create active citizens who are capable of participating in the social life of the community. It is only when an individual's capacity for co-operation, communication, creativity, initiative and flexibility has been strengthened that he or she is also prepared for working life.

Apprenticeships linked with basic school education could provide an incentive to young people to go to school without the fear that such education will deprive them of the skills required for earning a living. It could also facilitate productive and higher-income employment in the future and help to combat the exploitation of child labour in the long run. Apprenticeships have often been viewed as an aspect of working life rather than of education. The issue is therefore one of converting the cheap workforce model into a model in which active learning is designed to go beyond routine production tasks. Such on-the-job training needs to be recognised as part of the educational system.

As to the vocational education and training system, Adhikary proposes that it be integrated in community learning centres and linked to local level developmental institutions, since they know more about the local market needs. Titumir has called for the diversification of technical and vocational training. Although most vocational and training systems cater to micro-enterprises, what is needed are more comprehensive services to the latter. Apprenticeships and internships must be able to compensate for the income that young people and adults forgo while participating in them. The creation of National Skill Testing Committee has been an innovative effort in Nepal to encourage informal learners to become certified and be recognised for employment at various levels in both the private and the public sectors.

Gender Issues

Women need technical, managerial and social skills not only for their economic activities but also to enhance their participation in making decisions in the household and the community. Women and their families need to be helped to increase income and production capabilities, reduce household burdens and eliminate some of their fatigue and drudgery. Furthermore, women workers in the informal sector suffer not only from loneliness and alienation but also from insecurity and vulnerability. Silveira and Motasas examine the position of women domestic workers whose wages and social entitlements, they argue, have not improved despite the increase in modern lifestyles of high-income bracket families. Training programmes for such women in the informal sector usually include activities ranging from influencing macro-economic conditions, lobbying, making the market women-friendly, linking human rights to their economic rights to own assets and helping them to manage business, enter into contracts and certify skills.

Literacy training and basic education is an essential prerequisite for training self-employed women. It has been found that the benefits from education are likely to be much greater than those from vocational training alone. Since prior general education determines access to training, an approach to equalisation which is confined to training will produce only marginal improvements in the situation of disadvantaged women, who will still be over-represented in low-education, low-income occupations and among the unemployed. Skill development and enterprise training programmes for women need to be linked with educational and training institutions, where they could be developed further and made available to a larger group of women.

Training and education is not simply a matter of social justice or social welfare but also a question of how to enable women to get onto on the path of economic betterment and improved performance. In her case study on women construction workers, Nathan says that a higher order of technology is essential for uplifting female workers. This is not easy to implement, however, because, as she notes, men are usually given the first opportunities to gain training and retraining. Since most women are unskilled workers, the introduction of new technologies into the construction industry is more likely to make them redundant and force them back into destitution.

Likewise Silviera and Matosas place emphasis on the importance of developing new technological skills among women. According to the authors, the entrance of technology into the home has led to an increasing demand in the marketplace for home-based services. This has opened up a whole area of demand for new skills, which need to be developed and strengthened.

CHALLENGES

The Centrality of the Issue of Basic Education

Given the size of the informal sector and its importance for the survival and development of hundreds of millions of children, youth and adults, there is no question of the importance of a system of learning linked to its development. Learning in the informal sector should be studied, supported and reinforced (Corvalan, 1997). However, when considering what should be prioritised, the matter becomes complex. The present case studies indicate that it has proved very difficult to integrate the informal and non-formal learning which is relevant to the informal sector into the formal educational system. But this is the real challenge.

The role played by governments in non-formal education depends on their commitment to the basic education policy. The challenges of adult education and training relate not only to the changing world of work but also to educational policies whose action or lack thereof generate or fail to develop educational systems that meet the learning needs of youth. On the other hand, it is necessary to ask whether the lower end of the informal sector is better served by educational policies that are integrated in economic and social policies.

At present there are only a few major national initiatives bearing on the informal sector. Hence it is important for young people and adults to sensitise the government to their problems, to develop a multi-sectoral policy and to implement it in a decentralised way. While many countries are planning major national programmes for youth and adults who have not completed lower secondary school, in many other countries adult basic education has yet to be made a legal right and made available to all who want such education, nor has funding for basic education been provided.

Partnerships between State, Civil Society and Private Sector

While programmatic activity in the informal and the non-formal educational sectors may be seen as lying outside any formal policy framework, private sector involvement has not been particularly forthcoming in favour of education and training which reflects the conditions of street workers, garbage workers, self-employed women and women construction workers. There have been only a few cases in which sustainable partnerships have been possible between the business sector and the poor and in which these partnerships are guided by business interests rather than simply by charity.

In recent years partnerships between the state and civil society have emerged, but they still need to be forged at the systemic level if any amount of upscaling is to be achieved. The challenge lies in the capacity of collective bodies and community associations to present proposals to the state for training and education in the face of the new forms of the production and organisation of goods and services. One way may be for governments to invite interested parties to bid for public money to fund training and education for the informal sector and to participate in public policy.

There are good reasons for maintaining that governments should identify the most successful NGOs and groups to collaborate closely with them in training and skill development. Appropriate policies in this direction are urgently needed because it is not possible for formal institutions and governmental departments to undertake this task directly. While the state should mediate the functioning of the programmes, NGOs operating in the field should be assured that they will have relative autonomy.

Partnerships with civil society and the private sector are only possible if governments have a clear national policy on basic education for meeting the livelihood needs of the majority of the population engaged in the informal sector.

Continuing Education and the Demand for New Basic Skills

Many people in the informal sector, particularly those with few education and skill assets, still lack access to continuing training. The ongoing processes of globalisation and opening up economies as a result of liberalisation policies are likely to have a serious impact on developing countries. Most authors in this volume point out that the comparative advantage enjoyed by countries due to labour costs is seriously threatened under globalisation. Krishna and Mitra each emphasises, for instance, that the advantage of cheap labour and natural and local resources for small production units, which sustains a significant proportion of the informal sector, will not last long. The extent of new technologies, particularly in information and communication technologies, bio-technologies and micro-electronics, relevant to workers and units in the informal sector will depend on the level of skill adaptation in the sector. In light of this, the authors argue that it is value addition through technical change, skills, and organisational and entrepreneurial abilities which will increasingly determine the sustainability of livelihoods and businesses. It is here that the role of continuing or lifelong education and training strategies will determine the future of the informal sector. Training and education for the informal sector can no longer apply local standards, but must meet world standards. To achieve this, quality assurance frameworks will be required, as well as regulations, the assessment and verification of providers, assessors, the development of criteria, descriptors and benchmarks for quality assurance, and the establishment of means for attaining accreditation.

Not only globalisation and technological development but also the reality of poverty demands that new skills and technological literacy be facilitated with a view to promoting employability in the low income sector. This is necessary in order to prevent the emergence of further processes of social exclusion which threaten to result from merely addressing new targets of technological development. When embracing reform agendas, non-formal education providers therefore need to be alerted to the creation of new sectors of educational and social disadvantage. The recognition of skills and competencies, regardless of where they have been learned (formally or informally, at work or at home or in the community), is likely to improve lifelong learning for all.

Meeting these challenges will largely depend on the capacities of national and sub-regional capacity to embed education and training for the informal sector within comprehensive national and global development policies and systems. The major questions which governments and social partners need to address include: What are the policy and practical measures which need to be implemented in order to overcome basic education and literacy handicaps? How should education and training become part of the government's economic and social policies? How can education and training and skills be developed on a continuous basis? How can existing training practices in enterprises and other out-of-school learning settings be exploited in transforming education and training systems and the culture of learning? What are the respective roles and commitments of stakeholders to increase investment in lifelong learning opportunities that are accessible to all? What role should the international community play in promoting improved education and training for the informal sector?

This book is concerned with the ways in which education and skills development prepare individuals and communities for decent work and sustainable informal sector activities. It views this in the context of the importance of developing appropriate policies and a proper institutional environment. Most significantly this book is concerned with demonstrating that such a development can be successful only to the extent that it reflects the innovations, initiatives and approaches emerging from the informal sector itself and the directions already taken by it.

REFERENCES

Bagnall, R. G. (2003). *Enhancing income generation through adult education. A comparative study*. Brisbane: Australian Academic Press.

Burckhardt, G. (1997). The acquisition of competencies by women in the urban informal sector in Rwanda. *Education, 55–56*, 111–30.

Coombs, P. H. (1968). *The world educational crisis: A systems analysis*. New York: Oxford University Press.

Corvalan, O. (1997). Introduction. *Education, 55–56*, 9–21.

Delors, J., et al. (1996). *Learning: The treasure within*. Report to UNESCO of the International Commission on Education for the Twenty-first Century. Paris: UNESCO.

Commission of the European Communities. (2000). *A memorandum on lifelong learning*. Brussels: Commission Staff Working Paper.

Faltin, G. (1999). Competencies for innovative entrepreneurship. In M. Singh (ed.), *Adult learning and the world of work* (pp. 189–204). Hamburg: UIE.

Gallart, M. A. (2001). Poverty, youth and training: A study on four countries in Latin America. *Compare, 31:1*, 113–28.

ILO. (1998). *World employment report*. Geneva: ILO.

Institute for Scientific Co-operation (ed.). (1997). *Focus: Education and Training for the Informal Sector*, in *Education, 55–56.*

Ouane, A. (2002). Adult learning: Emerging issues and lessons to be learned. In M. Singh (ed.), *Institutionalising lifelong learning: Creating conducive environments for adult learning in the Asian context* (pp. 17–21). Hamburg: UIE.

UIE. (1997). *The Hamburg declaration and the agenda for the future*. Hamburg: UIE.

UNDP. (2001). *Human development report 2001: Making new technologies work for human development*. New York: UNDP

UNESCO. (2002). *EFA global monitoring report: Education for all. Is the world on track?* Paris: UNESCO.

UNESCO. (2000). *Dakar world education forum*. Paris: UNESCO.

UNESCO. (1990). *The Jomtien declaration on education for all*. Paris: UNESCO.

UNESCO. (1999). *Recommendation of the Second International Congress on Technical and Vocational Education*. Paris: UNESCO.

SECTION 1:

CROSS-CUTTING THEMES

SCHOOLING AND BASIC SKILLS: TRAINING PROGRAMMES AND CHALLENGES IN THE INFORMAL SECTOR: LATIN AMERICA

Enrique Pieck

LITERACY AND SCHOOLING LEVELS: WHAT ARE WE TALKING ABOUT?

The concepts 'literacy' and 'schooling' raise a number of questions concerning their relative importance, ranging from what is understood by literacy and schooling to what their purpose is in today's world and what their relationship is to the labour market. What are the benefits of schooling? To what extent does school prepare one for life? What are the implications of not being schooled or literate in this modern world? Schools are supposed to impart a variety of basic skills that will allow individuals to function adequately both socially and in the market place. To what extent have schools accomplished this? These are some of the questions addressed in this paper[1] on educational issues in the Latin American context.

A first consideration is to look at literacy and schooling from the perspective of those who lack it, that is, the most disadvantaged social groups, which also have the lowest levels of education. The so-called educational gap is the widest among the lowest income groups: almost 200 million Latin Americans over the age of 15 have not completed basic education, among them approximately 14 percent cannot read or write; in other words, they are absolute illiterates.

A second consideration addresses the question of equivalence that is assumed to exist among the terms literacy and schooling and basic skills, meaning the minimal knowledge and abilities (language, communication and mathematical skills) needed to cope in a social setting. In fact, literacy here relates to the extent to which the population with access to and several years of education has acquired basic skills or functional literacy. Along these lines, the findings of a recent research initiative conducted in seven Latin American countries reveal that 'in every domain, 50 percent of individuals who have completed six or seven years of schooling place in Levels 1 and 2—of the four levels covered by this research' (Infante, 2000, p. 180). Here literacy refers to skills and knowledge demanded by practically every country in the context of globalisation and technological development, including speaking a second language, computer skills and (at the very least) familiarity with a scientific language.

This paper focuses on several pivotal questions. How are the problems associated with basic skills management to be solved? If the lowest schooling levels and early insertion in the labour market occur in the lower income sectors, how well-prepared are these sectors to function adequately in the labour market? In terms of

Madhu Singh, (ed.), Meeting Basic Learning Needs in the informal Sector, 25-42.

basic skills training, what are the challenges that face the school system? What educational and occupational strategies have been implemented to help youth, adults, women, peasants, indigenous populations, migrants and other disadvantaged segments of the population to become productively integrated into the labour market? What lessons have we learned from them?

In order to address each of these basic questions, this paper has been divided into several sections. A brief introductory overview of a number of educational indicators in Latin America is followed by the challenges that skills training initiatives must address in this region. A third section briefly outlines the trend that has accompanied the recent concern with making occupational training programmes available in deprived sectors, with special emphasis on young people. In closing, this paper addresses the pivotal issue, namely key considerations for the formulation of productive insertion policies inspired by lessons and contributions emerging from various projects undertaken in the region.

A STARTING POINT: SHREDS OF LITERACY AND SCHOOLING IN LATIN AMERICA

Despite the important progress made in the 1990s, education in Latin America is still a rather gloomy affair. While basic education coverage has been recognised as near universal, important gaps in universal coverage still remain, particularly in rural areas. At present, educational systems seem more concerned with the quality of education and ensuring its relevance and capacity to deliver the skills that are necessary to fare well in life. However, statistics are not encouraging in this area. Brunner (2000), who synthesises the educational problems affecting the region, helps us to gain some perspective and reflect upon the challenges that have yet to be met.

At the regional level education lags behind, is underdeveloped or partly developed in the best of cases. In some countries coverage is wanting and exclusion is high; capacity to compensate for the cultural deficits of children and youth from underprivileged homes is scant; high repetition and dropout rates translate into substantial wastage; learning outcomes are poor; there are limited human resources and educational materials, which are usually mismanaged and/or misused within the system; articulation mechanisms among and between the various levels of the educational system and its environment are weak, particularly when it comes to the labour market; the educational level of the labour force aged 25 or older is mediocre (averaging five years) and 14 percent of the population is mired in illiteracy; there are marked differences in education between the richer 10 percent (11 years or more) and the poorer 30 percent (fewer than four years) of the population; and the generation of knowledge aimed at improving the teaching/learning processes and promoting public policies for the sector is scarce.

In light of a substantial increase in the educational coverage in a large number of countries, the percentage of the population currently accessing the middle level of education[2]—a level which in many countries represents the upper threshold for most—has also risen. The implications to be drawn from this fact seem fairly straightforward. Since this level frequently represents the last rung on the educational ladder, at least in terms of the lower income sectors, the challenges it poses and the support it calls for are quite evident. Research conducted in Mexico has revealed that while 12 percent of non-poor youth between the ages of 20 and 24 have completed tertiary education, in the case of disadvantaged youth this figure drops to 7.3 percent (Pieck, 2000). The challenge therefore lies essentially in providing basic skills training that facilitate successful performance in the workplace and in reinforcing this middle level through training which focuses on minimal occupational skills, which would help to improve early insertion in the market place. Clearly, investing in human resources training while the individual is still in the second cycle of formal education makes considerably more sense than investing later in compensatory education (ECLAC, 2000b, p. 109). Research findings on functional literacy levels point to the lack of quality that is evident in the delivery of basic and secondary education. Some have gone so far as to claim that completion of the school cycle does not necessarily guarantee that the individual will have a real mastery of reading, writing and mathematical skills, which is to say, the teaching imparted at schools is insufficient to cope with the demands imposed by the school's own environment (Infante, 2000, p. 181).

A report on an OECD study (quoted in Milos, 2000) which describes and compares basic adult skills in 20 countries revealed, in connection with Chile, the staggering fact that more than half of the adult population does not understand what it reads and is limited to making basic inferences from printed material. These deficits become more severe in the area of mathematical calculations, and one would expect to see even further deterioration in sections of the population where basic education is seldom completed or the quality of education is low—that is, usually in poverty stricken homes. If this is Chile's reality, countries with lower educational levels and living standards would fare even worse. What, then, is the good of receiving an education? What problems prevent the educational system from fulfilling its primary mission, namely delivering minimal basic skills? Additionally, if no guarantee can be given that schools do perform this basic function, what can we expect from sectors of the population which do not have access to education, or those which are forced to resort to a marginal source of education of dubious quality?

UNDER THE EQUITY PRISM

Seen from the perspective of equity, students from lower income families tend to exhibit the lowest levels of academic achievement. In the context of the existing relationship between education and the replication of poverty, studies show a positive correlation between the education of parents and that of their children. In other words, the likelihood of acquiring adequate minimal education is closely linked to the parents' educational background and income level in poor households. In the case of women's education, it has been shown that a significant correlation with improved family health and academic achievement exists. It has been found that parents of 80 percent of urban youths have completed less than ten years of schooling; in fact, between 60 and 80 percent of these adults fall short of the basic educational threshold required to access well-being levels (ECLAC, 2000b, p. 101). What, then, are the chances for individuals to forge ahead? Today only 20 percent of youths whose parents do not complete primary education finish secondary education. However, among individuals whose parents completed at least 10 years of education, this percentage rises to more than 60 percent.

Data from another regional research (Gallart, 2000) conducted in five Latin American countries point to the impact of poverty on the academic achievements of youth. The data highlight that the attendance rates, the average school years completed and the percentage of individuals with secondary education, is substantially lower among the poor than the non-poor. Attaining seven years of basic education is no small achievement in the region. However, here again the differences between the poor and the non-poor are dramatic: approximately twice as many disadvantaged individuals have failed to complete more than six years of education. In terms of employment, the poor also bear the brunt of unemployment, with doubling or more than doubling unemployment figures.

One of the major challenges is to facilitate the productive insertion of groups living in deprived areas. This requires that one reflect on the restrictions that currently exist in the formal labour market and question the extent to which the formal educational system prepares the individual for the world of work and the relevance of the skills acquired. It also evokes the traditional concern with the classic imbalance between the supply of education and the demands of the labour market.

A glance at the relationship between education and work reveals that a large portion of the gainfully employed population is not sufficiently educated to move beyond the income levels associated with the lower occupational categories. Also, even if educational inequities are high among social strata in the region, they are nevertheless lower than inequities regarding income levels (ECLAC, 2000a). An important question is how much schooling is needed in order to ensure a productive insertion that allows one to break away from the poverty cycle and move beyond the lower levels of occupational income? According to the Economic Commission for Latin America and the Caribbean (ECLAC), ten years of schooling represents the minimal threshold required if education is to play a significant role. It is no mere coincidence that the lower tiers of the labour market (unskilled workers, farmers, service sector workers) include individuals with less than ten years of schooling and whose incomes average approximately 2.5 times the poverty line. Based on estimates prepared by this ECLAC, it takes 12 years of education to have a 90 percent chance of staying out of—or moving beyond—poverty (ECLAC, 2000b, p. 105). However, as pointed out earlier, achieving seven years of basic education in the region is no small accomplishment (Gallart, 2000). Where does hope lie for these populations?

From the above it can be said that, in connection with the question of basic skills, the red flares lie in the underprivileged segments of populations. This sheds light on the acute problems in the educational system which prevent schools from assisting individuals, especially those from lower income groups, to acquire basic skills. It also highlights the fact that there are large segments of the population which never go beyond basic education and groups which are already part of the educational gap, have dropped out of school, or exhibit critical deficits in basic skills acquisition and find themselves in dire need of the skills that would ensure their insertion into productive activities. It has become painfully clear that the limited access of lower income groups to good quality instruction has restricted access to better paying jobs. It has also become clear that there is a need to formulate training, occupational and educational strategies to compensate for the educational deficits characteristic of these groups. How are we to deal with these challenges? What strategies should be used?

TWO ORIENTATIONS GUIDING SKILLS TRAINING POLICIES

The desire to impart critical basic skills implies that one first distinguish between two groups: (i) those who are part of the formal educational system and (ii) those who are not part of that system, that is, those who have dropped out and lag behind others from an educational point of view. Regarding the educational needs of the first group, the focus needs to be on basic skills and those abilities derived from the processes of globalisation and technological development. Regarding the second group, it is necessary to update basic skills and impart occupational training, since it is ultimately—though not solely—the labour realm which determines the educational demands and needs of this group.

For *those attending school, especially for more vulnerable groups*, the challenge is to establish a set of measures at the basic level of education. In recent years a number of programmes aimed at enhancing the quality of education have been formulated as a strategy to rid the educational system of inequality and inequity. Many of these strategies have been steered by a positive criterion of discrimination—giving more to those who have less—as a means of equalising the educational status of large groups of the population. In this field of education various initiatives have been undertaken by private stakeholders, popular education movements and NGOs, as well as by government institutions. The strategies adopted reflect the different ways the problem has been perceived. While some programmes have attempted to compensate for the impoverishment under which schools in lower income areas operate by upgrading their infrastructure, equipment and materials, others have been geared towards the teacher as a way of spurring better educational practices; still others have sought to incorporate curricular innovations; finally, there are those that favour economic support initiatives (scholarships, school breakfasts, and so forth) intended to mitigate the dearth of resources afflicting these groups and help prolong the permanence of the student population in the educational system by lowering repetition and dropout rates (Jacinto, 1999).

On the subject of quality and equity of the educational system it may be said that educational reforms may prove insufficient if limited exclusively to the internal curricular, administrative and financial aspects of a school. To assess their real impact and counteract the negative effects produced by poverty, wider links to social policies are needed (ECLAC, 2000c). Given the economic needs of lower income households, improving the quality of education alone is neither enough to keep youths from dropping out nor to prevent them from repeating.

Basic education initiatives seek to counteract the condition of exclusion and forlornness which has been imposed on some groups of the population living in poverty. Experiences such as 'Fe y Alegría' (Faith and Happiness), Colombia's Escuela Nueva and the educational activity of Mexico's Consejo Nacional de Fomento Educativo (CONAFE) represent alternative and compensatory modalities intended to offer these segments of the population a higher quality of educational provision and expand coverage in isolated areas.

For *those who have dropped out of the formal educational system*, their lack of literacy and schooling problems surface as severe deficits when it comes to the use of basic skills. Again, this condition affects essentially the disadvantaged groups, which face a different set of challenges regarding their integration into the labour market. Productive integration into the market represents a major and immediate challenge and entails in turn the provision of basic skills and occupational training. Therefore, any mention of schooling and literacy points to the need to educate members of these groups in life skills, that is, in abilities that bear specifically on the labour world.

Within this population group, young people represent a particularly vulnerable segment that demands prompt action and differential strategies. From a labour standpoint, their situation contrasts markedly with that of other groups, considering the fact that their unemployment rates have become twice that of the entire working population. According to a report on youth employment published by Panorama Laboral 2000 para América Latina (Cinterfor/ILO, 2001), in the 1990s both unemployment and underemployment rates among youth (aged 15 to 24) took a turn for the worse, rising from 7.9 to 16 percent in ten years. Of those fortunate enough to have joined the workforce, 6 out of 10 lost their jobs. Clearly insertion into the labour market poses tremendous problems for young people. The fact that for every 100 individuals hired during the decade 7 were youths and 93 were adults is quite disturbing. In addition, their average wages represent 43 percent of those paid to adults. It has been argued that one of the major problems confronted by young people entering the labour market is underemployment, a reflection of the minimal benefits derived from their acquired education (Muñoz Izquierdo, 2001). For disadvantaged youth, the most recurrent alternatives are found in the informal sector (where employment has risen to 2.5 percent) with the attendant problems associated with deficits in basic and occupational skills mentioned earlier. These problems make their insertion into the labour world even more traumatic and should be addressed in training programmes.

With regard to this group, initiatives have been advanced in the realm of nonformal education and training programmes and within vocational training institutes. The major task of these educational modalities is to facilitate the successful insertion of young people and adults from lower income groups into productive activities. What has been done in this area? To what extent have occupational training strategies focused on the lot of the underprivileged?

BREAKING NEW GROUND: IN SEARCH OF TRAINING STRATEGIES FOR THE DISADVANTAGED

Training programmes designed to meet the needs of young people and adults from lower income populations are not plentiful (King, 1988). These sectors have traditionally been excluded from such programmes. While vocational training institutes have neglected these sectors in their programmes, adult education has failed to incorporate the work component into its activities. With very few exceptions, and apart from a new-found concern on the part of some institutions to bring occupational training closer to poor, this kind of training has become a veritable 'no man's land' in underprivileged sectors (Pieck, 1998). Occupational training initiatives have been targeted primarily at the formal sector of the economy, forgetting that vast numbers of Latin Americans live in poverty (40 percent in Mexico, 80 percent in Honduras, to mention just two instances) and engage in some kind of economic activity, essentially in the informal sector. However, past failures have shown that programmes are urgently needed which are suited and responsive to the necessities and characteristics of the contexts of disadvantaged sectors (Leonardos, 1999; Pieck, 2000). Unfortunately, as pointed out by Bennell (1999), the role technical and vocational training may play in eradicating poverty has been underestimated within the framework of social strategies adopted by developing countries, even if rhetoric acknowledges technical training as an essential component of public policy.

In recent years—perhaps to counteract the structural adjustment programmes that typified the past decade—greater interest in developing programmes for these vulnerable groups has been evinced. These programmes range from those of an essentially compensatory nature to the more comprehensive initiatives that aim to incorporate these populations into their national development plans.[3] In time, the lessons learned have broken through narrow-minded views whose only strategy was to rely on mere training, the idea being that technical courses would have the necessary power to link the population to their labour world. These traditional occupational training projects have raised questions about the short-sightedness of training strategies, both in terms of programme design and objectives, especially in the context of volatile markets. Another matter of concern is the need to acknowledge that the demand for qualifications through training programmes have become insufficient as the sole criterion of positive discrimination, particularly in markets where the greater complexity of production technologies does not necessarily go hand in hand with higher qualification requirements (Valdés, 2001).

The need to think of professional training in a broad sense and not simply as occupational training alone has emerged from both past successes and past failures. Growing importance is being attached to focusing on cultural issues. Emphasis is being put on teacher training and on the need to design comprehensive curricula. Part of this new-found holistic approach derives from the need to integrate the objectives of occupational and social inclusion. In the past there was a tension between concerns of occupational objectives and those associated with housing, health, education and other social welfare concerns that are crucial for the success of training and productive strategies. There is a need to adopt a comprehensive approach to the actions undertaken and to establish co-ordination mechanisms among the various levels and stakeholders.

SOME CRITERIA FOR POLICY DESIGN

Some criteria can serve as guiding principles for developing training policies in deprived sectors. The following considerations are derived from experiences in various countries in Latin America.

Diversity, Equity and Quality: Relevant Answers to the Different Population Groups

The different kinds of populations, their cultural and social diversity and the nature of their learning demands require a more accurate definition of what is commonly understood by 'disadvantaged groups'. A diversity in the types of training intervention is necessary. In recent years the importance of addressing the heterogeneity of the population making up the underprivileged sectors has been pointed out repeatedly. While some initiatives carried out by government and non-governmental organisations have used focal strategies as a key criterion in the elaboration and development of programmes (some examples are INA, POCET, the Chile Joven Project, Brazil's Capacitacao Solidaria—see Box 1, below), a more global, longer-term strategy is needed which includes structured plans and actions, as well as a clear view of the target population and the features each programme should include in order to respond adequately—both in the long and the short term—to the educational needs of disadvantaged groups, be they peasants, migrants, rural women or urban youth. It implies the need to enrich the programmes with a view to maximising their impact on each of the target groups. Furthermore, it demands a clear understanding of requirements based on the needs and characteristics of the subjects and their environments. Clearly, a programme aimed at the occupational training of disadvantaged urban youth will require educational re-insertion and comprehensive vocational training strategies, complementary social programmes in fields such as health and recreation, as well as in work support programmes. Likewise, programmes aimed at attaining the productive insertion of indigenous women will need an accurate description of their contexts and potential, their age range and the nature of their expectations. It also requires the co-ordination of these programmes with their daily activities.

Educational policies thus conceived fall within the realm of positive discrimination and are underpinned by differential strategies (Schmelkes, 1996). In other words, they should take into account approaches that offer the lower income population a chance to access a quality educational supply that is sensitive to their needs and interests, while granting them an opportunity to advance by means of higher education and occupational training initiatives.

In this way underprivileged segments of the population would benefit from multiple educational opportunities through access to: (i) diverse programmes and alternatives in the various contexts, (ii) the possibility of moving freely among them and (iii) viable mechanisms to advance to higher levels of education.

Box 1. Capacitacao Solidaria and Voluntary Civil Service

Brazil's Capacitacao Solidaria and Voluntary Civil Service (SCV) programmes are examples of recent and innovative experiences in the area of occupational training for youths from lower income backgrounds who have not had much education. In Capacitacao Solidaria's programmes, articulation with the various institutions plays an important role since training strategies are supported by training organisations that help to identify the most suitable work opportunities. The courses offered are organised in various modules that seek to re-insert and/or prolong the permanence of young people in formal education and teach the theoretical and practical aspects of occupational skills. Likewise, the SCV combines strategies for the enhancement of education, professional training and delivery of community services (Leite, 2001; De Avila, 2001).

For Permanent Education

Permanent education implies the establishment of educational and training systems that favour lifelong educational strategies and are linked to the development of educational and training paths at various levels. It points to the necessity of filling a number of voids within the system—for example, by creating vocational training and general education paths beyond the compulsory stage, introducing work-related experiences at the compulsory stage, designing modular systems so that courses given at different levels and through modalities of education and training may be combined, establishing secondary education that allows for technical and academic achievement, opening diversified paths to higher education that interconnect with other systems and levels. Of crucial importance here is the development of technical education, an issue undoubtedly still unresolved in numerous countries and calls for the incorporation of important components of occupational training and culture into mainstream education. It suggests the importance of generating flexible and diverse links between the formal and informal sectors which are sensitive to the educational and occupational trajectories of underprivileged groups. Proposals of this sort are urgently needed in the region, particularly where vast segments of the population lack basic skills training and where the last years of basic education is nowadays the upper threshold in a large number of countries before people join the labour force.

The Two Sides of the Coin and their Demands[4]

Concern for formative strategies such as basic education aimed at productive insertion needs to be seen in the context of the dichotomous world where globalisation and polarisation coexist. There are two essential dimensions to the problems that socially disadvantaged groups have to confront: (i) international competitiveness and globalisation and (ii) social integration and exclusion (Gallart et al., 1996; Jacinto & Gallart, 1998). On the one hand, the mutations of the labour world resulting from the advent of new technologies and production patterns demand that special emphasis be given to an education that promotes skills and aptitudes which may facilitate both insertion into the labour market and social mobility. On the other, spiralling unemployment, a precarious labour market and endemic poverty levels point to the essential task of developing the skills that will allow men and women to become productive members of society. In developing countries, it is not just a question of finding work but also one of guaranteeing sustenance and sustainable livelihoods to all concerned.

In view of these two scenarios, the tasks that fall to technical and vocational training and education in underprivileged sectors should focus on: (i) adapting and responding to the various contexts and needs of marginalised sectors by making available relevant and high quality education, and (ii) facilitating access to new skills and technological literacy in order to promote employability among low income sectors and to prevent the emergence of further social exclusion processes. On the one hand, the idea is not to keep underprivileged groups from accessing new skills. Rather, they should be given the opportunity either to join the formal labour market or to continue on to higher levels of education. On the other, every effort should be made to offer lower income groups the tools they require to enable their productive insertion by providing them with high quality basic education which is congruent with local needs and labour characteristics.

Catering to the Impoverished Sectors: What Does It Entail?

While most training programmes represent the demands of the formal economy and market, attention must be paid to the fact that a large percentage of people, particularly the young, eventually settle in the informal sector of the economy. This sector calls for a very specific type of learning which training programmes will have to confront.

Among the underprivileged segments of the population, the labour world takes on a specificity of its own which will ultimately define the characteristics that any programme should have if it wishes to meet the training needs of this sector. Work acquires a specific meaning in poor areas, especially in rural areas, where it is closely linked to the physical environment and to survival strategies. In this distinct setting, productive insertion demands relevant training programmes capable of satisfying their particular economic survival (Pieck, 2000).

This type of strategy, particularly when directed at a population's underprivileged groups, makes necessary a reformulation of the notions of work, employment, employability and productivity. These terms do not necessarily follow the logic of the formal labour market, nor do they imply that the skills being promoted are necessarily linked to the technologically oriented sectors. The strategies must consider the characteristics and needs of the specific groups, and programmes must heed the nature and features of their contexts—as well as the particular training needs of the populations living in impoverished areas. Clearly, at this level quality becomes directly equated with the relevance of the contribution the programmes make to the specific needs of the various population groups. In other words, the success of a programme will be contingent upon how relevant the acquired skills actually prove to be in the workplace and whether individuals use these skills in economically productive ways (McLaughlin, 1990).

Problems Associated with Small Business Endeavours

On the subject of promoting small businesses in the informal sector, some precautions are in order, since training in the informal sector raises some questions worth reflecting upon. One of them has to do with the reproduction of self-employment under precarious conditions. We are well aware of its limitations in terms of age, work experience, lack of capital, limited social networks, etc., which often translate into high-risk and unrealistic ventures for low-income youths (Ramirez, 2000; Messina, 2001). Be that as it may, it is important to recognise that given the restrictions of the formal labour market a large number of young people will enter the informal sector one way or another. This implies that training programmes need to incorporate curricula elements designed to impart interdisciplinary skills that are common to both the formal and the informal markets.

In the case of adults, where there is a greater chance of finding technical skills and practical experience, training programmes must adopt on-the-job training strategies and be closely linked to the particular needs of the economic/productive activities of that sector of the population (Vielle, 1995). A training strategy thus conceived has the capability of responding to the actual concerns of the people, a feature not too often found in training programmes. Mexico's CIMO (see Box 2, below) and some of Colombia's SENA programmes illustrate cases in which training strategies have been transferred directly to the productive groups.

The Integral Dimension of Every Economic/Productive Activity

The integral dimension of any productive insertion endeavour is an essential component of any occupational training strategy. Meeting a project's immediate demands (e.g. loans, specific courses) will not accomplish much in the absence of a diagnosis that can provide a holistic solution to the problems affecting the various projects of a specific population. In this regard, addressing these projects from the point of view of dimensions such as organisation, production, commercialisation, technical processes, accounting systems and division of labour, regardless of the magnitude of the particular business endeavour, is of paramount importance. In some cases support may come to small operators in the guise of technical assistance, in others it may translate into accounting services for projects under consolidation. As a result, technical training becomes a training/consultantship effort, which approaches potential projects from an integrative perspective. That is to say, it does not merely offer an immediate response to a project's technical or economic need but emphasises the way in which the support or funds are being efficiently used. In other words, it becomes a response based on an integrated analysis of the economic and productive activity, and results in an improvement plan designed to contribute solutions capable of steering any business pursuit in the direction of an economic development project. The integrated perspective of training programmes evinces the insufficiency of technical training initiatives and funding strategies, taken as isolated components. This basic premise—an integral view of projects—has been conspicuously absent from the development of technical training programmes aimed at deprived sectors. This has resulted in an educational supply that elicits no interest beyond the boundaries of the course itself and, on occasion, appears irrelevant and apathetic to the impact of the promoted courses.

Box 2. Integral Quality and Modernisation (CIMO)

A meaningful experience in terms of how training in underprivileged sectors has been conceived and is applied is Mexico's Calidad Integral y Modernización (CIMO). Its strategy—a novel approach in the realm of training strategies—is based on previously conducted integral diagnoses, availability of training courses and process-related advisory services (accounting, organisational, and commercialisation and consultantships), features that set it apart from other institutions. The starting point is a strategy that focuses on a work initiative, which revolves around the various projects developed by the very people living in these areas. However, the difference is that it not only supports the specific training needs of a particular project but provides training based on an integral view of the economic project. Meeting a specific technical need or mobilising financial resources through loans is simply not enough. The support provided must form part of an integral training strategy designed to shepherd the project through its various phases. CIMO's training strategy—clearly integral in nature—represents a spearhead in the field of adult education and occupational training. From the standpoint of adult education it creates an original link to productive endeavours, while in terms of occupational training it pioneers efforts in underprivileged sectors.

Articulation of Training with Basic Education

A key consideration in occupational training for deprived sectors is the importance given to basic education conceived as a pre-requisite for occupational training and as the cornerstone of permanent education. Basic education is the chief guarantee of the basic skills demanded by employability. In this regard, it is important that occupational training programmes include school re-insertion strategies, especially when one considers the deficits exhibited by youth from vulnerable sectors. It is important to articulate occupational training initiatives with basic education and to devise plans which create linkages between the different educational strategies and schools so that students in training may, at the same time, complement their basic education. In this respect, articulation strategies between both systems are indispensable. While this is a foremost preoccupation of the literature and research, much of the road still remains untraveled. With the notable exceptions, for example, of Honduras's POCET and Brazil's Capacitacao Solidaria (see Box 3, below), few undertakings have cared to incorporate basic education components into their curricular strategies and plans. In other instances this has been accomplished through informal institutional agreements whereby students fill in their basic education voids while involved in occupational training programmes. Building bridges between initiatives by both types of institutions—educational and training—are essential to the drafting of such agreements.

Box 3. Experiences Emerging from Mexico's Centro de Estudios para el Desarrollo Rural (CESDER) and Honduras's Programa de Educación para el Trabajo (POCET).

The significance of Mexico's Centro de Estudios para el Desarrollo Rural (Study Centre for Rural Development) lies in the double purpose it serves for youths living in impoverished areas. On the one hand, it represents a programme that allows the insertion and re-insertion of young people into the formal educational system in areas where these types of service are either in short supply or non-existent. Through this mechanism, young people are given the option to continue their education at higher levels if that is their wish. On the other hand, it incorporates into high school curriculum an occupational training option where the concepts of work and employability become relative and relevant through links with the local context. Therefore, the occupational training offered by the programme is not keyed to the formal labour market but to communal economic undertakings (e.g. farming and ranching activities and small business endeavours).

Within the Central American context, Honduras's POCET emerges as an attempt to narrow the links between formal and non-formal education and the world of work. This suggests the significance of understanding that formal education can only find solutions to part of the educational problem and, consequently, the importance that both systems, formal and non formal, reinforce their ties to the labour world and create internal mechanisms designed to complement one another. The project envisages education for work as a permanent and ongoing non-formal adult education process which, based on the characteristics and needs of the population, provides the formative elements human beings need in order to embark on productive endeavours. The methodological proposal has been geared towards the adult. From a strictly remedial educational approach, the project is metamorphosing into a type of functional education responsive to the needs and circumstances of adults, one that touches on occupational training and culminates in education for development through work-related initiatives.

The education for work proposed by POCET aims to combine literacy and basic education components with those characteristic of occupational training, while simultaneously ensuring the fulfilment of educational processes in productive work through concrete activities and the establishment of self-managed communal and inter-communal production associations. As with CESDER, a significant aspect of this experience is the value assigned to work-related practices in deprived environments. In the particular case of CESDER, the possibility of accessing a higher level of education it has opened to lower income youths is noteworthy.

The Necessary Confluence between Sectors

Among the training strategies aimed at underprivileged groups, the co-ordination of programmes with institutions from different sectors is currently considered a *sine qua non*. In fact it is the driving force behind the manifold possibilities of technical training. It is through co-ordination activities with institutions concerned with finance, organisational matters and commercial activities that the knowledge acquired through training will lead to productive insertion and the creation and development of small business endeavours. This crucial factor guarantees that the various programmes will have a positive impact on the expansion of economic activities and help in turn to improve the target population's living conditions. The importance of addressing the training of deprived sectors from an intersectoral perspective is supported by the basic premise that training in and of itself is not enough, and through the recognition that the promotion of social inequality is not restricted to the educational domain. Thus the importance of dealing with problems from various fronts (Valdés, 2001) is highlighted.

Along these same lines—and on the assumption that any educational process will be intertwined with various dimensions—integration becomes an indispensable component of training policies. Integration also points to the importance of acknowledging that the inherent complexity of the groups involved requires a multi-faceted approach whereby health, housing, recreation and so forth are also taken into account, since training alone or simple insertion in the labour market will neither guarantee social insertion nor the outcomes that training programmes anticipate. A case in point is the design of occupational training programmes aimed at marginal urban youths which rely on co-ordination efforts with social programmes to ensure that the curriculum will also contribute to the resolution of social and cultural issues. It is not simply a matter of integrating them into technical training courses, but one of seeking the participation of different sectors and organisations in the fields of education, labour and health. This becomes indispensable just as much as the creation of links to women, youth and peasant organisations, labour unions, etc. The idea is to formulate joint strategies and offer integral answers to problems that must necessarily be dealt with from various fronts.

Box 4. Integral Education Centre (CEI)

Brazil's CEI is a labour training centre catering to disadvantaged youths. Its programmes are supported by the integrity that characterises their actions and by intersectoral co-operation. The courses offered cover a range of possibilities which include driving instruction, music, mechanics, physical education instruction, etc. Thanks to various donations, in addition to the commercial links to private and public enterprises established by the different co-operatives created within the CEI, the centre does not depend on government funding. The CEI has also generated employment opportunities and supported its students with on-the-job training in public and private enterprises (quoted by Leonardos, 1999).

Tensions between Efficiency and Equity

A distinct tension between programmes is that generated by efficiency versus equity. The process of selecting young people who will participate in training and support programmes represents a typical case. It is a common practice that the filters used in the selection process—for the sake of the efficiency of the programme—place priority on youths who are not necessarily from the poorer sectors (Messina, 2001). Thus it is not unusual to find that that the rational criteria adopted by institutions, programmes and funding agencies are at cross-purposes with the guidelines for integrating disadvantaged youths. The rationales run counter to each other and call into question the scope and objectives of equity promoting programmes.

Practical Innovations: Upgrading Non-Formal Education

While non-formal education programmes contribute to alleviating the harsh economic conditions that prevail in these communities and may prove interesting to some target groups (such as women youth and adults), the marginal nature of these programmes has prevented them from both acquiring the required level of quality and becoming legitimate sources of occupational training. An interesting feature of these programmes is that they lie on the borderline that separates what constitutes occupational training from what does not—a fact that may lend the efforts needed to cross from one side to the other a certain amount of appeal and viability. All this should be part of a strategy intended to advance occupational training in these sectors starting from what is already there.

It could be argued, however, that innovations in the field of vocational and technical training and education could simply entail: (i) rethinking non-formal educational programmes, (ii) relying on local support and (iii) joining efforts through the combination of complementary services (Leonardos, 1999). This could well be the case of non-formal education in deprived areas—a marginal modality and the only training alternative in rural areas which are being imparted to low-income groups, involving courses of a domestic nature (cooking, manual arts, beauty-related) or trades (carpentry, blacksmithing), and are imparted to low-income groups usually in rural areas.

Raising the quality of these programmes demands inter-institutional collaboration that involves the revision of learning programmes, curricular models, teacher training initiatives and an improved infrastructure. This would facilitate the improvement of the profiles of graduating students and the generation of articulations that ensure continuous technical training, as well as the development of productive activities backed by financial, business, organisational and marketing assistance. These could be valid alternatives that could reach out to those living in that 'no man's land' represented by today's occupational training efforts in the poorer regions (Pieck, 1998; Bennell, 1999). Through their relationship with various institutions—health, early and basic education, nutrition, etc.—these programmes, rather than serving a merely social and political function, would take on real significance as a legitimate, relevant and useful educational supply, especially for rural and marginal urban women (Pieck, 1996).

Box 5. The Public Workshops of Costa Rica's Instituto Nacional de Aprendizaje

Costa Rica's Public Workshops, sponsored by the Instituto Nacional de Aprendizaje, have identified tracks for developing the potential of non-formal educational activity in deprived sectors. These workshops clearly show the viability of taking occupational training to the marginal sectors. Their underlying strategy goes beyond merely channelling technical courses to disadvantaged regions, as they perform diverse functions that include occupational training initiatives, the creation of self-employment opportunities and building links with the community. Some of the main features of the workshops are the flexibility of their teaching and learning processes, scheduling, learning sequences, and resources used. The model encourages a participatory curriculum wherein quality is narrowly associated with the relevance the imparted knowledge has to the reality of the students. Thus training can either transcend or have an impact on the creation of productive units based on the concept of self-employment. Another virtue of the Public Workshops is the support they elicit through substantial inter-institutional co-ordination activities where they function as a neural point of convergence for community-related activities. Lastly, an important aspect of these workshops is their incorporation into professional training centres, a feature that allows those so inclined to further their training. In the field of adult education, non-formal education programmes and the workshops and mobile units sponsored by professional training institutes would have a greater impact in deprived sectors if the needed modifications were actively promoted.

COROLLARY

The review of some experiences and indicators for designing educational and training programmes for disadvantaged segments of society suggests a set of considerations in connection with *sine qua non* aspects of policy formulation and with the myths surrounding such programmes. We have seen that basic education or enhancing the quality of training courses is simply not enough. Neither the mere delivery of technical training courses nor the positive discrimination criteria that ignore contextual variables is alone sufficient.

The lessons learned make it clear that an integral approach is indispensable. They highlight interventions in different sectors, and articulations among the different systems and subsystems. They also imply a greater appreciation of the role played by occupational training in responding to such antithetical needs as modernisation and poverty. They also stress the importance of taking into account the nature of and needs inherent in impoverished environments, as well as the urgent need for programmes to be relevant—particularly when the educational supply is being directed at deprived areas. Honduras's POCET, Mexico's CESDER and Costa Rica's INA, for example, represent training strategies that have remained true to this orientation. Perhaps one of the vital elements of these initiatives is the importance of combining the context with the learning needs. The inescapable conclusion is that occupational training in these sectors requires intervention mechanisms other than those intended for the formal market.

Finally, the evidence of deficits in basic skills and the resultant lack of employability make mandatory that any occupational training programme include articulations between technical and basic skills as part of its curriculum. Likewise, it emphasises the importance of developing articulations between educational and technical training systems, as well as between formal and non-formal modalities, in order to respond to flexible and shifting itineraries characteristic of a population that moves between one system and another, a population that has no other way of harmonising their own educational and labour trajectories.

Clearly what is needed today is a strategy capable of reconciling policy in the fields of education, occupational training and employment. Today's problems suggest the need for Occupational Training Councils which would include the following among their key functions: (i) orienting and co-ordinating the initiatives of the various institutions that relate to this field, (ii) setting up links between institutions of the various sectors (NGOs, the private sector, public organisations) and (iii) helping to design methodologies and strategies capable of meeting the training needs of the informal sector. This strategy would seek to quantify the conception and practice of occupational training on the basis of the confluence of actions and actors who at present neither identify themselves with this activity nor are part of it.

NOTES

[1] Some of the basic notions used in this paper were originally presented at the Ibero-American Forum on Education and Work, 'Formación de técnicos y profesionales competentes: un futuro deseable', organised

by the Organization of Iberoamerican States (OEI) in the framework of Pedagogy 2001 (Havana, Cuba, February 5–9, 2001).

[2] The middle level is that level of schooling that follows the completion of an average of ten years of formal education.

[3] Some examples of this type of initiatives are Honduras's Programa de Educación para el Trabajo (POCET), Costa Rica's Public Workshops organised by this country's Instituto Nacional de Aprendizaje, Uruguay's Training Centres and Colombia's SENA initiatives (see below).

[4] Some of the information used in this section has been borrowed from Pieck, 2000.

REFERENCES

Bennell, P. (1999). *Learning to change: Skills development among the economically vulnerable and socially excluded developing countries*. Employment and Training Papers. Geneva: ILO.

Briasco, I. (Coord.). (2001). *Educación y trabajo para grupos desfavorecidos: Recomendaciones para la acción*. Madrid: OEI.

Brunner, J. (2000). Globalización y el futuro de la educación: precisiones, desafíos y estrategias. *Seminar on Educational Prospects in the Latin America and Caribbean region* (Santiago, Chile, August 23–25, 2000).

Cinterfor/ILO. (2001). *Informe Panorama Laboral 2000*. Montevideo: Cinterfor/ILO.

De Avila, C. M. (2001) 'Programa Capacitacao Solidaria. Una contribución para el fortalecimiento de la sociedad civil'. In E. Pieck (ed.), *Los jóvenes y el trabajo: La educación frente a la exclusión social* (pp. 269–301). México: UIA/IMJ/Cinterfor-ILO/UNICEF/Conalep/RET.

ECLAC. (2000a). *Panorama social de América Latina 1999–2000*. Santiago: ECLAC.

ECLAC. (2000b). *Equidad, desarrollo y ciudadanía*. Santiago: ECLAC.

ECLAC. (2000c). *La brecha de la equidad: Una segunda evaluación*. Santiago: ECLAC.

Gallart, M. A., et al. (1996). Adolescencia, pobreza y formación para el trabajo. In I. Konterllnik & C. Jacinto (eds.), *Adolescencia, pobreza, educación y trabajo* (pp. 95–130). Buenos Aires: Losada/UNICEF.

Infante, I. (2000). *Alfabetismo funcional en siete países de América Latina*. Santiago: UNESCO/OREALC.

Jacinto, C. (1999). *Programas de educación para jóvenes desfavorecidos. Enfoques y tendencias en América Latina?* Paris: IIPE/UNESCO.

Jacinto, C., & Gallart, M. A. (1998). *Por una segunda oportunidad: La formación para el trabajo de jóvenes vulnerable*. Montevideo: Cinterfor/RET.

King, K. (1988). Training for the informal sector in developing countries: Issues for practitioners. *Adult education and development*, *30*, 18–30.

Leite, E. (2001). La construcción participativa de una política pública: La experiencia del Servicio Civil voluntario. In E. Pieck (ed.), *Los jóvenes y el trabajo: La educación frente a la exclusión social* (pp. 303–329. México: UIA/IMJ/Cinterfor-ILO/UNICEF/Conalep/RET.

Leonardos, A. C. (1999). *Non-formal vocational training programmes for disadvantaged youth and their insertion into the world of work: Towards a framework for analysis and evaluation*. IIEP, Occasional papers. Paris: IIEP/UNESCO.

McLaughlin, S. (1990). Skill training for the informal sector: Analysing the success and limitations of support programmes. In D. Thurnham et al., (ed.), *The informal sector revisited*. Seminar on the informal sector revisited. Paris 7-9 September, 1988. Paris: OECD.

Messina, G. (2001). Modelos de formación en las microempresas: En busca de una tipología. In E. Pieck (ed.), *Los jóvenes y el trabajo: La educación frente a la exclusión social* (pp. 401–428). México: UIA/IMJ/Cinterfor-ILO/UNICEF/Conalep/RET.

Milos, P. (2000). *Una metodología para el desarrollo de competencias básicas en procesos de formación laboral para jóvenes de escasos recursos*. Santiago. (Photocopy.)

Muñoz, I. C. (2001). Implicaciones de la escolaridad en la calidad del empleo. In E. Pieck, (ed.), *Los jóvenes y el trabajo: La educación frente a la exclusión social* (pp. 155–200). México: UIA/IMJ/ Cinterfor-ILO/UNICEF/Conalep/RET.

Pieck, E. (1996). *Función social y significado de la educación comunitaria.* México: UNICEF/El Colegio Mexiquense.

Pieck, E. (1998). Educación de adultos y formación profesional: Incidencia y posibilidades en sectores de pobreza en América Latina. In C. Jacinto & M. A. Gallart (eds.), *Por una segunda oportunidad: La formación para el trabajo de jóvenes vulnerables* (pp. 187–224). Montevideo: Cinterfor/RET.

Pieck, E. (2000). Educación de jóvenes y adultos vinculada con el trabajo. In OREALC/CEAAL/CREFAL/INEA (eds.), *La educación de personas jóvenes y adultas en América Latina y el Caribe. Prioridades de acción en el siglo XXI* (pp. 102–142). Santiago: OREALC/CEAAL/CREFAL/INEA.

Ramírez, J. (2000). *La formación laboral de jóvenes pobres desempleados: Necesidad de una estrategia consistente y de un marco institucional sostenible.* Montevideo: Boletín Cinterfor/ILO # 150 (September–December 2000).

Schmelkes, S. (1996). Hacia la equidad: Innovaciones en el medio rural en América Latina. In CONAFE (ed.), *Encuentro Latinoamericano de Innovaciones Educativas en el Medio rural* (pp. 23–40). México: CONAFE.

Valdés, T. (2001). Empezar a trabajar en sociedades sin empleo: Apuntes para la orientación de los perfiles profesionales de inserción. In I. Briasco (ed.), *Políticas para grupos desfavorecidos: Recomendaciones para la acción* (pp. 21–24). Madrid: OEI.

Vielle, J. P. (1995). El trabajador del sector informal como sujeto de la educación de adultos: Un intento por redimensionar la categoría de 'pobre' en la perspectiva de una estrategia renovada de educación para el trabajo. In E. Pieck & E. Aguado (eds.), *Educación y pobreza: De la desigualdad social a la equidad* (pp. 373–396). Mexico: UNICEF/El Colegio Mexiquense.

INFORMAL LEARNING AND THE ROLE OF SOCIAL MOVEMENTS

Bernd Overwien

This essay is concerned with informal[1] learning as a form of learning integrated into practical living. The point of departure is the banal enough fact that although the learning subject can be supported in his or her learning activities by organisational contexts, these activities do not of necessity have to take the form of school. Learning also takes place outside of this institution. Without doubt, forms of school can also play a positive part for working children and adolescents, but so far traditional school concepts have resulted instead in their exclusion. The question thus arises where and how young working people can acquire competencies that are useful for their life perspective. In attempting to answer this question, we must look at informal learning in everyday life. Hitherto educators have given too little attention to this form of learning. In the following, therefore, we shall first take up the fundamentals of informal learning. Then we shall consider the 'informal apprenticeship', a widespread form (not only in Latin America) of the acquisition of occupational skills. Against this backdrop, initial answers are developed to the question of whether there is an alternative way of learning from the movement of working children and young people and how such an alternative is to be formed in co-operation with them. Comparatively little is known so far about how learning takes place within social movements as a 'learning environment' (Lave, 1991). To what extent can people's education (*educación popular*) as the educational theory of social movements (Liebel, 1994) be connected with occupational, work-oriented training? The discussion of these questions will be complemented by thoughts on informal apprenticeships in small firms and the discussion of a concrete example, inspired by people's education, on the use of the 'informal apprenticeship' for working children and adolescents.

The discussion of informal learning is not as new as it might seem in view of more recent publications, especially from the USA. The significance of this form of learning was already discussed some 20 years ago. However, the debate took place in relatively isolated 'development policy' contexts. At the same time, it is not surprising that informal learning was talked about to begin with above all in the context of education and the 'Third World'. Precisely in the less industrialised countries, formal and non-formal education continue to be of less importance for various reasons—for instance, lack of resources. Informal learning is predominant; it leads to the acquisition of occupational or employment-relevant competencies. By contrast, the proportion of persons who acquire corresponding abilities and skills by formal or non-formal education is relatively small.

Madhu Singh, (ed.), Meeting Basic Learning Needs in the informal Sector, 43-59.

To clarify definitions, the term 'formal education' is used here for what takes place in schools and educational institutions, with classes normally arranged by age group. 'Non-formal education' includes all organised learning that takes place outside of school (Sandhaas, 1986, p. 399). Both terms are used in a different sense from 'informal education' and 'informal learning'. When distinguishing these terms, it is helpful to proceed from the learner and to refer to the degree of organisation of the learning concerned (Coombs, 1974). The concept 'informal education' should be avoided where in fact 'informal learning' (from the viewpoint of the subject) is meant. 'Education' suggests intentionality, whereas 'learning' can also take place without intention. The notion 'informal education' should only be used for those instances that involve the creation of special contexts for informal learning. In the context of one British approach to informal learning, the intention is to link up with the lifelong process whereby people learn from everyday experience. However, according to this view, the notion 'informal education' also includes non-formal education as organised pedagogical activity outside of schools and training institutions. Educational activity is also included in the framework of 'community education', as well as social advisory work. The representatives of this approach expressly invoke problem-oriented social education of German provenance (Jeffs & Smith, 1996). Here 'informal education' supports informal learning. 'Informal education' refers to the conscious introduction of learning inputs into informal learning situations. On the other hand, 'informal education' also means the opening up of learning strategies for and through the learners. 'Informal education' should be separated in definition from 'non-formal education' and used when informal learning is to be rendered possible, supported, reinforced or structured. 'Informal education', then, always involves a deliberate intervention related to informal learning. Without doubt, informal learning is at the same time essentially self-determined learning.

Already the UNESCO Report on *Learning to be* (Faure et al., 1972) stressed that the consequences of the scientific-technological revolution and the increasing flood of information will cause great changes in traditional educational systems. These developments 'have expanded the functions of autodidactic education and raised the value of active and conscious learning attitudes' (Faure et al., 1972, p. xxxii). At first with reference to 'primitive societies' the Faure further observes: 'These natural, non-institutionalised forms of learning and apprenticeship have prevailed to the present day in vast regions of the world where they still provide the only form of education[2] for millions of people.' With regard to 'modern' societies, it is noted: 'Furthermore, things do not happen so differently as might seem at first sight in contemporary school-going societies, for it remains true that children—and adults—receive a large part of their education from the environment, their family and society, drawing directly, existentially, on experience' (Faure et al., 1972, p. 5). It is further stated that 'education' until recently in all societies was part of everyday life, either in the family or in groups, in community work, in the relation between craftsman and apprentice, or at play.

The Faure Report—which was concerned with the realisation of informal learning potential, while lacking a learner-oriented perspective—stated that informal learning comprises about 70 percent of all human learning. The Commission demanded that conditions be created to make this form of learning easier (Faure, 1972). The Delors Commission of UNESCO resumed this perspective in 1996. It placed particular emphasis on people's potential competence, which lies fallow and must be mobilised. Formal and informal possibilities of learning, it states, should as far as possible be linked by an integrative overall system. The role of teachers should also be newly formulated. The Delors Commission called for a turn away from knowledge-dominated learning to competence-developing learning, thus stressing the learner's abilities. The development of key competencies is expressly mentioned (Delors, 1996).

Within the context of an essay written in 1986, Berstecher proceeds from the assumption that the 'formal education system in developing countries' had already been researched in detail, but that there was a lack of research relating to 'informal educational activities' (Berstecher, 1986, p. 227). The author therefore calls for the removal of the separation of learning and acting:

> The inclusion of the living environment in the educational process, learning from coevals, older or working persons, etc., would also mean relativising the value of professional teachers, school premises and books. The abolition or weakening of the formal entitlement system would both give a large boost to the sphere of non-formal learning and promote the integration of learning and practice. (Berstecher, 1986, p. 229)

The fact that anticipatory learning continually grows more difficult is an argument for ceasing to regard work and education as opposites. Precisely what this could mean for 'developing countries' remains unclear. However, it is remarkable that Berstecher's remarks related to the 'Third World' of 13 years ago are now highly relevant to industrial countries, though doubtless for other reasons. The lack of recognition of informal learning is presumably connected with the fact that educational planners continue today to proceed excessively from objective needs and too little from the potential of the learner. Thus, although the potential of informal learning has repeatedly been debated, a consistent change of emphasis and perspective to the subject of learning processes has yet to be made. Only after this has occurred will it be possible to link informal learning meaningfully with other forms of learning.

The predominant discourse on informal learning as expressed in North America is to be treated with caution, a discourse that is by no means confined to education or the social sciences, but has also become a part of debates on economic theory. From this perspective the debate on the recognition of informal learning is closely tied to economic cost-utility thinking (Garrick, 1998, pp. 5ff.). In the context of this discourse, which is closely linked to the debate on learning organisations, informal occupational learning has a highly instrumental character. As Garrick shows, informal learning within the competence-based approaches contains a hidden curriculum. In light of the reconstructed experiences of six persons learning within such a context, he criticises the messages concealed within the promise of empowerment. These approaches reflect the employers' contention that informal learning is a way of making the labour force more useful. This runs counter to the overt aim of expanding the knowledge of the individual. In this context, those who exceed the bounds of the firm's community spirit will easily place themselves outside of the 'learning organisation'. It is also significant that there are distinct limitations as to the subject matter of informal learning in the context of the firm. Social questions such as the division of labour according to gender, the distribution of social wealth, the production of products harmful to the environment, etc., are not addressed (see Garrick, 1998, pp. 20ff.).

Thus what is presented as informal learning often serves the interests of the employer rather than the learner. However, it can be turned to the advantage of the latter provided there is a 'demasking' (Garrick, 1998) of the intentions that lie behind 'human resource development' approaches.

INFORMAL LEARNING: THE EXAMPLE OF INFORMAL APPRENTICESHIP

In the sphere of occupational employment-oriented learning, informal methods play an important role. These learning processes are everyday practice in many parts of the world, but are still largely ignored by education research (see Overwien, 2000). For example, informal apprenticeship exists traditionally in many countries in Latin America as a means of acquiring occupational competence. What takes place here is more than merely learning the trade. The notion of informal apprenticeship combines two rather contrary components, which is why their relation to each other is a tense one. 'Apprenticeship' refers to a planned learning process which is at least roughly structured. Learning processes are informal when they are not planned in a professionally educational manner (Schöfthaler, 1981, pp. 97ff.). An informal apprenticeship, which is common in small firms, involves learning processes that are not exactly planned but are at the same time more or less clearly structured in line with the given firm's production requirements. Beyond that, many small firms are places of socialisation for the young people working there, and not only where these are family firms. The connected learning processes are also generally termed 'informal' (Nestvogel, 1978, p. 64).

Considerably more young people acquire occupational competencies through an informal apprenticeship than would be possible in the framework of state projects and programmes or those organised by non-governmental organisations. It would no doubt also be hardly possible to finance training measures comparable in their effect given the existing political will of the decision-makers. The structures within which this training takes place do not need to be established with much effort and cost, but already exist. Often this kind of competence acquisition is more relevant for employment effectiveness than many training programmes, although it is also necessary to recall that working conditions are often extremely poor. Informal apprenticeship is a traditional form of competence acquisition with varying degrees of commitment, which, however, is generally assumed by all concerned (Overwien, 1994, p. 188). Under conditions that are arranged more or less by agreement, young people gain the competencies required for a given field of activity. The duration of such informal apprenticeships varies considerably. It depends not only on the skills and abilities required for the occupational field concerned but also on the subjective judgement of the workshop owner, who assesses the progress made and the economic benefit derived from the labour of the informal apprentices. Apart from certain gender-specific fields of occupational activity, the informal apprenticeship system involves particularly young males in the field of craftsmanship.

Not all informal learning processes are equally complex. Frequently, individual skills can be learned more or less in isolation and then brought together in the production process. However, there are also production processes that require more complex skills and abilities from the start. Greenfield has studied how weaving is traditionally learned in an indigenous population in Southern Mexico. She stresses the cultural and particularly the social interconnections of learning. In the context of a guided learning process, learning takes place from the start in practical action, with direct checking of errors. Greenfield draws attention to the particular character of the process, described as 'scaffolding', by which the instructors withdraw progressively from the learning process (Greenfield, 1984, pp. 129ff.).

Informal apprenticeship fits into the social structures of the sphere of small firms. Young people are integrated into working life at an early stage. They learn chiefly by imitation and identification (see Bakke, 1995; Overwien, 1994). From varying tasks in the context of the existing division of labour within the firm, it is often the case that experienced workers are also involved in passing on activity-related competencies. It can be assumed that the higher the degree of identification of the informal apprentices with the economic as well as ethical and social objectives of the other employees—but especially those of the master-craftsman—the more learning becomes self-motivated. Theoretically, however, the other pole of an assumed continuum is that of the shallow practising of only a few skills that are essential for the firm concerned.

Traditional or informal learning processes are usually considered excessively from the perspective of the European or North American middle-class, with its learning models derived from the small family and the school (Nestvogel, 1988, pp. 32ff.). The concept of imitation applied against this background, which is in any case burdened with negative associations, sets off strongly devaluing associations relating to narrow limits to learning. For this reason it should be separated from the schemes of thought connected with imitative school learning. In small firms, after all, learning does not take place in a static, abstract and artificial sphere, but on the basis of concrete models in the social and economic environment. These manifest themselves in the work of the adults in the context of their shared activities with young people. Overall, the notion of 'participatory experience' (Nestvogel, 1988, pp. 31) in this context is more precise than that of imitative learning. But it should once again be stressed that in this connection we need to ask how the quality of the informal and traditional apprenticeship can be improved and how bridges to the formal education system can be created.

EMPLOYMENT-ORIENTED LEARNING FOR WORKING CHILDREN AND ADOLESCENTS

After concluding an apprenticeship, whether formal or informal, young people will hardly be in a position to start a business, even a small one, themselves. Further learning, in the context of long-term experience of work and life, is required in order to become familiar with work processes, costing, staff management and other aspects of running a business. The individual path to becoming a small entrepreneur is thus a long one. Frequently, it takes many years (Singh, 1997; Bakke, 1995; Boehm, 1997, p. 24; Overwien, 1994). Particularly where young people are concerned, it is necessary to think of different ways of organising work, preferably co-operatively. Acquiring the necessary competencies for a micro-business requires certain personality traits (frequently already marked during the process of socialisation), as well as key competencies drawn from school and non-formal education, in combination with the training and work experience in the firm. It becomes quite clear, then, that a separation of working and learning is counterproductive from an employment perspective. A number of research studies on the acquisition of employment-relevant competencies for the field of micro-enterprises in various countries in the 'Third World' confirm this (see Karcher & Overwien, 1997).

Training for working children and adolescents—or, to use the Spanish acronym, NATRAS (*niños y adolescentes trabajadores*)—whose learning experience is generally rather informal in nature, must therefore proceed from their everyday lives and their working and learning situations. Their learning habits, especially the practice of learning by doing, are of particular importance for the shaping of educational processes. Since the focus needs to be on the acquisition of competencies appropriate to their situation, a subject-centred learning process needs to be organised in which the emphasis is on the learners rather than on the curriculum or the teachers. Their previous experience must be suitably taken into account, and they themselves must as far as possible steer the learning process. Otherwise they may become alienated from the training and even decide to break it off. For this reason much attention must be paid in the process to the participation of the NATRAS. Furthermore, the matter to be learned needs to be chosen so as to be predominantly practical and partly productive, so that the learners can earn money as soon as possible by applying what they learn. With regard to the great importance of key competencies, the learning opportunities need to be broader than is usual for limited instrumental competencies. The learning courses should be integrated in the activities of social movements or local organisations, since the processes then become more continuous and effective. In the sphere of social movements, however, their objectives and the means for achieving these are in the forefront. The question of what the individuals involved derive as learning experience is frequently only a marginal question in the awareness of those involved. Where the objectives are only partly achieved or not at all, the competencies acquired can also fall on the debit side. In the case of success, they are too little regarded as learning experience that can have further application. Educators in the role of learning advisors can and should contribute to making informal learning potentials more conscious and thus more applicable for those involved.

Informal learning and a learner-related approach demand an unfamiliar role from teachers. Educators are rather organisers of learning processes; they act as assistants to learners or learning groups to a greater extent than was hitherto normal. The role of the educator in *educación popular* satisfies these needs in many ways. After all, in education for liberation it is into consideration from the start taken that the participants already possess abilities, as well as relevant knowledge gained from experience, even without certificates. In *educación popular* learning proceeds from the subject. This applies not only to literacy courses for adults, but also to work with children and adolescents. The children's movement in Latin America, as a part of *educación popular*, also lives from the constant construction of relevant learning environments. The processes of self-organisation for the purpose of representing their own interests can only come about via concentrated informal-organisational learning. As becomes clear, informal learning cannot be separated here from social learning. For outward-directed work, the preparation of cultural activities and the expression of political views, a high degree of informal learning is necessary.

The effectiveness of informal learning presumably depends greatly on key competencies, such as organisational or communicative abilities. In the context of people's education it is precisely these competencies that are promoted. It is obvious that informal everyday learning often takes place in the form of dialogue. Adopting this approach helps to remove superfluous barriers to learning. Following Freire's approach, teachers, who act rather as co-ordinators, withdraw increasingly in the course of the dialogic learning process (Freire, 1972). The process of dialogue in the group enables the learners to approach the goal of their learning process as subjects, learning together informally. The learning process takes place in this case between the subject concerned and the object of learning, but also between the subjects themselves (Freire, 1973). It is essential that the learners develop ordering structures to classify what they have learned. If we assume, with Freire, that achieving awareness of the alterability of the world is a step towards liberation, then clearly this realisation is a pre-condition for all really self-intentional learning.

In this context Liebel reconstructs *educación popular*, in synthesis with approaches to street education, as an educational social movement. He traces a close connection between educational approaches critical of political rule and a practical approach proceeding from people's need for survival (Liebel, 1994, pp. 159ff.). Apart from this, there are few research findings on (informal) learning within social movements. One interesting study stresses the connection between learning in social movements and the existence of social networks. Monkman studies the migration-related learning processes of Mexican immigrants in California. Her enquiry focuses on possible ways of supporting the informal learning of the immigrants by means of units of non-formal education. For this purpose the author carried out biographical interviews and gave the results depth with participatory observation in the context of meetings with immigrants. The development of what she calls 'transnational' identities essentially takes place within longer-term learning processes linked with social networks (Monkman, 1999, p. 369). Although details are not given of the underlying learning processes, the persons interviewed repeatedly emphasise their relevance.

In the context of people's education against the backdrop of unalleviated poverty, it will become increasingly necessary also to discuss questions of the economic future of the participants. On the educational level Gibson attempts to give relevant suggestions on the basis of a comparison. The author examines parallels and differences between the education of Paulo Freire and 'enterprise education', which is practised above all in Great Britain. This latter sets out to promote small entrepreneurship in the education sector as well, and in this way to point out employment alternatives. This is not directly applicable to people's education, where what is involved is the individual and the collective and their role in overcoming oppression. 'Enterprise education' focuses only on the individual and his or her economic possibilities. We do not wish here to separate off elements of people's education as a 'method' and thus to deprive them of their political content. The question is rather how elements of 'enterprise education' may be included in an expanded horizon of *educación popular*. Gibson sees the parallels especially in the context of the educational process. In both approaches, the learners are in the foreground and a process orientation is given preference over a knowledge orientation. In both approaches, too, the teachers accompany the process. A problem orientation with the discussion of solutions is also among the parallels. Further aspects are the strengthening of the personality and the self-confidence of the participants (Gibson, 1994, pp. 49ff.). Contradictions between the two approaches can be seen particularly where what is aimed at is a collective orientation together with the strengthening of the subject, on the one side, and only the strengthening of the individual in the economic process, on the other. Portions of 'enterprise education' could provide an impetus for informal learning in the structure of *educación popular* insofar as a view of people as also economically acting subjects is more strongly acknowledged. However, as a rule it will have to be a question of co-operative economic activities if considerable contradictions are not to arise between the educational approach and practical action.

A POPULAR EDUCATION PROGRAMME IN NICARAGUA[3]

The question now arises as to how the type of education outlined above can be put into practice. Hitherto there have been few documented examples, but those we do have give indications of a corresponding problem-oriented and practice-related debate in the context of the Central American children's movement (Liebel 1993). This includes the consideration of the use of informal learning structures in small firms for NATRAS. In Managua the NGO INPRHU collaborates with corresponding firms. The same organisation is endeavouring to connect informal apprenticeships and *educación popular* in Esteli in the North of Nicaragua. Although employment-oriented learning here is likewise not directly integrated into the structures of the children's movement as a social movement, the liberation-education-oriented educators of the NGO build upon concrete learning experience of the NATRAS in the movement of working children. This is clearly shown by the formulation of the young people's selection criteria. Yet the selection itself is made not by NATRAS but by educators. The staff of the NGO do not carry the movement approach consistently further but act largely in the context of conventional socio-educational practice. Nevertheless, the learning and empowerment processes from the movement of working children are taken up. Most probably they are even a precondition for successful training in small firms. Without an individual strengthening of the NATRAS within collective processes, an apprenticeship for them in the largely hierarchically structured firms would presumably be hardly thinkable.

The economic possibilities in Esteli are quite limited. The town has 100,000 inhabitants, of whom 70,000 live in the town itself and 30,000 in the rural environs. Out of the 70,000 inhabitants, 53% are below the age of 15. The context for the project is favourable, since constructive collaboration with the municipal administration is possible. The fact that the administration is Sandinist is not so important. What is important is rather the attitude of politicians and authorities, which is oriented to local questions.

The number of young people engaged in training is dependent both on the economic possibilities of small firms and on financing by organisations from Norway and Spain. The money is needed for educational guidance and for a grant as a compensation for income not earned during the period of training. The NATRAS attend to training in building timber or furniture-making shops, metal workshops, saddler's or hairdressing and beauty salons. Training also takes place in smithies. In the context of the project, training places are sought locally in order to provide training in accordance with local structures, both economically and socially. In the context of a second training variant, work is done in a nursery garden, in which plants for reforestation, decoration and fruit trees are grown. This firm belongs to Instituto de Promoción Humana (INPRHU). More than in normal small firms, there is the opportunity here for the NATRAS to contribute their experience. In the context of the project work, experience has shown that a working child or adolescent cannot move from one day to the next from working in the street to a more-or-less formal kind of work, such as that in a hairdresser's or a carpenter's shop. Therefore, it is meaningful for many NATRAS to work in a sphere more open to their needs and experience.

Selection of the trainees is made according to various criteria. First of all, the workshop owners take no one under 13 years of age. As a rule it is assumed that younger children lack the necessary physical strength. A further important selection criterion is previous participation in experience processes within the framework of the overall project. This involves above all a certain level of identity and self-awareness within the organisation. Furthermore, the young people should be able to try out social relations in the framework of the assisted groups that differ from those of the street. They should develop a self-critical attitude and think over their work experience in the street. Overall, what is involved is a process of becoming conscious whereby the expectations of the new work acquire a proper foundation. A permanent process of reflection begins in the preparatory groups and accompanies the change from the street to the workshops. Further criteria for selection include 'psycho-social' factors such as the role of the NATRAS in the context of their family economy. Basically, family contact is regarded positively. Sometimes, however, difficult family constellations result in patterns of behaviour that hamper training.

Most of the NATRAS have been able to acquire enough schooling to be able to read and write and perform basic mathematical operations. There is no school or school-type institution integrated into the project; there is, however, close co-operation with schools. Here co-operation takes place only with schools whose teachers contribute a sufficient background of thought about the life of young people in the street. The founding of a special project school has been rejected for political reasons; it is the state's task to provide schooling. The educators involved in the project see themselves as mediators between the NATRAS on the one hand and families, schools, workshops and political or administrative instances on the other.

Basically, the project works within the context of local structures. Thus the idea also arose for training in existing workshops. By gearing it to existing structures of the labour market, it becomes possible to identify local employment possibilities for working children and adolescents. The workshops in Esteli have a simple level of craftsmanship and mostly work for the local market. The educators see it as their role initially to speak with the workshop owners and sensitise them to the problems of the working young people. They then visit the workshops and initiate a dialogue on the life of the NATRAS, an exchange of ideas on the thinking of the young people such as the latter could hardly carry out in this form with the workshop owners. In the course of the discussions, the small entrepreneurs are asked whether they could imagine giving work to NATRAS. In this process, it is of special importance to learn something about the attitudes of the workshop owners towards the NATRAS, since this is decisive for the success of co-operation.

Most of the owners of the small firms already have experience with young people, since there are numerous apprentices employed informally who learn a trade within a few years, training for which they receive no wages to begin with. They often have the status of apprentice for three, four or five years, after which they receive a relatively low paid job as assistants. In the workshops in which there are other apprentices in addition to the NATRAS, there have been no problems so far. The other young people are aware that the NATRAS are only able to obtain training with the aid of grants, whereas they themselves are financially enabled by their families to work as informal apprentices. One difference between the NATRAS and the 'normal' informal apprentices is that the former have experienced life on the street and are correspondingly stigmatised. They have experience of violence, both from others and from one another. Towards the end of the week there is sometimes drinking in the workshops, arguments occur and the tone frequently becomes fairly rough. By reason of their previous experience, the NATRAS are often not prepared to expose themselves to such structures again. Since these are part of the reality of life, however, they need to learn to cope with them in their own way.

Only one of the 24 workshop owners with whom the project currently co-operates learned his trade in the framework of formal training. Even in the field of hairdressing and beauty care, training in Esteli is frequently informal. In other towns, professional non-formal courses are offered. In some cases the hairdressers in Esteli have attended such courses in other towns, but most of them have trained informally. In the workshops, learning takes place alongside production. There are no programmes or curricula. A structure results from the production that happens to be in demand. Likewise, as noted, the owners of the workshops also have no systematic training.

The workshops with which co-operation exists are relatively small, with hardly more than three to five employees. Most of them are formalised insofar as they pay taxes. It is important for the workshop owners to declare to state authorities that when they employ the NATRAS they are not doing so in order to obtain more workers but to perform a social service. To this end, there must be a formal contract to prove this to the ministry of labour.

The advantage of training in the daily practice of the workshop is the closeness to the reality of the firm and to the market. Thus learning takes place with the tools available locally and with products that can be sold locally. The quality of the products and services is, however, usually not very high, or at least depends greatly on the individual experience of the workshop owner concerned. The success with which the apprentices are able to learn in the context of such workshops certainly also depends on this experience, but also on the didactic ability of the workshop owner.

Another problem is the economic situation. Young people who no longer work in the street, sell in the market or clean shoes, need an income. They cannot afford to train without reward. In contrast to the other informal apprentices, who are bound within a more-or-less functioning financial family structure, the NATRAS usually lack such support. Therefore, they receive about $40 (1998) per month as a grant. This grant is below the income that they would as a rule be able to get in the street. However, it must be taken into account that the situation of the NATRAS is considerably improved in the context of training. Thus, for example, they only work four hours a day, instead of from six in the morning to five in the afternoon. They work either in the morning or the afternoon and can go to school the rest of the time. Furthermore, they are not exposed to physical violence, ill-treatment and so on. These improvements in their living conditions have a positive effect on their self-esteem. In this connection, it is also important that work takes place within the group and creates social bonds. Thus, while the NATRAS earn less than before, they have a number of advantages. One problem frequently is that they were used to getting a daily income in the street without having to wait for it. Now they are confronted with receiving their pay only at intervals, for instance fortnightly. For many of them, this is a problem, since they obtain credit, for instance, in the small shops in the quarter and thus can fall into a vicious circle of debt. On the other hand, members of their families see this comparatively fixed income coming in and attempt to share in it one way or another. In the families it is expected that the NATRAS pay their share of the household costs. Whenever water or electricity bills arrive, corresponding demands on the young people are made. However, since they had been used to disposing of their income alone and making no contribution to the household, this can lead to tension. In this regard, the moderating influence of the educators is important.

Every one to two weeks, there are meetings with the NATRAS to discuss the situation in the workshops. They discuss the problems they have encountered, how learning has taken place, etc. At the same time, there are also meetings with the mothers. Most of the NATRAS have some contact with their families. Young people that only live in the street are not included, since too much instability is seen here. A process of negotiation always needs to take place in order to restore the relationship between NATRAS and their families and thereby to create a certain stability.

Most of the educators engaged in the project are former teachers, with years of experience. However, when selecting them it is important that they have retained a critical attitude towards their activity as teachers and are also integrated in the development of the community. They are former teachers who saw their work at school as involved with the community, proceeding from their political convictions. It is a fundamentally important approach within the project that all those involved go through mutual learning processes. The teachers also expect to learn from the NATRAS. This means that the roles on both sides are different from those in school. In the everyday process of work, conscious reflection on the experience is important. To some extent, this experience is also recorded in writing. One important function of the teachers in accompanying work in the small firms is to have regular conversations with the NATRAS about the situation with regard to relations on the level of the firm. When there are difficulties with the workshop owners or colleagues, suitable intervention immediately ensues. Not infrequently, situations arise in which problems involving the families of the workshop owners need to be addressed.

At the time of writing this essay, there are 44 NATRAS in training, which lasts between one and one-and-a-half years. Work is done in the workshop for four hours a day from Monday to Friday. Every Saturday, there are meetings for evaluation and planning. Most also still attend school; a few who work eight hours a day are unable to do so, but these are adolescents of 17–18 years of age. In the context of the grants programme there have been no fluctuations, apart from some initial problems. However, at times the NATRAS become involved in family activities, for instance, during the coffee harvest; they return to the project, however. Out of 124 apprentices, 22 (20%) have meanwhile obtained a more-or-less stable job in the trade they learned. Two returned to the street. Most of the rest work in the context of the family economy or as occasional workers in informal employment. Most, then, are not directly employed in the field in which they trained; but it should be noted that it is relatively common in Nicaragua to change jobs when the occasion arises in order to improve income. A fixed identification with certain trades does not exist to the same extent as in, say, Germany. For example, at the moment the production of tobacco is being resumed in Esteli. Money can be earned in the cultivation and also the production of cigars. The cultivation of tobacco and the production of cigars in a *zona franca* (a zone of production largely free of taxes and other contributions, with very limited rights for those employed there) offer the possibility of obtaining a (small) income under very poor working conditions—but at least a comparatively regular income.

From the perspective of the project, it is regarded as a considerable advantage that the young people attain psycho-social stabilisation. Even when they subsequently do not work in the same trade, there is a considerable boost to their self-confidence, and the development of an individual, positive identity can be observed. Regarded from a psycho-social perspective, the project is a success. The training is also important for the role of the NATRAS in their various family environments. Their personal esteem by others is considerably enhanced. Initially, there were problems in a carpentry workshop with an owner who gave one young person the same work continually for six months. The owner was then talked to and the situation resolved. Such initial experiences were of importance for later work, since such cases can be avoided nowadays. Other problems include avoiding situations in which the NATRAS have nothing to do but clean out the workshops. Sometimes there are problems in relations with other workers who wish to exert power, etc. Within the project, there are examples in which young people from the street came to employment via a lengthy process. Pepe entered the project at the age of 13. At this time, he was strongly *callejizado*, that is, he had almost broken off contact with his family, slept in the street or in houses with friends with whom he sniffed glue, was involved with drugs, stole in buses, etc. Through the involvement in the movement of working children and adolescents and the project, a lengthy process was initiated in the course of which he not only concluded elementary school but was able to be integrated into a business dealing in spare parts for automobiles. In time, the owner of the business developed so much confidence in this young person that he even gave him the day's earnings to take to the bank. When the owner died, problems arose as to his further prospects. Workshop owners frequently demonstrate readiness to support the project; however, they must see and accept that there is an organisation in the background that intervenes and supports.

A nursery garden founded by the organisation INPRHU, whose inception was preceded by a market study, is of a somewhat different nature. On the one hand, this firm has more socio-educational supervision than is possible in smaller firms. For this reason, work is carried out here with NATRAS who come comparatively directly from the street. It can perhaps be compared with many training projects in Germany in the sphere of work with socially disadvantaged young people. One point of emphasis is on the psycho-social reinforcement of the NATRAS. However, from the beginning one hope has been that a number of youth will later be able to become independent with activities from the field of work of this nursery school for forestry and decorative plants. Thus from the start an awareness is created as to which raw materials and half-finished goods must be used, the part played by working hours, how sales can be implemented, and the amount of the final profit. In practice there are, of course, contradictions between this market orientation, that is, the question of profitability, and the requirements of working with young people. Additionally, the economic and thus employment structure of Nicaragua permits only limited predictions concerning a subsequent integration into the market. On the practical level, the solution to this is that the educator and co-ordinator in the nursery has a double qualification: in addition to his educational training and experience, he also has business knowledge. At the same time, for educators involved there is permanent further training, including in economic matters. Within the nursery garden, above and beyond the informal learning in daily work, special courses are also given. In the context of the nursery garden, the founding of one's own firm could also take on collective forms.

CONCLUSION

To sum up, this approach contains a number of promising aspects for the future. The young people involved are working children, or 'street children'. They are now working in local craft firms or trades, in car-centre shops, bakeries, a nursery garden, etc. They receive a small grant as compensation for the loss of income in the street, where they previously earned money, though by means of activities with little perspective. The owners of small firms pay their 'normal' apprentices no wages, which means that it is the training they are interested in. Relatively independent young people such as the 'street children' do not always find it easy to tolerate these structures. This is possible finally only because the process of the 'informal apprenticeship' is accompanied by varied educational activities oriented towards *educación popular*. These activities are geared to the requirements of the young people.

Studies carried out by the NGO itself concerning the success of the project have shown that a relatively small proportion of those who complete the training subsequently work in the field of activity of the firms in which they trained. But the great majority are able to pursue independently an activity that guarantees their survival, either alone or together with others. The reason for the relative success appears to be the connection between informal learning in an environment which is not always experienced as pleasant but which is the world of real life, and educational activities that are consciousness- and subject-oriented and largely participatory. Thus people's education can certainly be connected with the attainment of an income perspective, since the occupation takes place in perfectly normal small firms. Yet the previous experience of the young people within the movement of working children and adolescents also seems important for success. The learning experiences from this social movement and the strengthening received, which can be termed 'empowerment', have certainly been important pre-conditions for the success of the project. It can therefore be asked whether an approach of this kind with young people of similar biographical background can function at all without the influence of a comparable social movement.

From this perspective further experience needs to be evaluated for the thorough clarification of the possibilities and limits of a link between people's education and employment orientation. It would be important to aim at a combination of the corresponding approaches. For example, the Chilean Organizaciones Económicas Populares (OEP), which originated during the period of resistance to Pinochet's dictatorship and were founded by slum-dwellers with the goal of producing and distributing goods and services, have yet to be studied with regard to learning. Meanwhile, materials from the Programa de Economia del Trabajo, a Chilean NGO, clearly show that politico-economic activities on the level of this social movement were consciously connected with learning inputs (e.g. PET, 1990). Overall, the means and competencies available to the individual members of the organisations were thematised and pooled. The activities were not only concerned with direct survival production but also with work on self-identity and participation in the changing of political and social structures, combined with an improvement in the quality of life of the members. The involvement in this movement was not confined to a small group of slum-dwellers in Santiago de Chile. In 1982 there were about 280 OEPs in and around the capital; by 1991 the number had grown to almost 2400, involving 80,000 people. Community vegetable gardens and soup kitchens had been founded, but also co-operatives in various fields. All these groups had in common that they were engaged in economic activity within an economy based on solidarity (Nyssens, 1997, pp. 63ff.). In the mid-1980s Möller studied the work of a women's group in Venezuela whose initial goal was to provide common education. Out of this activity, little by little, production activities of many kinds have developed (Möller, 1986). Using an example from Argentina that is oriented to *educación popular*, Rudolph shows that an orientation to everyday life and simultaneous practice-related employment-oriented work with young people can be successful (Rudolph, 1997).

Such examples should be examined systematically with regard to concrete modes or procedures for the combination of social movement and informal learning. Relevant indications are provided by the Nicaraguan example, but overall it remains unclear what institutional and organisational requirements of informal learning in social movements exist and how precise the learning that takes place is. Apart from this, non-governmental organisations frequently develop dynamics of their own that can endanger many of the aforementioned principles of people's education. For instance, the interest in guaranteeing stable jobs with corresponding influence sometimes collides with the need of the 'basis' for democratic structures. Further, there is the question of the spectrum of learning potential of social movements and possible bridges to formal education. Also to be discussed is the exact role of educators in light of the attention paid increasingly to informal learning. The question of whether and which key competencies (Negt, 1997) are important for informal learning, and how they are acquired, is equally important. Here too the question of whether they transfer to other life situations arises. The role of motivation to learn in the case of informal learning also requires investigation.

This list of open questions is doubtless incomplete; tackling it also presents methodological challenges. By reason of the complexity of the subject, studies of informal learning need to be interdisciplinary in approach. Apart from a certain number of studies in the field of education in the narrow sense, studies in the field have chiefly been carried out in ethnology, anthropology and psychology. Findings from cultural, cognitive and socialisation research should also be adduced. In the context of anthropology and ethnology, there are a number of studies (especially from the USA) which deal with the dependence of learning on culture and examine learning processes on the level of an ethnic group or in the context of a village. In the field of museum education, too, informal learning processes are being studied. These studies need to be examined with regard to their applicability to the field of social movements. It is important to stress that, although the cultural contexts may differ, methodical approaches may also be relevant in other contexts.

NOTES

[1] The adjective 'informal' is used above all on three levels. The first is that of social relations, e.g. in the case of informal groups or informal relationships. Another level is economic. Initially applied to 'Third World' countries, the informal (economic) sector was defined in contradistinction to the formal sector. The formal sector embraces medium and large, frequently multinational, enterprises, which make use of capital-intensive technologies, together with the field of public services. The 'informal sector' is a blanket term for extremely heterogeneous activities mainly of small enterprises, whose common denominator is the fact that they stay largely outside of state control—which makes them informal rather than formal. It is on this third level of the application of the term that this essay will concentrate. In contrast to formal and non-formal learning, the term 'informal learning' is used, particularly in the literature in English.

[2] Sandhaas (1986, p. 404) draws attention to a problem of (also cultural) translation: Frequently in German-language publications on international education questions, the English word 'education' is equated

relatively arbitrarily with the German words *Bildung* or *Erziehung*, since it covers either and sometimes both of these. (The same problem also arises in French and Spanish.)

[3] This section is based on an interview with Carlos Gonzalez, the Director of the NGO INPRHU-Esteli, in March 1998.

REFERENCES

Bakke, S. (1995). *Competencies in the informal sector in Lima, Peru: An empirical study of selected production and service trades*. Dissertation Universität Bremen.

Berstecher, D. (1986). Zur Diversifizierung des Bildungswesens in Entwicklungsländern. In H. Thomas & G. Elstermann, *Bildung und Beruf. Soziale und ökonomische Aspekte* (pp. 227–239). Berlin/Heidelberg/New York/Tokyo: Springer.

Butrón, M. E., Callejas, E. & Qoaquira S., David, S. & Coaquira, S. (1995). *Microempresa y capacitación. Diagnóstico de necesidades de capacitación del sector informal urbano*. La Paz: Centro de Fomento a Iniciativas Económicas, Area de Formación y Desarrollo Empresarial.

Coombs, P., & Achmed, H. (1974). *Attacking rural poverty: How non-formal education can help*. Baltimore: John Hopkins University Press.

Dehnbostel, P., Molzberger, G. & Overwien, B. (2004). New Forms of Learning and Work Organization in the IT Industry: A German Perspective on Informal Learning. In Bascia, N., Cumming, A., Datnow, A., Leithwood, K. & Livingstone, D. (eds.). *International handbook of educational policy*. New York : Kluwer (forthcoming).

Delors, J. (1996). *Learning: The treasure within*. Paris: UNESCO.

Faure, E., Herrera, F., Kaddura, A.-R., Lopes, H., Petrovski, A. V., Rahnema, M. & Champion Ward, F. (1972). *Learning to be: The world of education today and tomorrow*. Paris: UNESCO.

Freire, P. (1972). *Pedagogy of the oppressed*. Harmondsworth: Penguin.

Freire, P. (1973). *Education for critical consciousness*. New York: Seabury Press.

Garrick, J. (1998). *Informal learning in the workplace: Unmasking human resource development*. London: Routledge.

Gibson, A. (1994). Freirean versus enterprise-education: The difference is in the business. *Convergence, 27*, 46–57.

Greenfield, P. (1984). Theory of the teacher in the learning activities of every day life. In B. Rogoff & J. Lave (eds.), *Everyday cognition: Its development in social context* (pp. 117–38). Cambridge, Mass.: Harvard University Press.

Heaney, T. (1995). Issues in Freirean pedagogy. At http://nlu.nl.edu/ace/Resources/Dokuments/Freire Issues.html.

Illich, I. (1971). *Deschooling society*. New York: Harper and Row.

Jeffs, T., & Smith, M. (1996). *Informal education: Conversation, democracy and learning*. Derby: Education Now Books with YWCA George Williams College. See http://www.infed.org/space/w-inf3.htm.

Karcher, W., & Overwien, B. (1997). On the significance of general competencies in the urban informal sector and conditions for their acquisition. *Education, 55–56*, 43–55.

Lave, J., & Wenger, E. (1991). *Situated learning*. New York: Cambridge University Press.

Liebel, M. (1994). *Wir sind die Gegenwart*. Frankfurt a. M.: IKO.

Möller, S. (1986). *Berufsbezogene Erwachsenenbildung in Venezuela. Ein Beitrag zur Reduzierung von Armut und Marginalität?* Frankfurt a. M.: IKO.

Monkman, K. (1999). Transnational migration and learning processes of Mexican adults constructing lives in California. *International Journal of Educational Development, 19*, 367–82.

Negt, O. (1997). *Kindheit und Schule in einer Welt der Umbrüche*. Göttingen: Steidl.

Nestvogel, R. (1978). *Verstärkung von Unterentwicklung durch Bildung?* Bonn: Verlag Neue Gesellschaft.

Nestvogel, R. (1988). Einheimische und westliche Bildungsformen in Schwarzafrika. *Unterrichtswissenschaft, 1*, 28–42.

Nyssens, M. (1997). El germen de una economia solidaria: Otra vision de la economia popular. El caso de Santiago de Chile. *CIRIEC-Espania, Revista de Debate sobre la Economia Publica Social y Cooperativa, 25*, 63–82.

Overwien, B. (1997). Employment-oriented non-formal training for young people in the informal sector in Latin America. *Education, 55–56*, 146–57.

Overwien, B. (1994). Micro-enterprise in the informal sector of Managua and the long road to vocational competence. *Adult Education and Development, 42*, 91–108.

Overwien, B. (2001) Informal learning, social movements and acquisition of competencies for self-determined working and living. In M. Liebel, B. Overwien & A. Recknagel (eds.). *Working children's protagonism: Social movements and empowerment in Latin America, Africa and India* (pp. 247–267). Frankfurt/Main, London: IKO (in preparation).

PET (Programa de Economía del Trabajo). (c. 1990). Cómo podemos formar nuestro taller laboral: Cartilla de Capacitación Popular. *Constitución Juridica de Organizationes Productivas*. Santiago de Chile: Programa de Economía del Trabajo.

Rudolph, H.-H. (1997). *Jetzt Reden Wir! Jugend, Lebensweltbezogene Bildung und Gemeinde-entwicklung in Lateinamerika.* Frankfurt a. M.: IKO.

Sandhaas, B. (1986). Bildungsformen. In H.-D. Haller & H. Meyer (eds.), *Ziele und Inhalte der Erziehung und des Unterrichts* (*Enzyklopädie Erziehungswissenschaft 3*) (pp. 399–406). Stuttgart: Klett-Cotta.

Schöfthaler, T. (1981). Informelle Bildung. In *Zeitschrift für Pädagogik*, Supplement 16: *Die Dritte Welt als Gegenstand Erziehungswissenschaftlicher Forschung* (pp. 97–115). Weinheim/Basel: Beltz.

Singh, M. (1997). Processes of education and training in the context of local self-help organisations in the informal sector. *Education, 55–56*, 56–69.

Welton, M. Social revolutionary learning: The new social movements as learning sites. *Adult Education Quarterly, 43*, 152–64.

THE INFORMAL SECTOR: NON-FORMAL EDUCATION SETTINGS FOR WORKING CHILDREN

Laila Iskandar

The growing trend towards globalisation has led to a growth of consumption, production and trading patterns that seem to be slowly eroding respect for popular knowledge and to value mega-trends led by a few powerful giants in the global economy. These giants, by and large, have thus far demonstrated little respect for local knowledge, nature, or indigenous patterns of consumption, production and learning. Yet, while learning in the formal economy is transferred across boundaries by governments and private sector conglomerates, local knowledge survives with verve in local communities and struggles to transfer its richness via a vast network of informal sector markets in the developing world.

The informal sector has been providing settings for non-formal learning, which has been exploited by the non-profit sector in some parts of the developing world. It has provided the poor with a rich world of transformative learning in which children, youth and adults engage. This world—the informal sector—has brought the realities of adults and children into one common place: the informal sector workplace. Whether driven by the poverty of their adult parents or working alongside other adults, children and youth are increasingly finding themselves plunged into a world in which they learn and earn in very adult contexts.

BACKGROUND

Research findings indicate a clear link between aspects of child deprivation—in fact deprivation of basic children's rights—and child labour. Numerous studies have identified a triangular relationship between poverty, deprivation of education and various forms of child vulnerability, including child labour.

In explaining why their children worked, parents questioned whether basic education was relevant for providing their children's need to gain experience. Others complained of the burden of school expenses. Family economic pressures come out clearly in the study. Results indicated that a child's contribution to the family budget ranged on average between 22.8 percent (mothers' estimates) and 30.7 percent (children's estimates).

Female-headed households are often among the most vulnerable groups and rely to a great extent on child labour as a source of income. The table below compares female-headed and two-parent households in a sample in Egypt. For children from female-

Madhu Singh, (ed.), Meeting Basic Learning Needs in the informal Sector, 61-73.

headed households, economic factors were much more important reasons for work. These findings are indicative of the vulnerability of such households, a fact which calls for policy consideration.

Table 1. Reasons Given by Children (under 15 years) for Working: Comparison between Female-Headed and Two-Parent Families		
Reason*	**Children in Female-Headed Households %**	**Children in Two-Parent Households %**
Contribute to family income	61.8	39.9
Earn own money	43.6	33.0
Educational failure	42.3	49.6
Learn a profession	38.5	45.2
Other	5.1	6.7

*The respondents were permitted to state more than one reason.
Source: Child Labour in Egypt Survey (1991)

Data from the Social and Health Status and Educational Achievement of Adolescents in Egypt Survey (ASCE) (1998) indicate that for working adolescents (10–19 years old), the most important reason for working was to help the family (without pay). This pattern is prevalent in rural areas where children and adolescents work in family cultivation.

Table 2. Distribution of Working Adolescents (10–19 years) by the Reasons for Starting to Work	
Reasons	**%**
Help family without pay	36
Provide income for family	19
Has spare time	16
Cover own needs	9
Likes to work	9
To gain experience	6
Poor scholastic performance	5

Source: Social and Health Status and Educational Achievement of Adolescents in Egypt Survey (ASCE) (1998), Cairo, Egypt

NON-FORMAL LEARNING FOR WORKING CHILDREN

What opportunities are there for the estimated 100 million children world-wide who are currently out of school? What must be done to address that challenge in a world of continued environmental degradation and poverty? A world in which 1.3 billion people live on less than US$1 a day and in which 884.7 million adults are illiterate and caught, for the most part, in a cycle of educational failure, poor health, social exclusion and exploitation? (UNESCO Education for All Week on the EFA website, April 24, 2004).

Innovative methods of non-formal basic education have come to the forefront of this global issue and promise to provide learning opportunities for those who are caught in the poverty trap and cannot access formal schooling.

Non-formal education is, by definition, dispensed outside of any established or structured formal system of learning; it is adapted to each group, its culture, and its aspirations, its daily realities and learning needs. Freed of the constraints of time and place, and built on the reality of local communities, this type of learning upheld by UNESCO integrates the natural learning processes of young people trying to survive in difficult circumstances.

Since one of the main reasons people are excluded from formal schooling is the necessity of working, be it in the fields, in workshops or in the home, non-formal education inherently links the learning process to work-related and income-generating contexts. It seeks to anchor learning in local practice and indigenous knowledge of how to work, earn income, trade, access credit, and organise communities.

Non-formal education is grounded in the popular economy. But so is work in the informal sector. From that arena it creates a vast 'school' or 'learning space' within the informal economy. In large measure it revolves around self-employment, such as street-vending or crafts co-operatives, barter, exchange, local production, family-owned businesses, etc. These are ideally suited as vehicles for non-formal education since they are based on community relations and sharing, as well as on the adoption of appropriate technologies, such as recycling, to create local products. Linking non-formal education closely to the reality of exclusion has many advantages: educational tools and materials can be made out of almost anything: learning content is based on local needs and knowledge; the learning place is the living space; the distinctions between learners and teachers are blurred as both come from within the community; and organisation of the learning experience reflects the community's structure.

Learning schemes grounded in local systems of economics and culture allow youth to create their own path towards sustainable development, a path on which even the most excluded can lead the way. Basic non-formal education, and by extension practical skills training in the informal economy, remain among the few means of addressing the dire situation of excluded youth.

THE EGYPTIAN CONTEXT

In Egypt, Community and Institutional Development (CID) has been piloting experiments to transform informal sector working places into non-formal islands of learning. These have largely centred around recycling communities in Egypt. These communities defined what they wanted from education in the following terms: an education that would lead to lifelong earning skills; an educational setting that was flexible, fluid and involved earning while learning; an experience that valued them as individuals and built on their skills of sorting and recycling waste; an experience filled with dignity and respect for their knowledge; an education that would not alienate them from their families and their trade.

PRINCIPLES OF NON-FORMAL INSTRUCTION

The broad principles upon which this concept is based are that: non-literacy-based instruction can be a powerful tool towards the eventual acquisition of literacy; learning in the world of work in the informal sector is much more relevant than learning in the world of the classroom; development projects which bring about transformative life situations provide a rich field for curriculum design and content; the key to economic and educational empowerment is to link the two in one nexus where they meet, that is, the informal sector; the learning experience can be enriched by viewing the conditions of poverty and informal sector work as a springboard from which to draw the lessons of life, literacy and community; and the institutions proposed for the implementation of such concepts are more effective if they are community-based, grass roots in nature and use local channels chosen by indigenous people in consonance with their culture. The informal sector provides autonomous learning that is vibrantly linked to culture, music and the arts of local communities.

HOW IS COMMUNITY-BASED NON-FORMAL EDUCATION CONNECTED TO THE ENVIRONMENT?

In the heart of Mokattam, a neighbourhood in which 20,000 Cairo garbage collectors live, a deliberate and conscious decision to link the natural, social and cultural environments to basic education was made in 1988. This was under the auspices of the Association for the Protection of the Environment (APE), a community-based NGO in the neighbourhood. The textile industry surrounding Cairo became a major partner in providing clean remnants (rags) to the non-formal recycling school for young girls and women, free of charge.

The *natural environment* was one of garbage—a dirty environment of man-made waste where people had survived on their sorting ability to recover as much as was humanly possible, to process it, re-manufacture and trade it. This had exposed them to a social environment of untold health hazards and unspeakable human indignity. It had made them one of the most severely excluded groups in society and had deprived them of basic human rights of education, health and civic participation. It had made them incredibly stoic, resourceful and determined to survive. But it had also left them with a deeper experience of injustice and oppression than any other group in Egypt. The *cultural environment* was one of building on ancient models of production, conservation and materials use. These realities all went into the design of a basic education programme revolving around the collection, transport, recovery, recycling and trading of man-made waste. The design of this experiment followed the following arguments.

The natural environment had to consist of clean man-made waste. The educational programme could not revolve around an undignified learning setting or learning situation. However, the curriculum would be based upon the very focus of their activities and their lives: sorting garbage. Therefore, the physical environment of *clean* rags would elevate the sorting expertise to a learning setting that would lead to the highest level of aesthetic and cultural expression: handmade crafts from organic fibres of the world's best-known, unique cotton—Egyptian cotton—made by the world's most unique, renowned people—the garbage collectors of Cairo, and with the same hands that had suffered unspeakable indignity by having to sort rotting filth manually 365 days a year.

The *social environment* would have to be one that not only protected the learners' health from hazards of man-made waste. It would also be one that taught about how to protect ourselves from the health hazards of handling Cairo's garbage at home. Thus the health education component became of paramount importance at the rag-recycling centre. Indeed, learning about health was celebrated in a festive mood at the Monday noontime 'parties', where prizes (towels, soap) were awarded and new things were learned about health.

The non-formal school used culture and theatre to learn about health. The girls and women produced puppets from rags, made up their own plays, presented social dramas and composed songs and poems around health themes.

The social context of oppression and exclusion dictated that the admission policy specifically target those who were illiterate, had never gone to school and were utterly poor. Children who went out on the garbage route therefore were given first priority. They were extracted from a situation of oppression and placed in a healthy, dignified situation of 'learning and earning'. Observers from the West, from formally schooled economies and contexts, called this 'child labour'!

The design deliberately planned to transfer learning to the home and to ensure that the 'schools' maintained power over students by overcoming the usual perception of school/centre's walls and instead enlarging the area of the 'school' or 'learning place' to include the home, the street, the community at large. Thus the students continued to produce at home, came to school for their 'homework assignments = production orders' and then returned to school for 'grading homework = quality control.

Justice issues were further incorporated into the design by ensuring equal access to education. The smarter ones—that is better producers—did not get more work assigned to them, but 'pay = grades' was based upon merit. Thus the concept of excellence in education was upheld since the producers did not compete among themselves but against a 'standard', that is, quality.

The cultural imperative of conserving the earth's non-renewable resources meant that the design had to make use of every scrap of rag we received and that we would not purchase rags to make quilts. We would only *recycle* what the textile and garment industry discarded.

The emphasis on culturally appropriate tools led to the use of a handloom to weave rag rugs. This ancient Egyptian piece of technology was not supplanted by more modern technology imports. Cultural production models of collaboration rather than competition were the rule. Weavers who had no room in their homes for a loom could weave at a cousin's or girlfriend's if her parents approved.

Cultural patterns of women's mobility were observed. The school—that is, the NGO—sent a truck to collect and transport the rags from the formal sector textile industry to the centre. The centre was located in the heart of the neighbourhood. Women and girls would go out to local sales events always accompanied by a volunteer from the educated classes. Men were not be allowed at the training centre, so that husbands and parents would not fear sending their wives or daughters into socially 'dangerous' situations.

Publicity was made about the school and people were encouraged, indeed urged, to visit the centre. Shuttle buses would facilitate and assure a steady stream of admirers and shoppers. Self-awareness, pride, new self-perceptions and valuation would result. Not to mention increased sales and full pockets!

The elements of this design rested upon finding new solutions to the learning and development dilemma by finding a direct relationship between local indigenous knowledge and formal scientific knowledge. Why erase and replace the old with the new? What parts of the old could contribute to the new in a dynamic, innovative way? Where were the linkages between the two? How could we connect them?

We obtained the rags from the business sector. These constituted in essence the 'waste' of the rich. The poor wove them into world class handicrafts of the highest quality and sold them back to the rich. And in between a curriculum was woven into the transformational elements of the craft. Thus, from the rich to the poor and back to the rich, formal and informal markets criss-crossed, formal and informal knowledge fused through the mediation of a deliberate design to provide poor, working children and youth with work extracted from an informal sector ethos and transformed into community learning and earning.

After six years 500 girls and women had graduated. They had been selected based on need (economic and dispersion from different homes so that a target of 500 graduates would be placed as developmental 'seeds' in 500 homes out of the 700 in the neighbourhood, over a six-year period. Of those:

250 continued to be regular producers, earning from L.E. 80 per month to L.E. 350 (1 US$ = L.E. 3.34 in 1996). This income was spent on nutrition for children, health care, education, clothing for feast occasions, household appliances, in that order. Sixty-four percent of the women were practising family planning. Fifty-six percent said they would not circumcise their daughters who had still not been circumcised. Seventy percent of the single girls said they would not circumcise their daughters when they got married.

Over 250 girls had achieved functional literacy in 1996 (measured by tests administered by the centre and not by the national literacy examination). The people—girls, women, men—and their institutions (NGOs) had begun teaching others their trade. APE established a training department in 1997 and began training trainers to spread the 'gospel' of recycling to Egypt and indeed, to the whole world. Partnerships with other NGO's in North Africa (Tunis and Morocco), the Middle East (Gaza), Africa (Senegal) and Latin America (Columbia) served as conduits for the exchange of learning. A South-South dialogue had begun.

The rag-recycling centre was designed as an alternative education delivery system, which offered learning in out-of-school settings, and earning in out-of-formal sector or 'sweat shop' settings.

REPLICATION

Currently learners in CID's projects in Egypt are trained in four recycling schools: two in Cairo, a third in Tenth of Ramadan and a fourth in Nuweiba, South Sinai. All are managed by community development associations that are deeply rooted in the life of the community.

In Cairo the Association for the Protection of the Environment (APE) in Mokattam established the first non-formal basic education for girls and women around recycling rags. Learning was immediately and directly linked to income-generation and the local environment. Literacy was introduced and reinforced as a very natural means for weighing quantities on machines, numeracy was developed as a means for weighing quantities of recyclable material, and hygiene was brought in as a prerequisite for obtaining clean finished products. Culture and the arts, recreation, and community mobilisation were essential parts of the curriculum. The second recycling school was established in the same neighbourhood, Mokattam, in 2000 and was funded by partners from the donor agencies (UNESCO), the private sector (Groupe Schneider Electric, Proctor and Gamble, Tetra Pak) and business associations (Rotary Sunrise Cairo). It is run by a local community based group, the Association of Garbage Collectors for Community Development (AGCCD).

In 1992 and 1996, APE experimented with a source-separation initiative in two neighbourhoods in Cairo and found it to be successful. The Egyptian Environmental Affairs agency hesitated to introduce it city-wide and thus lost an opportunity to design a waste management system for Cairo based on local, indigenous knowledge and practice. Youth trained in this project set out for the South Sinai, where they taught hotels, shops, restaurants and residents source separation of municipal waste leading to more ecological ways of waste collecting and sorting. The young people of Mokattam established a sorting plant on the South Sinai part of the Red Sea Coast in the town of Nuweiba and with a new partner NGO—Hemaya for Community Development. They trained young Bedouins in the ways of recovery and recycling, while also trading in recovered non-organic household and hotel waste, where the most deprived and marginalised become key actors in the preservation of the environment.

Many cities and towns in Egypt have no official system for solid waste collection. The Tenth of Ramadan town is a new industrial complex, which houses large to medium industries. It has also become a residential town for industrial workers, managers and government employees. The Hope Village Society acquired large premises in the Tenth of Ramadan city. Since 1988 it has catered to the needs of street children, providing them with counselling, shelter, education and vocational skills. Through its active board members and community support from local officials, that NGO has acquired land on which it set up a recycling learning centre along the lines of the one established by the APE team in the Hemaya NGO in the town of Nuweiba, South Sinai and by the youth in AGCCD in Mokattam. Thus the transfer of learning technology, content and process, were transferred from Mokattam, Cairo, to Tora, Cairo, from both to Nuweiba, South Sinai and back to Tenth of Ramadan, 50 kilometres northeast of Cairo.

PROJECT STRATEGY AND IMPLEMENTATION METHODOLOGY

The design CID (Community and Institutional Development, Cairo) draws combined solutions for children and youth working in the informal sector who have been deprived of a formal education; it works to combat environmental degradation, as well as generate income, around a curriculum which combines theatre arts, music and joy of learning. It is a complex design, which requires the expertise of non-formal educators, solid waste specialists, institutional building know-how and grass roots development practice. It is the marginalised, out-of-school working children and youth and street children who are the main learners in these learning islands. Learners thus come from the informal sector with a rich reservoir of knowledge about labour markets, trading, credit, local technology, survival strategies, social capital, community solidarity, etc.

The innovativeness of the 'schools' lies in the combination of research and action, carried out by the learners themselves. Young people participate directly in the needs assessment and in the running of the projects. This approach is further reinforced by the fact that it is the learners who eventually become the teachers of other children and youth.

The main method of instruction is hands-on instruction in which artisans or facilitators work directly with learners. Numeracy, literacy and business accounting skills, etc., are transmitted through structured, non-formal learning initiatives involving specific activities. Accounting skills are introduced to diversify learners' knowledge so that rather than becoming specialists purely in one skill, they can learn to calculate and manage a business, whatever and whenever it may be. The local environment and its opportunities are used to the greatest extent possible as a source of material and inspiration. Thus trash which is otherwise perceived as a 'nuisance' becomes a valuable commodity and a focus of curriculum design.

NGOS AS AGENTS OF CHANGE AND NON-FORMAL SCHOOLS

Non-formal learning travels best through and among NGOs which work closely to exchange experiences, transfer technologies and learn at the same time as the youth engaged in the experiment. Thus both individuals and institutions learn. They create a working network among them, delineate roles and provide the inputs which move the transformation along among all partners.

NGOs have been found to play a dynamic role in the following areas. They inventory resources a community possesses rather than dwelling on the baseline indicators of need and marginalisation, that is, counting the material resources available in the community (for example, seeking to determine how they currently earn an income, what their economic activities, their marketing outlets, their technical skills level, their expertise, their mobility, their knowledge, their traditional positive practices are); identify potential catalysts within the community and without; target and select youth as the critical participants in the project; promote the idea within the defined locations and present it to the stakeholders; and allocate teachers and trainers for this project. They also work with CID on upgrading the skills of project trainers and teachers; establish recycling learning centres in their towns and neighbourhoods; work on integrating the experience and capabilities of youth with the recycling system; mobilise youth into formal sector companies for new waste management systems; identify the external resources available to the community, such as government clinics, patrons, funding sources, volunteers and markets; and provide the premises for training and administration of the project.

RESULTS

Through non-formal learning programmes for the rag-pickers of the informal sector it has been able: to strengthen, establish and make sustainable training and recycling centres in central geographic points with a high density of marginalised and out-of-school youth from the informal sector; to train educators/facilitators for the training of these youth and introduce functional basic education (literacy, numeracy and business accounting) into activities at workshops and youth centres. Local people with skills have been contracted to train youth in recycling and producing goods and have created market openings through a co-operative system. Youth have been trained in various marketable skills, crafts, sanitation and corresponding technologies. It has been possible to set up a marketing infrastructure and strategy for selling products within national and international industries (with links to tourism) and a co-operative system for young artisans for the sale of products. A coherent packet of training and learning materials relevant to the needs of deprived youth and their communities has been tested and researched by young people themselves. Community events have been held for the improvement of living conditions: environmental awareness days and neighbourhood upgrading schemes. There has been a close partnership with the media, which have continuously given their support by promoting the key issues involved in non-formal basic education.

NON-FORMAL LEARNING PARTNERSHIP WITH THE BUSINESS SECTOR

While most multinationals in the waste sector have been waste management companies which have sought to supplant native processes with their inappropriate Western technologies and systems, the design of the latest non-formal school found a nexus in which the interests of multinationals came to bear upon the preservation of indigenous recovery models. The Association for Garbage Collectors for Community Development (AGCCD) from Mokattam, Cairo is the home of most recent recycling school established by CID with funding from UNESCO and DANIDA.

The Genesis

In 1996 CID conducted a study on Brand Name Fraud for seven multinationals suffering from the problem of their empty brand name containers leaking back onto the informal market and being fraudulently refilled. This is a prevalent Third World phenomenon. The study concluded that a large volume of these empty bottles could be halted at the first link in the market chain, the Mokattam Garbage Settlement. Concurrently, many children had been noticed leaving this settlement on foot, with sacks on their back and venturing out onto the streets of Cairo to scavenge large municipal bins and recover cardboard, aluminium and plastic. These boys were surveyed and were found to come from the poorest of the poor among the garbage collectors. Their parents sometimes did not even own a donkey-pulled cart and suffered from poor health. Thus they were unable to work in the recycling workshops that dotted the neighbourhood and provided income for the families. As a consequence, they were forced to send their young children out to scavenge the bins on the streets of Cairo. This exposed the children to unimaginable health hazards and forced them to forfeit a chance of receiving an education.

Mokattam was identified as the first station for shampoo containers disposed of by affluent residents in Cairo and recovered by the garbage collectors to trade with other merchants. These merchants connect to a complex web of trading networks in the city which include people who refill the bottles with fraudulent products and pass them back on to the market as brand name shampoos, creams, etc.

Curriculum Design

The concept and design of this project are based on requiring 'learners' from among the children to bring to the school recovered empty shampoo containers which are sorted by them according to the expertise developed by their peers and parents in the neighbourhood. A standard form is used for recording their day's 'pickings'. Each learner is required to be able to read it, fill it in, calculate his day's earnings based on the market value of these empty containers and then have the literacy and recycling instructors sign off on it. Each month the consolidated sheets and forms each learner fills out reflect the monthly 'earnings' and recovered shampoo containers. The shampoo multinationals receive these sheets, pay AGCCD for them and it in turn reimburses the learners for the recovered valuable trash. In intervening period, a curriculum is interwoven with the focus of the work. The school and curriculum incorporate learning, working, environmental protection, poverty alleviation and earning into one neat package to give children lifelong learning and earning skills and afresh outlook on life. It keeps the bottles emanating from the seven multinationals from being refilled fraudulently, thereby protecting the companies' reputable product from being tarnished and the companies from great losses due to reduced sales.

The multinationals pay the youth and children who recover the empty shampoo bottles for the value of these items, which are 'destroyed' on the spot. The sheet which records the receipt of the empty bottles constitutes the core of the arithmetic and business math curriculum to be taught at the school. Thus, in essence, big business supports an innovative buy back scheme which creates a learning 'island' in the middle of a neighbourhood marked by trash, stench and small piles of burning residual waste. By being granulated and not simply destroyed, the bottles contribute to the creation of learning curriculum and livelihoods for youth. This process builds on existing networks of recyclers in the neighbourhoods who provide a ready market for the granulated plastic, which enables the school to become a self-financing learning institution—for the poor, by the poor—which protects the business interests of both rich and poor. Waste is upheld as a 'commodity' in keeping with indigenous practice and not perceived as a nuisance the way these same businesses generally perceive it in their countries of origin; local informal markets provide a ready distribution network for the granulated product; and price fluctuations keep the school watching the 'market' in much the same way as big business watches the stock market. Thus learners are not disconnected from the real world of business, trading and credit, and learning is much more relevant than in formal school settings.

Learners go on to learn how to acquire credit from neighbourhood sources in order to buy greater quantities of empty shampoo containers if they are unable to get enough from their own household collection route or street containers. Protective gear is worn during all stages of the sorting and recycling process. For children need to be empowered with income generating opportunities which do not threaten their lives or health and which at the same time provide them with the learning opportunities they were not offered in formal schooling. Thus, while children in this school come from among the poorest of the poor, who have no choice but to work in the worst imaginable circumstances, they end up receiving quality, relevant education at no cost to their families or to the government. They create self-financing schools and can claim to have paid their way through school.

Conclusions and Social Impact

This paper has described non-formal education programmes in Egypt which have reflected the importance of combining work, learning and indigenous knowledge. These interventions have been shown helped to improve the lives of working children in poor and disenfranchised garbage communities in Cairo. Such improvement has been made possible, on the one hand, by setting up an educational system for children who could not go to school and who have to work in difficult and dangerous circumstances in the informal sector and, on the other, by designing and implementing appropriate schemes for the recovery of bottles which could potentially become refilled with fraudulent products. The evaluation of these programmes has shown improvements in the nutritional and health situation of children and their marginalised parents. Children from poor rural areas have been provided with greater ability to face life's challenges. Literacy is acquired—in all its senses. Research has shown that working children are better nourished than poor non-working children. Greater vaccination coverage of mother and children has been achieved, and lifelong learning opportunities through literacy, primary health care, social activities, recreation, etc., have been provided. Support schemes provide learning opportunities for children in the recycling trade. Environmental learning projects have been implemented specifically to address the safe, clean recovery, recycling of unsoiled non-organic waste. These results can be achieved by creating a more sustainable partnership between the business sector and the poor based on business interests rather than on charity.

REFERENCES

Azer, A., & Ramzy, N. (1991). *Child Labour in Egypt*. Cairo: The National Center for Social and Criminological Research and UNICEF-Egypt.

Assaad, R., & Rouchdy, M. (1999). *Poverty and poverty alleviation strategies in Egypt*. Cairo Papers in Social Science, *22*, Monograph 1. Cairo: American University in Cairo Press.

Assaad, M. & Moharram, A. (1995). Unpublished Final report on the separation-at-source scheme as implemented by the association for the protection of the environment. Submitted to the Ford Foundation, January.

Adriaanse, A., et al. (1997). *Resource flows: The material basis of industrial economies*. Washington, DC: World Resources Institute.

Boyden, J., & Myers, W. (1995). *Exploring alternative approaches to combating child labour: Case studies from developing countries*. Innocenti Occasional Papers, Child Rights Series, *8*. New York/Geneva: UNICEF International Child Development Centre (ICDC), New York, and the ILO, Geneva.

Community and Institutional Development (CID). (1998). Unpublished *Study on brand name fraud*. Commissioned by Chemonics/Ahmed Gaber Associates.

Freire, P. (1987). *Pedagogy of the oppressed*. New York: Continuum.

Iskandar Kamel, L. (2002). Ecological education in the living environment. In J.-P. Hautecoeur (ed.), *Ecological education in everyday life, Alpha 2000* (pp. 21–43). Toronto: University of Toronto Press and UNESCO Institute for Education in collaboration with the Canadian Commission for UNESCO.

Iskandar Kamel, L. (1999). *Cairo: A city that learns from the Mokattam recyclers*. Unpublished paper presented to the Social Research Center at the American University in Cairo, Egypt.

ASCE. (1998). *Social and health status and educational achievement of adolescents in Egypt survey*. Cairo: Population Council.

UNEP and HABITAT. (1997). *Implementing the urban environment agenda, Environmental Planning and Management (EMP)*, Source Book, *1*. Nairobi: UNCHS (Habitat)/UNEP, Kenya.

UNESCO Education for All Week on the UNESCO website, April 24, 2004 http://portal.unesco.org/education/en/ev.php-URL_ID=30299&URL_DO=DO_TOPIC&URL_SECTION=201.html.

INSTITUTIONAL SUPPORT STRUCTURES AND MODES OF SKILLS TRANSMISSION

V. V. Krishna

Four components, namely skills training, funding or finances and market avenues, form the core of the institutional arrangements relevant for young people and adults in the informal sector, particularly in a developing country such as India.

STATUS OF FORMAL INSTITUTIONS RELEVANT FOR TRAINING AND SKILLS DEVELOPMENT IN THE INFORMAL SECTOR

When we consider the formal institutions relevant for training and skill dissemination specifically in the informal sector, we find a number of initiatives mainly from governmental agencies and institutions. The importance of training and skills requirements in the informal sector has increasingly come to the attention of policymakers in the past decade. Consequently, a number of programmes sponsored by various ministries and government departments are directly or indirectly relevant to the informal sector. As Mamgain and Awasthi (2001) point out, there are a number of inadequacies in the conventional skill development system which the government initiatives are beginning to address. For instance, these inadequacies are: (a) the existing system's inability to cover the entire spectrum which the informal sector population needs for skills and training for employment generation; (b) traditional apprenticeships leave gaps in the job-related knowledge of workers in various technical trades; and (c) conventional skills development systems do not address the changing business management skills required for the informal sector. However, before we begin to explore the problems underlying the subject at issue, it is necessary to review briefly the status of formal institutional sources of training which are relevant to the informal sector.

The salient features of the different formal institutional sources of training programmes and schemes available in the informal sector are as follows:

Vocational Training: Three types of programmes are available in the vocational training offered by the central government: for secondary school level, 10+2 level and the first-degree level. The vocational training schemes from the government are aimed at reaching both the formal and the informal sectors. 'Formal' here means regular schools. The informal sector is reached mainly through the NGOs or specially designed programmes from government institutions which are offered intermittently. The main pur-

Madhu Singh, (ed.), Meeting Basic Learning Needs in the informal Sector, 75-90.

pose of the secondary school level programme is to develop vocational interests among students. Thus far 56 NGOs have received assistance for reaching out to the informal sector, and the programme is reported to be in operation in about 652 schools.

At the +2 level of vocational training, there are about 150 vocational courses introduced in the fields of agriculture, business and commerce, engineering and technology, health and paramedical services, etc. The government is planning to enrol about one million students in such training and thereby reach out to 25 percent of the secondary school level students by 2000. This programme provides three years training, one of which is devoted to apprenticeship under the Apprenticeship Act.

The vocational training programme for people at the first-degree level commenced in the mid-1990s. It aims at enabling students to set up their own small enterprises. The scheme is mainly designed to train teachers of vocational subjects in universities and colleges and is in operation in 1,356 colleges, as well as in some universities.

In 1977 a vocational training programme for women was initiated with the assistance of the ILO and SIDA (Swedish Agency for International Development). This programme is carried out by a network comprising one national and 10 regional training institutions. So far about 1,900 training positions have been created and 17,462 women have been trained in various subjects.

Shramik Vidyapeeths *and Community Polytechnics*: These two programmes operate under the auspices of India's Department of Education. In 1998, 58 institutes were set up under the scheme of *Shramik Vidyapeeths*. The main thrust of this programme is to impart multi-dimensional training and education in urban areas in order to develop skills and upgrade skills for income generation and its enhancement. The scheme offers about 225 different vocational training programmes ranging from candle- and *agarbatti*-making to computer courses.

Community Polytechnics is a two-decades-old programme which aims at rural industrialisation through the application of science and technology. This programme aims to improve the quality of life by providing location/culture-specific, need-based, short-term training in skills and vocational trades. The target groups are generally unemployed youth, school and college dropouts and other underprivileged segments of the rural population.

Schemes under the Ministry of Rural Areas and Employment: A number of programmes—including the Employment Assurance Scheme for the Development of Women and Children in Rural Areas (DWCRA) and for Training of Rural Youth for Self-Employment (TRYSEM) under this Ministry—aim providing training in various skills in order to help trainees to secure employment and income generation in rural areas. The DWCRA was initiated in 1982. Under the Integrated Rural Development Programme, it aims both at imparting skills for income generation and at promoting various activities among women for improving their social and economic status. The programme groups 10–15 women based on their skills, aptitudes, etc. NGOs with the aid of CAPART (supported by the Ministry) have been the main actors in implementing this programme in rural areas. TRYSEM was initiated in 1979 and has as its objective the development of technical and entrepreneurial skills among rural youth aged 18–35 who come from families below the poverty line. The programme trains youth in Community Polytechnics and extension centres, *Krishi Vigyan Kendras*, state institutes involved in rural development and other institutions, including ITIs, depending on the needs of the area. These training programmes generally last about six months.

Schemes under the Department of Women and Child Development: There are two programmes specifically for women in rural and urban regions which provide training in various fields. The first is the Support to Training and Employment Programme (STEP), which is also implemented by NGOs; the second is the programme that combines employment and income generation with the setting up of production units and is assisted by the Norwegian Agency for Development Co-operation (NORAD). In the latter programme training is given to women and school dropouts in non-traditional trades, such as electronics, watch-making and assembly, printing and binding, handlooms, weaving and spinning, garments, beauty related work and typing. Financial assistance is given to grantee organisations for renting premises, machinery and equipment and daycare centres for women's children. There is also a programme of intensive courses of education and vocational training for women administered by the Central Social Welfare Board.

Training Centres under the Khadi and Village Industry Commission (KVIC): This is one of the oldest organisations involved in the development of rural industries by supporting training and imparting skills. There are about 51 training centres, as well as some production units. Training is provided in 120 courses in the areas of artisans, entrepreneurships, textiles, accountancy and marketing, etc.

Schemes under the Ministry of Rural Development's Council for Advancement of Peoples Action and Rural Technology (CAPART): Its objective is to facilitate the implementation of sustainable rural development projects, to act as a national database on voluntary action, to act as a national nodal agency for the development and dissemination of appropriate rural technologies, to promote participation and voluntary action, and to network with national and international institutions. Some of the major support initiatives sponsored by CAPART which are directly relevant to the informal sector are as follows:

Public Co-operation Scheme: This is an omnibus scheme aimed at promoting innovative and integrated projects and programmes not already covered by one of the existing governmental schemes. Micro-finance, health and sanitation, education, rural energy, sustainable development, disaster management, housing and environmental protection are some of the areas and fields in which innovative projects are offered to voluntary organisations which can assist either a village or *panchayats* (local village government) for comprehensive development for a period of three years by holding Participatory Rural Appraisal sessions with the respective *gram sabha* (village committee).

Rural Technology Scheme: This is a scheme implemented in consultation with Technology Resource Centres (TRCs), which are mainly located in rural areas and focus on upgrading technology and skill developments, to transfer technologies already developed by national laboratories and institutions. The technologies identified include rural housing, water conservation, village industries, food processing, herbal medicines, bio-mass utilisation and handicrafts.

Disability Action Scheme: This provides projects for the support of the disabled in order to help them to become economically independent and partners in developmental processes. The emphasis is on voluntary agencies with the capacity to work in the field and which are mainly oriented towards development.

Young Professionals Scheme: This project seeks to recruit young professionals on campus for work in rural and micro-enterprises. It offers trainees a stipend of rupees 8000, 25 percent of which is to be borne by the voluntary organisation for which the trainee works. After the training, the professionals can start their own voluntary organisation or NGO to implement CAPART's schemes.

As is well known, there are formal institutions—such as the *Khadi* and Village Industries Commission under the Ministry of Industries and other institutions in the Departments and Ministries of Rural Development, Child Welfare and Women's Development—which were created to aid the development of village, cottage and small sectors, including the informal sector. But as the above studies, and particularly the recent survey by Raghunandan (2000a–b), show, the direct relevance of such formal institutions to the development of the informal sector has been minimal, though they do organise workshops and sponsor training programmes mainly through NGOs. One can also include here other formal institutions in higher education, Industrial Training Institutes, science and technology including the Department of Science and Technology (DST), national laboratories under the Council of Scientific and Industrial Research (CSIR). While much of the work of the CSIR, DST and other institutions is concerned with the demands of industry, as well as of science and technology, only a small proportion of their efforts prove to be relevant to the needs and demands of the informal sector. But even here, such limited relevance has taken on greater significance in the last decade due to the intervention of some dedicated NGOs (see Raghunandan, 2000).

As to agricultural development in rural areas, the Agriculture Universities and Indian Council of Agriculture Research has run *Krishi Vigyan Kendras* (education centres for farmers) to educate farmers. Similarly, the CSIR laboratories for leather, food processing, mechanical, electronics, drugs and pharmaceuticals, chemical and biological research, provide technologies and skill development packages which are relevant to the informal sector, but CSIR and other such agencies are constrained to disseminate these technologies to the informal sector directly. There are very few training programmes offered by these agencies to the informal sector. They become relevant through mediation of NGOs. Training aimed at skill development, vocational education and other support activities of CAPART and other government agencies is offered through NGOs.

The DST's Science and Society Division (SSD) embarked in the mid-1980s on a programme to develop new approaches and perspectives, based on the previous history and experiences, aimed at the development of rural artisans and poor producers who have traditional technical skills and knowledge. An important objective of the SSD was to undertake the development of skills and traditional knowledge in collaboration with NGOs. The DST was not alone in this endeavour. The national laboratories of CSIR in food processing, leather, mechanical engineering, chemistry, drugs and pharmaceuticals, etc., which have developed a large number of technologies relevant to the poor and micro-enterprises in the informal sector needed NGOs to make their knowledge and technology relevant to the informal sector. Worthy of mention here are also groups such as Application of Science and Technology to Rural Areas (ASTRA) of the Indian Institute of Science, Bangalore. There are other formal institutions whose objective is to reach clients in the informal sector, for example, the Gandhian Institute of Studies in Varanasi, the Planning Research and Action Division of the Planning Institute in Lucknow and the Centre for Science in Villages in Wardha, Madhya Pradesh.

The most recent initiative of the DST in collaboration with the NGO Honey Bee Network, Ahmedabad, India, is the establishment of the National Innovation Foundation (NIF) in Ahmedabad in 2000. A central objective of the NIF is to document rural and community grassroots innovations based on indigenous knowledge systems in all fields and sectors of the rural economy and to safeguard their intellectual property. The importance of the NIF and of the DST's initiative lies in their linking of the formal and informal sectors to document all grassroots innovations country-wide and then to make institutional efforts to make these innovations commercially viable by creating enterprises wherever such potential exits. This linkage, however, is carried out by intermediary science-based NGOs and agencies which play an important role in the imparting and enhancement of skills in the process making the innovations commercially viable and, at the same time, in the education of rural communities concerning the importance of their valuable traditional knowledge, which could be transformed into intellectual property.

A predominant proportion of the educational and training resources, including the materials and financing from the formal institutional structure, is directed to formalised industry sectors and the 'upper end' of medium- and small-scale enterprises. When we begin to explore and document the relevance of formal training providers to individuals, groups and communities in the informal sector, the situation is not very encouraging. This is somewhat of a colonial legacy, which is reflected in the neglect of vocational and other forms of training and education in the post-1947 period, as has been convincingly shown in a recent study (Singh, 2001). Over the last two decades, other studies and surveys have also underlined the 'step-motherly' treatment of people in the informal sector in addressing their educational and vocational training, people who make up a significant proportion of active labour force (see Altbach & Kelly, 1978; Tilak, 1988; NCERT, 1990; Kundu & Sharma, 2001).

For instance, the KVIC, which is one of the oldest institutions for the development of small and medium enterprises and village industries, including the informal sector, has come under sharp criticism from a recent study by the Institute of Applied Manpower Research (IAMR). Based on this study, Mamgain and Awasthi (2001) point out that, apart from not being employment-oriented, the KVIC's training programmes do not appear to encourage the self-employment of youth in rural areas. The study also notes that the quality of training is 'poor' and that many of the courses designed by the KVIC are outdated. Furthermore, this study throws light on the inadequacy of the equipment and infrastructure support in the training centres and on the fact that the teaching staff is under-qualified. On the other hand, the ministry-administered programmes and schemes such as the Department of Women and Child Development and the Ministry of Rural Areas and Employment get entangled in bureaucratic and rural-political interests, which tend to overshadow the real needs and demands of informal sector workers. For instance, whereas the bulk of workers lack minimum education, skills and other means of supporting their training needs, there is little to no emphasis in the existing ministry programmes in rural and urban areas on addressing such pressing needs. Again, as some surveys and studies indicate, the manual labourers and wage earners who wish to improve their education and skills or to obtain training find no relevant schemes to compensate them for the loss of wages they would suffer while seeking such training. This is a real problem for the majority of workers in the informal sector. A 'vicious circle' of sorts holds such workers hostage: they have to improve their skills if they are to enhance their income and climb the socio-economic ladder; yet they cannot do so for the lack of schemes which really compensate them while they pursue the requisite training.

While there are several research studies conducted by universities and research institutions on the social, technical and economic aspects of the informal sector, very few of these have impacted on the lives of workers through practical training and education programmes for that sector. Much of the problem of the relevance of formal institutions arises from the lack of intermediary institutional processes of training and education for the development of skills and upgrading pre-existing artisan skills. It is here that NGOs become crucial as intermediary agents, linking the formal to the informal sector, particularly with regard to training and education in social and technical skills, capabilities and competencies. In science education, it has been especially NGOs such as Hoshangabad Science Teaching Programme (HSTP) in Madhya Pradesh and Kerala Shastra Sahitya Parishad (KSSP) in Kerala which have initiated informal teaching to expose children and adults who have dropped out of school to 'scientific methodology' and the 'scientific mindset'. Although much of the energy of these programmes has been devoted at catalysing popular science movements in India (see Krishna, 1997), they have had played a large role in launching adult education and literacy programmes through Ministry of Education, programmes which are still in operation today.

The major shortcoming of formal institutions run by government departments responsible for the informal sector is that they are not directly involved in the training at the micro-enterprise level of the informal sector. Much of the training and education which has been organised and exists at the level of schools, universities and specialised institutions is directly geared to the needs and demands of industry and the organised sector. For example, there are several important formal institutional structures, including governmental ministries and departments, CAPART, KVIC, CSIR, DST and others, but none of them have an institutionalised training programmes which takes direct responsibility for the informal sector. Their reliance on NGOs for training and education has become inevitable in many ways. It is in light of this state of affairs that the present report has sought to investigate some relatively successful cases in the informal sector (see boxes 1–5 in Table 1 below for the case studies examined in the present study) and the role of NGOs therein. As mentioned earlier, the objective of this study on Northern India is to develop an understanding of how training and skills development is given to workers in the informal sector, to map interesting cases of skill transfer which combine social and technical learning processes and to draw lessons that may be pertinent for the design and implementation of policies and programmes. In the following section, we shall explore the key features of and some processes underlying the success of these cases. But before doing so, it is necessary to spell out some of the methodological issues involved in the selection of the case studies and NGOs for this study.

When we look into the core elements of the relevant, existing institutional arrangements, three aspects come into view. First, the existing institutional structure is largely dominated by and geared to the needs and demands of the formal sector, both in the public and private domains. Second, while over the years the state, actors and agencies in the private sector have created some institutional support structures which may be said to be relevant to the informal sector, their relevance is again limited to the 'upper end' of the informal sector. Lastly, in the Indian context only a very small or residual component of the formal institutional structures (both pubic and private) is addresses the learning needs and demands of that part of informal sector where the problem actually lies—that is, the 'lower end' of the informal sector. For the sake of convenience, the 'upper' and 'lower' ends of the informal sector may be termed the 'modern' and 'traditional' segments, respectively.

While some level of education (minimum of primary/secondary) and endowment of skills (a mix of a both modern and traditional skills in carpentry, bricklaying, mechanics, electrical and painting, including the repair of various materials and equipment, computers, retailing, designing, real estate, building, auto drivers, hair cutting and style) characterise the upper end of the informal sector, the persons at the lower end are characterised by illiteracy to below-primary level of education and have mostly tradition-bound skills, such as cooking, cobbling, or they make shoes and are caste-based, micro-level vendors selling on the streets and 'bazaars', domestic workers, helpers working in shops, rickshaw pullers, etc.

LEVEL OF EDUCATION DETERMINES THE ABILITY TO LEARN AND UPGRADE SKILLS

Formal institutional structure for training and skill transfer, as things stand, appears to be irrelevant to the needs of the informal sector (lower end) unless aided by some mechanisms or the intervention of other groups.

Some relevant case studies (see, e.g., my paper in Section 2 of this volume) undertaken in Northern and Southern India (which are relevant to our concerns here) reveal the necessity of 'intermediary institutional processes' for training and skill transfer, economic and social empowerment and catering to other needs of workers in the informal sector. In many of the cases studied in India, it is revealed that NGOs, trade unions, community groups, missionaries and other actors have assumed the role of intermediary agencies, which give relevance to the formal institutional structure of training and skills for the informal sector as a whole (both upper- and lower-end spectrums). Given the transitory nature of the operation of NGOs and other groups and given the fact that these groups operate and are driven by the funding patterns of public and private agencies, intermediary groups such as NGOs prove to be relevant only for the short or medium term. There is an urgent need to institutionalise groups, actors and agencies which will perform intermediary institutional functions within both the public and the private domains and cater to the needs of the informal sector for the long term.

The case studies of the Barefoot College, Tilonia and the Annapurna Mahila Mandal (AMM), New Mumbai (see my paper in Section 2 of this volume) are instructive in this regard, for these institutions have been operating successfully for the last 30 years or so as intermediary institutions for training and skill transfer, financing micro-enterprises (in the case of AMM) and creating new market avenues for the products of and work in the informal sector.

IMPORTANCE OF INTERMEDIARY AGENCIES

While NGOs and other groups are relevant for short-term solutions, intermediary agencies which are institutionalised and devoted to the needs of the informal sector (such as the AMM and the Barefoot College) appear to provide long-term perspectives for addressing the needs of the informal sector on the one hand and forging important links to the formal sector on the other. One such intermediary NGO, to which we referred above, is the Honey Bee Network, which was initiated and is led by Anil Gupta and which seeks to identify and document grassroots innovations in the domain of indigenous knowledge systems in the informal sectors of the Indian economy. Over the past decade and a half, this network articulated 'social and ethical capital' at the grassroots level and initiated a 'movement' to safeguard the intellectual property of grassroots innovators and rural communities. In collaboration with formal institutions such as DST and the Gujrat state government, this network is also codifying rural innovations and patenting their intellectual property on behalf of the communities which have made the innovations. The work of Honey Bee Network does not stop there, however. In 1997 it created Gujrat Grassroots Innovation Augmentation Network (GIAN) with the assistance of the government. The main task of GIAN is to perform the important intermediary task of linking the formal and informal sectors of the knowledge economy to benefit rural communities and grassroots innovators. It performs the significant task of mobilizing and providing risk capital, making technical skills and know-how accessible to potential entrepreneurs and training rural people in appropriate skills in the process of commercializing potential grassroots innovations. The creation of small and micro-enterprises based on such innovations is a central objective for the Honey Bee Network and GIAN. These NGOs have transformed several innovations into products and filed patents on behalf of grassroots innovators over the last three years (see Gupta et al., 2003).

The limitations of NGOs and other agencies, from the perspective of their short-term relevance, should not be taken to mean that their role has only residual importance. On the contrary, they play a very important role in the short- and medium-terms by raising or improving the skill levels of workers in the informal sector. This institutional process of raising the educational or literacy levels of workers is important insofar as it determines the mobility of workers.

While people in the informal sector have little or no access to 'formal entitlements' in education and training for a number of economic reasons, there are hardly any formal and public institutions which are directly involved in running programmes for these workers. Consequently, the groups which are most active in skill development and educational and training programmes for workers in the informal sector are the NGOs, trade unions, community groups and others. However, since most of these groups involved in training and skill development are dependent on governmental agencies and ministries of rural development, women's welfare and development, etc., for funds, the government should develop appropriate policies for promoting such NGOs in their 'task' of education, training and skill development in non-formal institutional ways for the informal sector.

A worker's level of education determines his ability to learn and upgrade his skills, and thus his ability to move from the 'lower' to the 'higher end' of the informal sector. NGOs, SHGs, and trade organisations appear to be better endowed than formal institutions to penetrate the life-world of workers in the informal sector and to design employment-oriented educational programmes that meet their needs.

PRIVATE SECTOR AND INDUSTRY ASSOCIATIONS: EMERGING AS KEY PLAYERS

Economic reforms followed by liberalisation and globalisation have created a new demand for skills in a number of new areas, sectors of the economy that depend on workers with knowledge and sophisticated skills. Closely related to the upper end of the informal sector, these new areas of the economy range from information and communication technologies, the entertainment industry, the leisure and travel industry to mobile catering and fashion design (covering a range of products, including jewellery, leather goods, garments and ceramics). Catalysed by the information revolution, these new areas of the informal sector are based on new institutional structures. Many firms and individuals operate from home or small offices, with flexible working hours and are connected with a variety of clients through information technology and computer-based networks.

When we examine the source of institutional structure of support (that is, the core elements noted above) for the new areas of the informal sector, we find that here again the relevance of formal structures in the public domain is quite limited. To a large extent the private sector and industry associations are emerging as key players regarding the provision of institutional support to the new informal sector of the economy.

Knowledge and new technical skills, coupled with the emerging demand for upgrading existing skills, pose new institutional challenges for both the generation of new skills and mechanisms of their dissemination. At the core of these new institutional challenges is the spectrum of learning processes and training methodologies for workers in the informal sector. A radical shift in knowledge and technology is taking place across the wide spectrum of manufacturing sectors and in small- and medium-scale enterprises, including industrial districts (which contribute about 40 percent of India's GDP and are dominated by workers and firms from the informal sector), which threatens the survival of workers in the informal sector.

VALUE ADDITION THROUGH TECHNOLOGY AND KNOWLEDGE

The comparative advantages enjoyed by developing countries like India due to comparatively low labour costs is seriously threatened by globalisation. Small sector units which are dependent on micro-level informal sector units are already facing tough competition from a range of imported manufactured goods. In other words, the advantage of cheap labour, combined with the reserves of natural and local resources for small production units, resources on which a significant proportion of the informal sector depends for its survival, will not last long. The relevance of new technologies, particularly information and communication technologies, biotechnologies and micro-electronics, to workers and units in the informal sector will depend on the workers' level of skills and their ability to adapt them. A debate is already emerging on the question of inequalities and new technologies in India. In the long run, it is technical change, as well as the upgrading of skills and organisational and entrepreneurial abilities, that will increasingly determine business and economic prospects and hence the sustainability of any enterprise. It is here that educational and training strategies will determine the future prospects of India's informal sector.

Cheap manual and low-skilled labour and natural resources are unlikely to give comparative economic advantage for long. In the fast-changing economy marked by policies favouring liberalisation and globalisation, it is value addition through technology and knowledge that is going to play the decisive role in sustaining the existing markets for a range of manufactured products from the small- and medium-scale enterprises.

The existing knowledge institutions, including science and technology institutions and universities, have largely remained somewhat isolated from the needs of the small- and medium-scale enterprises based on the economy's informal sector. As the demand for new skills and the upgrading of skills and knowledge increases, the goals and structures of these knowledge-based formal institutional structures must be recast in order to meet the needs of the informal sector.

SOME ASPECTS RELATING TO DELIVERY OF TRAINING

Much of the training in technical and social competencies undertaken by NGOs is given in on-the-job training and apprenticeships where 'learning by doing' and 'learning by interaction' play an important role. The 'new role of NGOs' for imparting outside-job training and skill development programmes should make use of the existing formal schools and institutions in the evening or 'out of office hours'. Not only is the Barefoot College's night school programme the most appropriate example along these lines, but the Barefoot College itself is the most relevant model for evolving policies directed at institutional innovations in adult and non-formal education in the informal sector. *There is no shortcut to aiding and developing the informal sector; the only way to succeed is to provide training and skill development by non-formal means.*

Another important lesson taught by the experiences of Barefoot College is the way in which the college has been able to 'demystify technology' for ordinary people in rural areas and train barefoot solar engineers, hand-pump mechanics, communicators, construction engineers, etc. The college has successfully 'demystified' the conventional assumption that 'technical competencies' and 'technical learning' can be transmitted only through professional and formal institutional mechanisms and means. Here one thinks of a whole range of technical and installation procedures involved in the technologies and devices used in the rural context of industrialisation. By training barefoot engineers and skilled personnel in a range of trades, the college has established a new institutional and conceptual basis for understanding how 'learning by doing' and 'learning by interaction' work in the case of technology dissemination in rural contexts.

Demystifying Technical Competencies and Learning

The Barefoot College has successfully 'demystified' the conventional assumption that 'technical competencies' and 'technical learning' can be transmitted only through professional and formal institutional mechanisms and means to workers, firms and agencies in the informal sector.

By the same token, the experiences of the AMM also holds many lessons concerning areas of micro-credit and the development of women entrepreneurs for micro-enterprises (in the meals and Tiffin supply networks). The AMM has provided micro-credit for women for the past 25 years. In a very innovative manner, this NGO has shown how the objectives of training in 'social' and 'collective' competencies (including leadership) can be combined with micro-financing in the informal sector by designing appropriate methods of loan disbursement to groups of women from a particular local area. These methods also give new insights into the recovery of loans by means of an intra-group accountability system orchestrated by the group's leader and other group members. Recurring loans of higher amounts to group members are tied to the repayment obligations of members in the group. This is said to have reinforced the accountability system. The experiences of the AMM and a well-documented case of SEWA, Ahmedabad, have demonstrated the sustainable role of NGOs in micro-credit finance for the informal sector, which formal financial institutions have yet to penetrate due to several bureaucratic problems regarding guarantee mechanisms. These NGOs have, each in its own way, evolved appropriate methods for the disbursement and recovery of loans at much lower rates of interest than formal financial institutions. These provide relevant examples in micro-credit finance for the development of policies and their promotion in the much larger context of the informal sector, where it is particularly pressing that women workers be trained in entrepreneurship.

One of the major problems in diffusing relevant technologies (e.g. in leather, food processing, building and manufacturing) available or developed in the formal science and technology institutions to enterprises in the informal sector concerns a whole range of extension services, including scaling down the technology to suit micro-level enterprise, upgrading traditional skills to manage technical processes, training in suitable alternative technical processes to traditional processes and networking with formal technology support institutions for 'venture capital' and 'risk aversion' funding. CTD/STD and PRADAN have demonstrated that NGOs are better placed in accomplishing the task of technology diffusion to the informal sector since these organisations have developed certain 'organisational core competencies' which are not generally possible for formal institutions. For example, in the case of diffusing improved vegetable tanning processes for leather, which replaced the traditional and more cumbersome process, the aforementioned organisations helped to establish flayer co-operatives and networks so as to eliminate 'middlemen' in Uttar Pradesh and Himachal Pradesh. In the case of CTD/STD, it combined the training in developing social and technical competencies in the artisans and created nodal tanning centre at Mandi which served as a model to replicate self-sustaining tanning centres in more than 20 towns and villages in India. Without the intervention of CTD/STD, the impact of CLRI technology to improve and sustain the social and economic conditions of flayers and tanners in Himachal and other states would not have been possible. The case of CTD/STD in leather and food processing clearly demonstrates the new role of NGOs in 'consultancy for technology diffusion to the informal sector' and in bridging the 'communication and structural gaps' between the formal and the informal sectors.

Another important problem confronted by the informal sector units is the lack of adequate support for business opportunities through branding of products and marketing channels. In our case studies, CTD/STD as a nodal NGO, which is co-ordinating the activities of several independent small NGO enterprises in leather and food processing had taken upon itself the responsibility to register common brands (ARTISAN'S for leather products; and FARMER'S for fruit and vegetable processed products). But discussions held with various actors involved in the informal sector, reveals the need for co-operative marketing channels promoted by local or state governments and a certain quota of assured procurement of products. The individual state governments and central agencies also need to provide a space in the state controlled mass media for advertising the products from the informal sector till such time the industry is able to absorb the advertisement rents. Rather, training, 'de-scaling' technology to suit small enterprises or upgrading traditional technology, co-operative marketing operations including quality control measures need to be organised in the mode of clusters at the regional level. So far, the support of government agencies is only limited to promotion of products from the small and cottage sector at exhibitions in India and abroad.

Need for Institutional Mix

Case studies of the Indian context clearly demonstrate the need for an institutional mix, that is, the need for multiple institutions (government, NGOs, intermediary agencies and community groups) to generate relevant technologies, transfer skills and techniques and to deliver training (with a correspondingly certain division of labour) in the informal sector.

While the private sector, or the agencies within it, is already geared to the changing needs for training and upgrading skills at the upper end of the informal sector, particularly in the new areas and sectors opened up by globalisation, it remains necessary to concentrate on the 'lower end' of the informal sector.

For the 'upper end' of this sector, there is already a new partnership evolving between trade and industry associations (in the private sector) and formal institutions in the government and semi-government sectors for the training in and transfer of relevant skills. However, the real problem lies at 'lower end' regarding the organisation and regulation of training and skill transfer. Experience shows that there is an urgent need to expand the actors in intermediary agencies and to institutionalise potential NGOs and other groups for the long term. To achieve this, it is necessary to replicate the 'best practices' and 'models' of such groups as the Barefoot College, CTD and the AMM. The work of NGOs such as the Honey Bee Network and GIAN, referred to above, provides important examples, as does that of the CTD and the Barefoot College. In many ways, these science-based NGOs have placed the relevance of indigenous knowledge systems, or what may be called 'subaltern science', in the centre of the debate on development, thereby reflecting Gandhian economic philosophy. Furthermore, one can gain many insights and draw several policy implications from them on how to meaningfully bridge 'formal' and 'informal' sectors of the economy, society and knowledge systems in such a way as to sustain rural communities in developing countries.

Table 1. Different Formal Institutional Sources of Training Programmes, Schemes and Initiatives

for the Informal Sector

S. No	Training Programmes/Schemes	Sponsored/Offered by	Fields/Topics	Other Details
1	Vocational Training: Lower school 10+2 level, Degree level Vocational training programme for women.	Central Govt. Department of Technical Education through ILO/SIDA.	Agriculture, engineering technology, business, commerce, health, home science, services, etc.	Lower school training in 652 Schools; 56 NGOs used this scheme at 6500 schools with 150 vocational courses Introduced in 1356 colleges in 35 subjects.
2	*Shramik Vidyapeeths* (Non-formal, adult and continuing education, for urban community in imparting skills) Community Polytechnics.	Department of Education, Government of India.	225 different programmes: in incense stick and candle making, computer design, construction, plumbing, fabrication, welding, etc.	The aim of the programme is to develop skills and upgrade income generation. 516 community polytechnics (83 for women alone).
3	Employment, Assurance Scheme Integrated Rural Development Programme, Development of Women & Children in Rural Areas (DWCRA), Training of Rural Youth for Self-Employment (TRYSEM).	Ministry of Rural Areas and Employment.	DWCRA for any economic activity of women; TRYSEM is for entrepreneurial skills for youth, 18-35.	DWCRA is implemented by District Rural Development Agencies. TRYSEM training is for six months imparted through ITIs or other centres in the districts.
4	Provision of Support to Training and Employment Programme (STEP) NORAD-assisted programme Intensive courses of education and vocational training.	Department of Women and Child Development.	Electronics, watch-making, weaving and spinning, garment-making, beauty, typing, etc.	51 projects sanctioned so far; Focus on non-traditional areas; given to women aged 15+ years.
5	Training Centres.	*Khadi* & Village Industries Commission.		12 Multidisciplinary; 12 *Khadi Gramodyog vidyalayas*, 24 village industries and 10 training-cum-production centres owned by societies. 120 courses given in different areas/fields.
6	Public co-operation scheme, Rural technology scheme, Disability action scheme, Young professional scheme.	CAPART, Ministry of Rural Development.	All manufacturing sectors in rural and urban areas.	Co-ordinates training and skill imparting activities through NGOs and other institutions.
7	Prime Minister's *Rozgar Yojana.*	Ministry of Rural Development.	Entrepreneurial training.	Specifically for unemployed persons aged 18–35.
8	National Innovation Foundation.	Department of Science and Technology.	Grassroots innovations/ Indigenous knowledge systems in all sectors.	Imparting skills, commercialising grassroots innovations and creating enterprises.

REFERENCES

Altbach, P. G., & Kelly, G. P. (1978). *Education and colonialism.* New York: Longman.

Gupta, A. K., et al. (2003). Mobilising grassroots technological innovations and traditional knowledge, values and institutions. Articulating social and ethical capital, *Futures*, *35*, 975–87.

ILO. (1998). *World employment report 1998–99 – Employability in the global economy: How training matters.* Geneva: ILO.

Krishna, V. V. (1997). Science, technology and counter-hegemony: Some reflections on the contemporary science movements in India. In T. Shinn, J. Spaapen & V. V. Krishna (eds.), *Science and technology in a developing world, sociology of the sciences yearbook* (pp. 375–411). Dordrecht: Kluwer Academic Press.

Kundu, A., & Sharma, A. N. (eds.). *Informal sector in India: Perspectives and policies.* New Delhi: Manohar Publishers.

Mamgain, R. P., & Awasthi, I. C. (2001). Technology and training for informal sector: Need for new initiatives. In Kundu & Sharma (eds.), *Informal Sector in India*, 363–380.

National Council of Educational Research and Training (NCERT). (1990). *Vocationalisation of education: Achievements in the seventh five-year plan.* New Delhi: NCERT.

Raghunandan, D. (2000a). Best practices in technology dissemination for rural industries: National scenario in India. Paper presented at APCTT Workshop on Best Practice for Technology Delivery aimed at Promoting Rural and Small Industries, Bogor, Indonesia, 1–2 December.

Singh, M. (2001). Reflections on colonial legacy and dependency in Indian Vocational Education and Training (VET): A societal and cultural perspective. *Journal of Education and Work*, *14:2*, 209–25.

Tilak, J. B. G. (1988). Vocational education in South Asia: Problems and prospects. *International Review of Education*, *34*, 255–57.

GENDER AND THE INFORMAL ECONOMY IN LATIN AMERICA: NEW CHALLENGES AND POSSIBLE ANSWERS FOR LABOUR TRAINING POLICIES

Sara Silveira and Anaclara Matosas

The role played by the informal economy, which in most cases represents the only employment opportunity for an increasing segment of the Latin American population—particularly for women who are heads of households—means that people have to resort to informal activities to survive and mitigate the effects of poverty. The interdependence of the precariousness, lack of protection and low income levels in the vast majority of Latin American informal jobs means that women's participation in the labour world is still characterised by conditions of inequality and economic and social vulnerability. Thus, reducing the 'decent work' deficit[1] is, at the same time, the greatest and most urgent regional challenge, and one of the most powerful mechanisms against exclusion and marginality.

This article[2] elaborates the design and implementation of two programmes: the FORMUJER (Regional Programme to Strengthen the Vocational and Technical Training of Low-income Women) and the Programme for the Promotion of Equal Opportunities for Women in Employment and Vocational Training (PROIMUJER), which aim to promote employability and gender equality in Latin America, with special reference to women in low income jobs. The programmes adopt an approach which includes strengthening regional institutions, promoting innovative methodologies, improving the quality of training provision and enhancing the competencies of employability and citizenship of women and men. Above all, they seek to integrate the gender perspective in all aspects of the teaching and learning process. This paper presents the main methodologies developed, results reached and lessons learned by these programmes. The methodologies have proved relevant to national policies on vocational education and training designed to combat poverty by increasing opportunities of work insertion and access, especially for the informal sector and young people, and other vulnerable and discriminated segments of the population. We begin by giving an analysis of the distinctive characteristics of the employment situation and women's role in the informal economy in Latin America.

THE NEW EMPLOYMENT[3] SCENARIO

Globalisation causes a compression of time and space: it reduces economic and cultural distances, and it means that decisions and activities on any part of the planet have effects on and redefine national and regional development processes. While it generates opportunities, it also causes a certain precariousness.

Madhu Singh, (ed.), Meeting Basic Learning Needs in the informal Sector, 91-118.

Human labour is now based on contextualised and pertinent knowledge. Education has become the centre of the new society, and it definitely distinguishes the rich from the poor, both as regards people and as regards countries. Poverty does not only mean having less capital but also less knowledge and of a poorer quality. Those who are not able to produce or consume relevant knowledge run a very high risk of being excluded. On the other hand, women are not a secondary labour force anymore; they have consolidated the 'double presence' model, facing up to the difficult combination of the working cycle with family life. This involves the emergence of new identities, new lifestyles, and a reconfiguration of men and women in public and private matters and the corresponding gender relationships.

The well-known model of increasing, predictable and permanent employment and mass labour has entered into crisis. In the modern world temporariness coexists with short-term projects. Mobility between enterprises, formal and informal employment, the alternation between periods of employment and unemployment, the appearance of alternative labour relationships (part-time jobs, work at home, task jobs) are the new characteristics of the world of labour.

Urban informal labour has become a substantial part of employment, because of the new entrepreneurial organisation practices and also as an escape valve for the slowdown in the rhythm of growth of formal employment.

Employment is generated in small amounts (almost one job at a time) and small- and medium-sized enterprises (PYMES), micro-enterprises and local development processes become particularly important in the creation of jobs. This broad field of action requires that organisations and people be capable of adapting and transforming continuously so as to be able to face the labour world and to position themselves advantageously as regards the various available modalities.

At the same time, new activities related to sustainable development, information technologies and communication have emerged, as well as the new needs born of social changes.

The entrance of technology into homes (modernisation) and the shift of domestic tasks to the public space have led to an increasing demand in the market for traditionally home-based services. This opens up a whole world of alternative insertions which demands new skills that have to be strengthened and/or acquired.

Thus we could say that the new labour aims at diversity, flexibility and instability; it requires intelligence, polyvalence, self-responsibility, initiative and a capacity for enterprise, as well as the ability to manage uncertainty and change. This is closely connected with local aspects and new fields of employment.

THE LATIN AMERICAN CONTEXT: HIGH UNEMPLOYMENT RATES AND THE INCREASE IN INFORMALITY

As reported by the International Labour Organisation (ILO), labour performance in Latin America during the last decade has been erratic. Economic recovery processes have been and still are interrupted by continuous crises, and unemployment remains resistant to any cure even at times when economies gain strength.

Currently, an estimated 19 million people are unemployed; the average urban unemployment rate in the region in the first months of 2002 was 9.2 percent. The impact of these unemployment rates is generalised since they affect all groups of workers, but mostly women and young people (ILO, 2002a).

Even though different countries show different trends and developments in urban unemployment, one can say there is a tendency towards a steady increase. Argentina, Brazil and Venezuela come first with a higher increase than the regional average, and in fact Argentina has been the most dramatic case, since unemployment leaped from 16.4 to 21.5 percent.

Among the most significant factors behind this situation is the extinction of the public sector as a net employer and the adjustment made through employment cuts in the largest enterprises due to technological innovations and organisational changes designed to increase productivity (ILO, 2002a).

The changes in the structure of employment are well-known. Employment was privatised (95 out of every 100 new jobs were generated in the private sector), the demand for workers—particularly for the unqualified—decreased considerably in the formal sector and outsourcing, informalisation and precariousness of employment continue to increase. Of every 100 new jobs, 83 are generated in the services sector, and of these, 55 lack social protection. Between 1990 and 2001, 69 percent of the new jobs were informal. This means that the informal sector created 2 out of every 3 new jobs. During the same period, formal employment decreased from 57.2 to 53.7 percent. In the informal economy it was observed that the category of self-employed workers—which includes non-professional self-employed work and non-paid family work—was the area that generated most employment, accounting for 32 of every 100 new jobs. This was followed by micro-enterprises (23 of every 100 new jobs). On the other hand, women are being incorporated into the labour force in massive numbers, and their participation rate is getting closer to that of men (ILO, 2002a).

It is common to use the criterion of registration or non-registration to delineate the boundaries of the 'informal sector' from the formal sector. By and large, all people or groups who work in the informal economy are not acknowledged or protected by legal and regulatory frameworks (ILO, 2002a).

The informal economy comprises a variety of activities and several types of labour relations. There is self-employment in subsistence activities (street vendors, rubbish collection, etc.), out-sourced work in the home, self-employment in individual micro-enterprises with family workers or apprentices or wage-earners.

When analysing the new features of informality in Latin America, two main causes for the spread that are interdependent can be identified: decentralisation of production and a decrease in formal employment, which result in the proliferation of micro- and small entrepreneurs. Another reason is the reforms of the 1990s in labour legislation which made the market more flexible and permitted a great increase in isolated contractual agreements, even in formal enterprises. The informal world is highly heterogeneous and has a close relationship with the formal sector: whatever happens in the informal economy exerts an influence on work in the formal economy, and vice versa.

A second characteristic which defines informal activity in the region is its high level of vulnerability, and this is mainly expressed in shortcomings in hygiene, health and safety at work. From this perspective, the lack of social protection is both a distinctive aspect and critical for social exclusion. Even though a lack of social security is also found in the formal sector—57 of every 100 new employees had access to social protection in 2001—those who work in the informal sector are the most affected—only 19 of every 100 new informal employees were protected. This is due not only to their job instability and lack of income security, but also to the fact that they are more likely to run serious risks as regards safety and health in a vicious circle of lack of protection and poverty (InfoSud-Belgique, 2002)

It is worth mentioning that not all informal employment yields low income. There are self-employed workers who earn more than others with no specialisation, or low specialisation, in the formal economy. Working in the informal sector does not mean recovering from poverty, but the situation of poverty, marginality and exclusion may force a person to accept any kind of working condition, including earning very precarious wages.

Since this kind of job is becoming the only possible opportunity for an increasing percentage of people, the informal sector enables them to survive and mitigates the effects of poverty. However, as indicated by the Economic Commission for Latin America and the Caribbean (ECLAC), the region has not advanced in the process of recovering from poverty. On the contrary, extreme poverty remains. Between 1999 and 2002 the poverty rate diminished only 0.4 percent, and extreme poverty grew 0.3 percent. Argentina and Uruguay are two of the countries that underwent the worst deterioration in the living conditions of the population. In Argentina the poverty rate practically doubled between 1999 and 2002, growing from 23.7 to 45.4 percent, and poverty indexes grew by a factor of five (6.6 to 29.9%). In the case of Uruguay, the evolution of rates showed an increase of more than 50 percent, from 9.4 to 15.4 percent. Besides this, poverty and marginality systematically affect more women than men.

DISTINCTIVE CHARACTERISTICS OF WOMEN'S PARTICIPATION IN THE INFORMAL ECONOMY IN LATIN AMERICA

As mentioned above, in the 1990s there was a considerable increase in the labour participation of women, and this has altered the role of women in the labour market from that of a 'secondary worker' to a consolidated position as co-provider, and in many cases the only means of support for the home. Women currently make up slightly more than 40 percent of the urban working population, with differing rates according to educational level, economic stratum, age and ethnic group.

When we relate educational level to opportunity for entry into the labour market, for both men and women there is, in general, a positive relation between the number of years of study and the opportunity to obtain a formal job. However, on average, women need more years of study than men do to be able to enter the informal sector. The gap is even wider between those who have post-secondary studies, and this comes as a consequence of professional segmentation by gender together with the loss of quality and relevance of general education.

Women who belong to the low-income socio-economic strata and who have less education, a higher number of children, and fewer opportunities of hiring support services for domestic chores, face greater difficulties of labour insertion and performance. In 1990 the participation rate of women in the low income bracket was 29 percent, that of medium-income women was 42.6 percent, and for those receiving higher incomes it was 55.2 percent. In 1998 the difference fell to 36.2 percent, 48.3 percent and 55.4 percent, respectively (Abramo & Valenzuela, 2001).

Furthermore, female labour is identified by the continuous process of outsourcing. Between 1990 and 2002, 97 percent of the new jobs for urban female labour were generated in that sector. In 2001, 85.6 percent of total female labour was concentrated in the services sector (community, and social and personal services), and 27.7 percent in the trade sector (ILO, 2001).

Another phenomenon worth noting is the difference in wages between men and women. Even though this gap has narrowed in recent years, women continue to earn less than men in almost all Latin American and Caribbean countries. Women's average income in 1998 was 64 percent of that of men, in the informal sector it was 52 percent, and self-employed women workers were the most affected of all. These differentials are even wider as the number of years of study increases. In the region, the average remuneration per hour for women with 13 or more years of training is 30 percent lower than that of men (ECLAC, 2002–2003). Among the factors that contribute to this gap we can again mention their massive participation in the services sector, which is usually the worst paid, and family strategies that make the woman the head of the family, which determines their entering or leaving the labour world and their preference of part-time jobs.

The growth in women's participation coincides with an increase in female unemployment—which exceeds the average rate by approximately 45 percent (ILO, 2002b)—which is equally segmented. The rate among poor women is five times higher than that among women with the highest incomes (ILO, 2002a). Due to the increasing importance of women as heads of households and self-sustainers, this increase in unemployment has serious implications for their lives, and these effects are becoming more visible. One example would be low self-esteem caused by long periods without a job, and this leads them to accept precarious jobs with low wages.

Another distinctive aspect of women's participation is their overwhelming presence in the informal sector. In 2001, 49.7 percent of female employment was informal, while for men the figure was 43.8 percent. At the same time, in the informal economy women are concentrated in the most unstable, unprotected and precarious categories; therefore their insertion quality is lower than that of men. Furthermore, they are especially prone to being employed in small economic units where their contribution is invisible and they are practically not taken into account. They also work in agricultural activities which in many countries are not even counted in the statistical data system. This leads us to reflect on the quality and conditions of female labour, since in order to compensate for low wages they have to work for longer periods, which means a greater physical weakening of workers who in general are undernourished and with limited time for rest or sleep.

In the informal sector, home work, self-employment and domestic work are proportionally the biggest categories in the total of working women.

Work at home offers women the best opportunity to make their domestic and family responsibilities compatible with remunerated activities (CIOSL/ORIT, 2002). A number of fields have been added to the traditional tasks of textile service and the clothing industry. These are new technological services (such as phone sales, consultancies, internet, etc.), out-sourced manufacturing productive processes, small machine assembly, and other activities that have to do with the transfer to the productive field of many domestic activities, and this generates a highly heterogeneous range both of conditions and rhythms and of educational and training requirements. In the activities that require more technological intensity and qualifications there are better conditions, such as written contracts, benefits and social protection similar to those provided to people working in enterprises and with remuneration which is competitive in the local market.

For women, *home work* is also at *home*, which means that the boundaries between remunerated jobs and domestic occupations become blurred. Men, by contrast, perform their jobs mainly in a place specially designed for work, which may even be located next to their home, and they normally have an assistant, which reduces their working day.

Self-employed workers have been leading growth. They generated 9 out of every 10 new posts for women. This growth was particularly high in the Andean countries: Colombia (33%), Ecuador (36.3%), Peru (35.2%) and Venezuela (35.6%), and in Central America: Honduras (40.7%) and Panama (33.2%). Greater instability in employment and a lack of social protection are concentrated in the sectors that have lower qualification requirements. In general, contracts are verbal and do not involve any type of social protection or minimum income, and remuneration is provided per piece or on delivery.

On the other hand, domestic work (the category with the lowest pay and social protection levels in the informal sector) accounts for 22 percent of new jobs for women generated between 1990 and 1998 (ILO, 1999). In analysing domestic work in the region, we should distinguish between the category of domestic work carried out by family members, which involves 30–50 percent of women over 15 years old, and paid domestic work, which, as mentioned above, involves a large proportion of the female population.

Although several transformations have taken place, the sexual division of labour still assigns domestic chores, home and family care, and the reproductive function to women. Furthermore, social and demographic changes are occurring, such as migration, an increase in divorce rates, and an increase in the number of women who are heads of families, etc. The impact of this division is expressed in the overload of work without social acknowledgement, lack of time available for training or recreation, and deficient access to information systems. This restricts women's opportunities for entering the labour market, and their possibilities of participating in social and political life and decision-making.

As to their *insertion in micro-enterprises*, there are fewer women working as employers or owners than as employees. They face more difficulties than men do in establishing their own enterprises, and, as a consequence, these are usually smaller and experience irregular growth, and this makes it difficult for women to draw a clear division between work and home. They mainly perform activities in the sectors that have fewer barriers to access, where rudimentary techniques are used, and where the labour force is poorly qualified, the income is low and the employment unstable (Gehriger et al., 1999).

Another important aspect of female employment is that, although there is no overwhelming or generalised link between poverty and woman heads of households, homes which are run by only one adult (80% of which are headed by women) are more vulnerable to poverty than those headed by two adults. It should be taken into account that the contribution of women to total home income, particularly in poor homes, is very considerable, because this has a positive impact on the reduction of poverty. Several studies along those lines have shown that women's economic contribution to their families makes up a higher proportion in low-income families than in families located just above the poverty line (ECLAC, 1995, quoted in Aguirre, 2003).

Deficient social protection is also connected with gender. The data presented by the ILO show that around 38 percent of wage-earning workers do not pay social protection contributions, and in the informal sector the figure is 72 percent. Since women are over-represented in the informal sector, the lack of social protection feeds back as exclusion and vulnerability.

The information presented above leaves no room for doubt about the following points:

- The role played by the informal economy, which in most cases represents the employment opportunity for an increasing segment of the Latin American population—particularly for women who are heads of households—means that people have to resort to informal activities to survive and mitigate the effects of poverty.
- The interdependence and feedback of the precariousness, lack of protection and low income levels in the vast majority of Latin America informal jobs means that women's participation in the labour world is still characterised by conditions of inequality and economic and social vulnerability.

Thus, reducing the 'decent work' deficit is simultaneously the greatest and most urgent regional challenge and one of the most powerful mechanisms for prevailing in the struggle against exclusion and marginality.

Work and income in developing countries are the main sources of protection and social inclusion. At the same time, work is a fundamental component of the project of life, self-affirmation and social esteem, for both men and women. But for women it involves the transformation from the assigned model of a life plan dedicated to reproductive and non-paid work, which becomes an additional impediment to overcoming social barriers and prejudices regarding their rights and capabilities, and this inhibits their equal participation in employment.

In this framework the search for solutions to the problems of the informal sector should countenance the promotion of policies that simultaneously aim at modernising and increasing productivity, improving working conditions and removing extra requirements, as well as at combating the discrimination against women which comes as a consequence of gender stereotypes in the labour world.

THE IMPACT OF CHANGES IN EDUCATION AND VOCATIONAL AND TECHNICAL TRAINING

Labour in today's context demands individuals who can actively determine their course of action, those with the capacity to identify and appreciate their own resources and skills, with an interest in searching for support and a will to overcome their limitations, which can position them as generators of their own employment opportunities. Furthermore, this is fundamentally important in the construction of new identities and new life and consumption styles, which are reflected in family relationships and which imply a new understanding of gender and its connection to what is private and public.

Uncertainty, diversity and heterogeneity can only be approached from autonomy, which is understood as the ability to think and act for oneself, and to make choices. For this we need self-knowledge, independence, responsibility and decision-making competency. These abilities are fundamental in order to enter into and remain in the labour world, as well as to be socially included and able to exercise the right to citizenship.

Education in general, and vocational and technical training in particular, play a vital role in the acquisition of these competencies and in the process of expanding opportunities, since they are a fundamental instrument to combat the exclusion and inequality that greatly affect women and female employment.

The educational system should be in charge of the acquisition of these basic competencies; hence the importance of quality in formal education. The great vulnerable point throughout Latin America is education. The region has the highest repetition rates of the world—around one-third of primary school students repeat every year—and a high proportion of students do not manage to finish primary school. This results in a high risk of unemployment for vast sectors of society. The rural ambit and native populations have improved far less than urban and dominant ethnic groups.

Furthermore, the gender dimension makes the situation worse. Latin American young women are the overall majority in secondary education—and in the South of the continent they are also the majority in tertiary education—and they finish their studies in shorter periods of time and with better levels of attendance at qualification and updating activities. At the same time, native populations on the continent are still systematically excluded from education, and peasant girls and boys are still hampered by the low value that their parents place on education, which explains the high female dropout rate in the rural environment (Silveira, 2001). Segmentation according to income levels is also very marked. There is a global trend towards a sustained increase in female attendance in education; the gap between girls from the poorest homes and those from the richest is 25 points (Silveira, 2001, p. 14). This is because when a family cannot afford to do without the labour contribution of their children, daughters are the ones who have to stay at home to help their mothers with domestic chores. Moreover, in times of crisis, when women enter the labour market, their daughters are also the ones who take over home responsibilities and are therefore forced to leave school.

At the same time greater emphasis appears to be placed increasingly on the intrinsic value of education, and a decreasing value on degrees and diplomas awarded by the formal educational system.

All of this completely changes 'what to teach' and 'how to teach', and in a very particular way it questions labour training systems in the sense that their responsibility lies in the acquisition of resources and abilities that people in the labour market should possess. There must therefore be a meeting point, a point of co-ordination between the requirements and needs of the productive system and those who produce, men and women.

If we consider this role, we are implicitly acknowledging that even though training policies cannot generate employment on their own, they can and should support people and transform them into 'opportunity detectors' (Sallé, 2000), so that they cease to be passive individuals who depend on external intervention to supply them with ever-scarcer jobs and learn to position themselves as 'builders of their own employability strategy'.

The proposal to incorporate employability competencies in the teaching-learning process involves the development of one's abilities to learn to start a business, and to do this from the perspective of gender equality.

Mainstreaming gender in training implies understanding that gender is a basic socio-economic variable on which a number of other variables (such as income, educational levels, capital, culture of origin, ethnic group, social class, and rural or urban conditions) exert an influence. Therefore, achievements in gender equality may well entail drawbacks insofar as other inequalities are perpetuated (FORMUJER, 2001).

Training for employability with the gender focus allows people to confront, in an integral and co-ordinated way, the conditions and competency requirements of today's labour market, the characteristics and demands of new occupational profiles and values and the development and strengthening of individual abilities. In other words, this joint approach focuses on the development of competencies which are essential for survival and for individuals and enterprises to grow. Therefore, it becomes particularly important that different communities should adopt this focus since they have different characteristics according to the different modalities of the informal economy in Latin America, and they require special support in order to improve their conditions of labour insertion and overcome discrimination and disadvantages.

STRENGTHENING EMPLOYABILITY AND GENDER EQUALITY AS GOALS OF LABOUR TRAINING POLICIES: THE FORMUJER REGIONAL PROGRAMME PROPOSAL

These considerations and convictions are the basis of the design and execution of the Regional Programme to Strengthen the Vocational and Technical Training of Low-income Women (FORMUJER) and the Programme for the Promotion of Equal Opportunities for Women in Employment and Vocational Training (PROIMUJER), which, although it has a specific institutional and financial framework, has adopted similar courses of action and methodological assumptions to FORMUJER. Cinterfor/ILO co-executes both programmes and is in charge of co-ordination and technical and methodological supervision. FORMUJER is co-financed by the IADB and executed as Pilot Projects by the Ministry of Labour, Employment and Social Protection of Argentina, the National Institute of Labour Training 'INFOCAL' of Bolivia, and the National Training Institute of Costa Rica. PROIMUJER, on the other hand, is executed and financed by the National Employment Board of the Ministry of Labour of Uruguay.

This joint initiative aims at promoting and strengthening the abilities of regional institutions in order to improve quality, relevance and gender equality in labour training, and thereby to increase women's and men's employability, paying special attention to the training and labour and the insertion needs of low-income women.

The *basic assumptions* are: (a) the conviction that in order to fulfil their role of co-ordinators between employment and individuals, training policies should be relevant and should meet the requirements of economic and social development, as well as becoming an instrument to fight against social exclusion and inequality; and (b) the adoption of a gender perspective as a conceptual framework and an instrument of critical analysis so that, as the differentiated and hierarchical social assignment of responsibilities and roles between men and women are made visible, it is possible to interpret the social relationships of power between them, as well as other discrimination or social exclusion mechanisms which reinforce them (such as poverty, individual and family education levels, rural or urban conditions, racism, violence, etc.). The gender perspective is based on the consideration of people as individuals located in a social reality which conditions them, but which they can change by taking into account learning and personal and collective strategies. It means starting from the integral acknowledgement of a person who takes advantages of the abilities and life experiences of knowledge, feelings and values which nourish both his or her physical, intellectual and social dimensions.

To fulfil their objectives, these programmes have developed an intervening approach with a shared conceptual and methodological framework at the regional level, but with differing strategies for implementation which are adapted to national and institutional realities (FORMUJER, forthcoming-a).

The *conceptual issues* include: (a) an *integral and systematic approach to training policies* in order to tackle, globally and jointly, the diverse environments and all the spaces and dimensions where inequality and exclusion operate; (b) the *strengthening of employability and competency training*, which apply to the conceptualisation of lifelong education and therefore of people as active individuals in a continuous teaching-learning process; and (c) the *spread of opportunities and the improvement of equality expressed in the adoption of a double logic*: (i) the mainstreaming of the gender perspective in order to consider the needs and special characteristics of women and men as an integral and permanent dimension of policies and institutional practices and (ii) the focus on methodologies and action in order to ameliorate the initial disadvantages of women, particularly of poor women.

From *the methodological point of view*, the intervening approach model has two chief components: (a) *Action in both regional and national scenarios*. Cinterfor/ILO identifies and fosters the most innovative courses of action and development which have been tried nationally or internationally in order to avoid duplicating efforts, and it gives technical orientation to the actions and proposals of the programme. In each of the participating countries, methodological and strategic proposals are tried out and evaluated which are totally or partially developed by national and regional co-ordinating units and executing institutions. The proposals thus developed are adapted, complemented or enriched every time they are implemented nationally and therefore bring about a collective increase in knowledge. (b) *A flexible, participatory, multi-actor and inter-institutional management model*, which is based on co-ordination and feedback, as well as on joint collaboration among countries and institutions.

Furthermore, this intervening approach embodies an understanding of *systemasation, the spread and transfer of methodologies and lessons learned, not only as a methodological course of action but also as an objective in itself.* In this way it seeks to maximise and accumulate human, financial and time resources, and provides methodologies, instruments and intervention experiences which have been tried out for those who are interested in implementing training and gender policies so that they can advance faster and with lower costs. The fact of being located in Cinterfor/ILO promotes this spread, and it is implemented by means of technical co-operation, training action, forums, and also a web page and the continuous publication of reference documents.

As is clear from the intervening approach model chart and in the following descriptions, these focuses are the basis for and are expressed both in the design and the components of the courses of action taken by the programme and in the methodologies and instruments prepared.

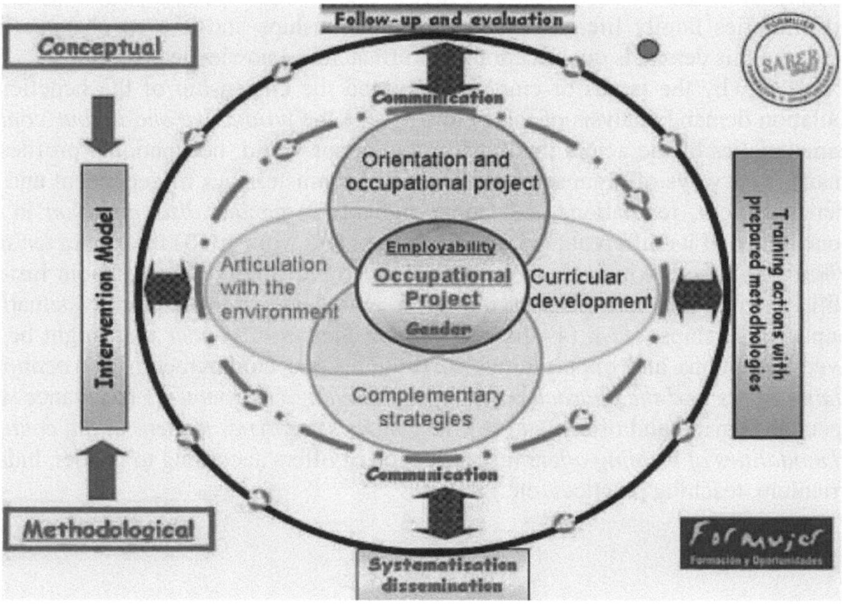

Training for Employability

Based on this referential framework, FORMUJER has defined employability as 'the aptitude to find, create, keep and enrich a job, taking over other jobs and thus obtaining personal economic, social and professional satisfaction' (Ducci, 1998). In this model, employability is connected with processes that occur at different levels—structural, economic, regulatory and cultural. Productive, organisational and gender relationship paradigms affect the demand for labour and the socio-educational position of people. Furthermore, the social representation of gender defines the labour force offer because some social groups, and particularly women, come up against greater difficulties to insert themselves and improve in the world of labour. But also affective and relational factors, and the life experiences of each individual, are coordinated within a specific context, thereby creating differences and inequalities in the possibility of access to resources, in employment opportunities, in the generation of productive activities and in participation and decision-making with regard to issues connected with the community or group to which they belong.

The personal, cultural and relational dimensions of employability need to be contextualised from a gender perspective and should be considered during the first stages of training and education. Training should not be reduced to a qualification; on the contrary, it should fulfil its essential function of contributing to social integration and personal development. Today training for employability is being linked with training for citizenship as never before. Democracy, development, and respect for all rights are interdependent concepts which are reinforced in both personal and relational dimensions of learning have a crucial importance. Furthermore, machines which require efficient reading and varied knowledge are being incorporated into everyday life and in our homes. The modernisation of urban life and of domestic work modifies family life and community relationships and it even changes lifestyles, and this demands qualifications and efficacious knowledge.

This is why the issues of employability and the citizenship of the beneficiary population demand analysis of the following: (1) the *productive and labour context* (characteristics of the actors involved in the labour world, occupational profiles in demand, new ways of organising work, special characteristics of dependent and independent work, regulations and labour rights); (2) *gender discrimination* in the labour field and its differentiated impact on men and women; (3) the *characteristics of those individuals* who wish to improve their employability (needs, labour history, abilities, skills and knowledge acquired in or outside of work, family situation, group memberships, etc.); (4) the *determining factors of gender* that might be involved in options and opportunities for training and employment; (5) *vocational training offers and the characteristics of the training environments* (relevance with respect to demand and offer); and (6) the *gender stereotypes present in the contents and modalities of training offers* (classification of offers according to gender, hidden curriculum, teaching practices, etc.).

Training Issues

On this basis FORMUJER works on the understanding that training for employability in today's context means (Irigoin & Guzmán, 2000): (1) Strengthening people's abilities so that they may improve their possibilities of labour insertion by means of the development of key competencies, which decrease the risk of obsolescence and allows men and women to remain active and productive throughout their lives, though not necessarily in the same position or activity. (2) Training for continuous and complex learning, which implies learning how to learn, how to be and how to do. (3) Providing support for people so that they may identify the internal and external obstacles which interfere with their achievement of goals and so that they may come to value their abilities and knowledge, as well as the demands and competencies demanded by the world of labour. This includes information and orientation about the educational and labour market which can indicate alternatives, demands and possibilities, in addition to eliminating stereotypes which define jobs as female or male, and implementing the search for and/or the creation of a job. (4) Stimulating and strengthening the ability of each person so that he or she may conduct his or her own professional itinerary, which is particularly necessary considering the environment of uncertainty in professional life now and in the future.

If we consider today's context of employment and of social organisation, as well as the barriers and the discrimination that women face, the question arises as to what the key competencies and the necessary knowledge would be in order to be able to tackle, with autonomy, reflection and flexibility, the problem of securing, organising and planning one's own job.

Fundamental Competencies

The *fundamental competencies* are the following: a) *Basic Competencies*, to 'learn how to learn' and to eliminate the old idea that learning is a one-off activity which takes place only in the classroom. Among these competencies are oral and written skills, applied math, even a second language, and also the ability to locate and critically understand information about reality in order to work out criteria for making choices and decisions. b) *Mainstream competencies*, the ability to 'learn how to do' in the sense of organising and adapting knowledge and abilities to new circumstances. These are particularly significant for women because they widen their range of alternatives and provide possibilities for horizontal mobility. These include the ability to anticipate threats and opportunities, to integrate and develop a systematic view of reality, to organise, plan and manage tasks, resources, and especially time and information, and to acquire a technological culture (to work with and to apply technology to tasks and to everyday life). Among these, one which stands out is the ability to start enterprises, since this is the basis of the formulation of a professional project, either one's own or someone else's. This involves initiative development, decision-making strategy, the ability to take risks and to take part (by means of the leadership development) in actively managing ideas and projects. This also contributes to citizenship culture and promotes democratic leadership. c) *Attitudinal competencies* are aimed at 'learning how to be', strengthening one's identity and eliminating self-limiting attitudes. For women, the development of these competencies is of fundamental importance if they are to overcome the mental and social barriers which limit their positioning and empowerment. Examples are personal skills (the reinforcement of identity and of personal and gender security, self-responsibility and being able to take on a leading role in the process of employment-training, and autonomy) and interpersonal and social skills (teamwork, responsibility, self-regulation, personal relationships, negotiation ability, knowing how to listen and communicate, emotional discrimination in labour situations, etc.). d) *Technical-sector competencies* contextualise and complement 'learning how to do'. For women, this means diversification, the valuation of old competencies developed in other fields and the creation of new competencies for the emerging demands of employment.

Only when 'equipped' with these characteristics can people approach today's challenges of generating and conserving work, and this is especially necessary in order to rescue the most economically and socially disadvantaged sectors of the population and to provide them with instruments by which they can acquire mobility and even the ability to seek their own labour opportunities by means of self-employment projects, micro-entrepreneurial work or any activity in which they can still be competitive in spite of their limited level of technological adaptation.

Training Modules

To support the development and strengthening of key competencies, FORMUJER developed the *Training Modules for Employability and Citizenship* (Irigoin & Guzmán, 2000), which consist of guidelines for the teacher and the corresponding pedagogical basis for a series of classroom activities which allow of flexible application and are adapted to different realities. This includes evaluation proposals and advice on their use and correction. The modules are aimed at developing abilities and fundamental capacities in order to acquire self-confidence, to strengthen the feeling of being part of a group, and to improve the ability to identify and solve problems (employability module), thereby strengthening personal autonomy and aspects related to participation and leadership (citizenship module). These have been designed for use in courses for women and men. Each activity can be adapted to the needs and specific experiences of the women and men involved so that the acquisition of abilities is processed together with a gender analysis which can be seen in practice and in the approach to problems.

These modules have been applied in an integral way or have been the basis for the preparation of a range of didactic materials. The integral and autonomous application was carried out in Bolivia. Costa Rica prepared the Manual with activities to foster employability from the classroom (Coto & Quiros, 2003) with an adaptation and correct application of the curricular development of *construcciones metálicas* (metal buildings), and the co-executors in Argentina used them as inputs in the construction of the occupational project.

Interfacing Gender Approaches and Competence-Based Vocational Training

After a process of exploration, development and experimentation with different approaches and methodologies, the FORMUJER programme adopted the combination of gender approaches and methodologies (FORMUJER, 2003a) as the conceptual and methodological framework of its project. The aim is to achieve the ultimate goal of improving employability, especially among poor women in the region.

Training based on vocational or labour competencies is understood as the process of developing curriculum design, didactic materials, activities and classroom practices. These are aimed in turn at developing a sum of knowledge, abilities, skills and attitudes which the person combines and uses to solve problems connected with his or her work performance, according to the criteria or standards set by the vocational field.

The gender interface and training by competencies make the following possible: (1) a double relevance for the context and the beneficiary population, where training is conceived of as a tool for the promotion of more inclusive and fairer social and economic development; (2) accepting individuals integrally, taking into account and appreciating their diversity and the diversity of the society which acknowledges them and promotes exchanges and learning; (3) the appreciation of different learning environments, the production of knowledge and the building up of individual paths which cater to diverse interests and equally diverse social contexts; (4) an appreciation of the importance of applying the criterion of quality in training for employment, which enables people to establish the requirements and conditions for the work performance of women and men in different contexts; and (5) the identification and removal of barriers and inequalities that stem from stereotyped visions of the role of different individuals according to their sex, origin, social situation, knowledge, etc., and that hinder free access to training and to jobs.

The interface of both approaches is systematically applied in all stages of curricular planning, and this makes it possible to design a training programme which is doubly relevant. On the one hand, there are the requirements and possibilities of the labour market; on the other, the profile of each individual, considering gender and giving value to formal and informal knowledge as competencies to be applied in performing a task.

The development and design of a study plan which incorporates the gender and competencies approaches can answer the following questions: Who is being trained? What are they being trained in? What for? Who trains them? How? When? All these questions involve gender problems that interconnect with problems of the socio-economic, educational, age, etc., profiles of the target population. It is necessary to be alert to such dangers in order to design the appropriate didactic responses for tackling them.

To apply this focus, it is necessary to develop an intensive training plan for planners, curriculum designers and teachers, so that they can take these approaches as their own and apply them. They must also remain alert, both during design stages and classroom practice, to the different expressions of the hidden curriculum where gender marks are developed unintentionally. This awareness training calls for self-reflection in order to be able to modify behaviour and the pedagogical treatment of discrimination. The ultimate aim is to bring about full inclusion.

To effectively construct a training plan which leads to inclusion, special attention should be paid to the gender perspective throughout the whole process, from the methodologies developed for the identification of an occupational profile to the execution and assessment of courses and their participants.

The experience gained through the processes of curricular development and revision, and through the systematic implementation of staff training, has given FORMUJER a group of instruments that systematise and guide the application of both approaches. Among these instruments, the following stand out: 'Collating lists for the incorporation of the gender and relevance approaches to the target population and the context of curricular development stages', and a *Guide for the Revision of Module Programmes with a Gender Perspective* (FORMUJER, 2003a).

The Teaching-Learning Process: Labour Orientation and Occupational Project

In the methodological proposal of FORMUJER, Vocational and Labour Information and Orientation are understood as components of the teaching-learning process, and not as an additional and random service. The task of orientation is to accompany and empower beneficiaries as they access the training institution. It offers support for their vocational option, information about the labour market and, above all, information about the possibilities and conditions of the different training profiles. In addition, during the development of training, orientation provides the beneficiaries with knowledge about the labour world and the behaviour and cultural guidelines which govern it, including support to facilitate work practice. Finally, in the last stage, orientation helps trainees by giving them instruments to search for employment and by accompanying them through the process of joining the world of work. Moreover, in order to promote the ongoing assessment of the quality of the training received orientation provides follow-up input for those who finish the courses. Throughout this process it is essential to incorporate the gender perspective since it helps to promote vocational diversification, to fight against segmentation, and even to increase the possibilities of insertion for women—so often blocked by stereotypes or ignorance—through dialogue with the productive sector. This is combined with a component of co-ordination with the prevailing social reality, plus a communication strategy and/or the involvement of employment intermediation services.

Labour orientation is given value as an element of the vocational training process, as a learning instance with a determinative role in increasing gender equality. In FORMUJER it has led to the development of a methodology, which is the *Individual and/or Collective Occupational Project* mechanism.

From the point of view of the participants, the occupational project is a didactic procedure for strengthening employability and promoting gender equality, since it brings together the reading of gender indicators in the productive and social environment, that is, the interface between gender and training by competencies. For training policies, it is an articulating focus for the teaching-learning process and a strategy which facilitates the personalization of training.

It is understood that through support for, and the strengthening of, each individual's abilities to define, prepare and manage a *feasible project of employment and training*, or an occupational project, there will be an increase in women's and men's aptitudes to obtain, develop, change and/or generate work.

The experiences that have been carried out within the framework of FORMUJER have proved that employability and the exercise of citizenship rights are strengthened when individuals are able to adapt their abilities, needs and knowledge to the competencies required by the labour context and when they can see themselves as creators of their own future, identifying their own skills, wishes, possibilities and difficulties and thereby make their way in life.[4]

For the participants in training and orientation action, the occupational project is the group of courses of action which are defined, planned, revised and re-planned by them and which aimed at achieving productive insertion or improving their employment situation. As a didactic strategy, it is based on the 'human capacity to design projects'. It seeks to boost key competencies in order to improve people's position in the world of work and production, particularly in uncertain labour contexts which require greater flexibility and autonomy. At the same time, it orients training and/or labour choices and paths, and it bolsters the exercise of citizenship, since it promotes the development of autonomy, a person's relationships with others and access to the public world.

The Occupational Project

The construction of an occupational project entails the development of the appropriate competencies to handle the following four stages.

1) *Self-diagnosis*: Where do I start? The result here is the identification and analysis of and the reflection on the individual's starting point as regards work and training. It means finding a balance which begins by acknowledging their own abilities, knowledge and competencies, whether acquired in work environments or in their own life context (domestic, community environment, etc.), reflecting on conditioning that is based on gender relationships or other differences and identifying subjective and objective aspects which may have an impact on the possibilities of labour or productive development. It also includes an analysis of the productive context, the natural (or other types of) resources which may constitute productive opportunities, as well as the real possibilities in the labour market and their requirements.

2) *Defining viable goals and strategies*: What do I want to achieve? After the self-diagnosis, goals in training and work are defined. This definition requires that one assess viability, analyse possible problems and design feasible strategies.

3) *Defining and planning activities*: How am I going to achieve that? Once goals and viable strategies have been identified, individuals begin to design a plan of activities in order to achieve them, that is, they develop their own occupational project.

4) *Executing, monitoring and assessing the project*: How am I doing? What have I achieved? When individuals understand the gap between the knowledge and competencies they already have and those they will need in order to perform in the chosen field, they can monitor their own process of development. Since the occupational project is a dynamic and open process, they can re-plan and adjust it. From the

didactic point of view, the occupational project becomes an instrument for assessment and self-assessment (FORMUJER/Argentina, 2001).

With a concept of the goals to be achieved in each of the stages in the construction of the project, competency units and elements are defined, as is the actual content that will be worked on by counsellors and/or teachers.

Implications for Training Policies and for Teachers and Counsellors

As explained below, from the point of view of training policies and for teachers and counsellors, the occupational project has several functions: a) It co-ordinates the different components and instances of the teaching-learning process: i) occupational orientation; ii) training action in terms of key competencies for employability and of the specific technical training for the occupational profile chosen; iii) dialogue with the actors in the world of work and in the community in order to define the profiles, extend and improve insertion opportunities of women, authorise practices or internships and even to negotiate labour insertion in formal work or with entities supporting micro-enterprises or self-employment; and iv) strategies to facilitate access to training for women in the beneficiary population groups (youth, micro-entrepreneurs, the informal sector, disabled people, workers in retraining).

b) It introduces individualisation in the training response in two dimensions: it focuses on differences and strengths, and enables each individual to go to different windows offering different courses and to select those technical, managerial or information aspects, etc., that he or she needs so as to implement his or her project.

c) It restores to the participant his or her main role in learning and in the ability to develop projects.

d) It makes up for the past, consolidates the future and creates a visible product.

e) It is based on the methodology of a process, with a beginning and an end.

f) It helps the teacher to have an influence on the elements regarded as important or worrying.

g) It promotes lifelong education.

h) It is a methodology and an instrument of assessment.

The construction of an occupational project may be promoted before choosing a working or training field, or it may be integrated into the training process for a predefined course of action. The second option is ideal since it means integrating in the training process the analysis of the employability and citizenship dimensions for the occupational field for which the individual has decided to be trained. Moreover, it means providing the individual with the instruments for constructing the occupational project oriented to increasing his or her employability in that field.

This would be a personal way of tackling an occupational project. However, the project could be collective, and this has been one of the most inspiring lessons learned from the experience of executing the FORMUJER programme. The design of collective projects to develop micro-entrepreneurial activities was unexpectedly intense in all the countries where the project was executed, and this holds particularly for Argentina and Uruguay because of the extremely serious economic crisis experienced by each country in 2001, which led to record levels of unemployment and poverty.

The developments of some entrepreneurial competencies have been included in the key competencies for employability. However, a scenario in which formal employment is the scarcest and most difficult space for the labour insertion of the target population made it clear that there was a need to extend the intervention in order to incorporate not only specific technical training in areas such as administration, accountancy and micro-entrepreneurial management, but also to adopt a broad and flexible set of strategies and resources to be applied in the practical stage of training and to cater to the requirements of the occupational projects of female beneficiaries, which could take the form of self-employment or micro-entrepreneurial work. With this work modality, the competencies that become more important include initiative, self-regulation, responsibility, organisational ability, planning ability, and continuous learning ability. But the projects should also incorporate the ability to carry out market and competency research, to develop a quality culture of the product or service to be offered and to maintain an openness to 'start new enterprises', which, among other things, means believing in one's own strengths and having a good measure of optimism.

Occupational project methodology has had to face two main challenges. In the case of individuals, it has had to incorporate the identification and development of the necessary competencies in order to diagnose, plan and manage the micro-entrepreneurial project, or the self-employment venture, with the participation of two or more individuals. Although this line still follows the process of the development of specific materials, there is already an *Orientation Methodology Guide for the Design of an Occupational Project for Independent or Self-employment* (FORMUJER, forthcoming-b).

For the conceptualisation of an Occupational Project for self-management, there has already been methodological development along the lines of recovering and adapting successful experiences and lessons from FORMUJER's intervening approach model. This methodological development derives from ENRED's Consultants and Direct Foundation, which was applied in the Veranera Programme[5] and in the Andalucia Equality Programme and is spelled out in the *Guide for Developing the Ability to Start Undertakings*. This methodology is structured around four basic variables: the attitude and aptitude profile of female beneficiaries (the individual), the group as a source of active support, the environment as a space where experiences are consolidated and business ideas/projects are the basis for the guided founding of viable and sustainable micro-enterprises.

This methodology advances the following proposals, consecutively or in parallel:

a) Work on the female entrepreneur: as a person and in the context of her environment.

b) Work on the project: starting by considering alternative ideas, evaluating them, going deeper into the best of them, looking for information and raising awareness about the most common mistakes and risks. Once the idea has been defined through methodologies for the design of projects and received the support of tutors, the participant begins to construct the project step by step and in a time sequence which starts with the client-market relationship, the information search plan and the definition of the offer. These are the steps and procedures that open the door to technical knowledge, and they are visualised with respect to the participant's need to find an answer. This is the monitored elaboration of a business plan.

c) Work on the enterprise: accompanying its opening and supporting its consolidation. Three major steps are taken: creation, infancy and development of the enterprise. In this step, resources and managerial and technical needs are visualised together with the risks or the most common mistakes. Once the business's infancy difficulties are overcome, it is necessary to gain support from others if the plan is to proceed. To that end, a mutual assistance programme is set up through workshops which help people to share and to learn collectively and with their tutors, relatives and environment, to train them, commit them and involve them. At this stage, the possibilities of setting up co-operation and network building strategies begin to be identified. The role played by the group in the motivation and reinforcement of and the feedback on the individual projects so as to generate shared learning and support common strategies is unquestionably a factor for success of the processes of improvement and change (Sallé, 2001).

But since the occupational project is also an institutional mechanism in which context-reading is expressed, it became necessary to redefine the role of training and, particularly in the FORMUJER program, the profile of the link component with the productive and social sectors.

For training to be consolidated as a bridge, as a route for individuals in the environment, it should acknowledge the potentialities and abilities of that environment, local development, different community organisations, etc. *Training has to assume a pro-active role, handling the environment through co-ordination with local development projects, support programs for micro-enterprises, enterprise promotion centres, etc. That is, it is necessary to change from the function of an environment reader to that of a promoter of labour insertion strategies and alternatives.*

The strategies implemented for the construction of the occupational project, and for integrating training with employability in the framework of the FORMUJER and PROIMUJER programmes, have been numerous and heterogeneous.[6] They have ranged from the inclusion of specific modules or workshops taught by counsellors (INFOCAL/Bolivia, 2000; FORMUJER/Costa Rica, 2002) teachers or even NGOs in co-ordination with training institutions, to their eventual inclusion in the (mainstream) national curricula. In each case, they have been received highly positive evaluations by participants, teachers and entrepreneurs who took on students seeking practical work experience. Significant changes are reported to have been achieved in terms of self-evaluation, the acknowledgement of knowledge, an increase in self-esteem and the incorporation of a pro-active activity for employment with efficient positioning and management of labour and social requirements.

Compensatory Strategies

In actions co-ordinate with orientation, and especially with the occupational project, the programme developed a support policy of an economic, cultural and organisational character to deal with the disadvantages and obstacles suffered by women due to gender discrimination, which makes access to and remaining in training more difficult. At first it was defined as a Scholarship System, but then it gradually went beyond the concept of mere assistance and was conceptualised as a collection of compensatory strategies. These served as didactic mechanisms for strengthening mainstream employability competencies and the ability of beneficiaries not only to manage themselves but also to promote the diversification of their professional options and access to areas of high technological content.

Participants defined support in that way within the framework of the action implemented by orientation and the occupational project in accordance with their real and differentiated needs. In many cases the answer to such needs was found jointly and co-operatively (e.g. having a day-care centre in the workplace run by participants themselves whose training schedules allowed them to do so or by unemployed participants). Moreover, institutions co-ordinated with the social context to solve different problems (childcare, transport, etc.). In this way the participants started acquiring experience and power as dynamic network agents and co-ordinators with the different actors and potentialities of the environment. This became a solid basis for the challenge of identifying and promoting labour insertion strategies through the sum of different efforts and resources from diverse sources (credit programmes, support programmes for micro-enterprises, technical training programmes which specifically focus on management, enterprise promotion programmes, etc.).

When compensatory strategies focus on individuals, they constitute a didactic methodology for strengthening mainstream employment competencies. The competencies they promote are the identification of problems in the family and public environments, the acknowledgement of the value of knowledge and resources, the ability to solve problems, the strengthening of decision-making about resources, the promotion of negotiation competencies, and empowerment. Here the person is regarded as being able to exercise his or her right to achieve tasks and to choose. The development of these mainstream competencies is confirmed in the proposals about the use of subsidies, in autonomous decisions about the use of the resources oriented to the project, etc. The conception of compensatory strategies invites the individual to identify the problem and see how he or she would solve it on his or her own, or with the co-operation of and in co-ordination with peers. In this way it promotes the potentiality of networks, both for individuals and for institutions. At the same time, the work with the local social reality and the possibilities that this offers for meeting the participants' needs and expectations is a clear message that there are dimensions of employability that depend on the individual alone, and that these dimensions can be influenced by the individual or by institutions.

To sum up, through FROMUJER a rich stock of experience has been accumulated which validates the importance and potentiality of a conception of compensatory strategy as a didactic tool incorporated into work by an occupational project. This replaces the dispensation of subsidies. It is therefore applied to emergency occupational programmes and programmes to combat poverty, as well as to programmes to promote equality. In addition to meeting economic and social needs deriving from poverty, such programmes may modify segmentation and discrimination in the sphere of gender, thus becoming an institutional message to promote proactive policies of stereotype-modification in the public labour space. Strategies may be defined both with respect to the needs of the population or with the intention to overcome the specific difficulties of a given sector.

Systematic Staff Training

The implementation of the approaches and guidelines that have been set out here can only be effected through a sweeping revision of institutional practices. Therefore, it becomes essential to get all staff members, in every category and in every function, to identify with the philosophy. Another consequence is a revision of the role of teachers: no longer are staff members the sole owners of knowledge; rather, they are facilitators and promoters of the learning process who acknowledge the knowledge, strengths and weaknesses of students. To accompany the occupational project, it is necessary to include and pay attention to differences and special characteristics. Moreover, it is necessary to monitor constantly the conditions and requirements of the labour world and one's own subjective views and how they are expressed in the classroom. Likewise, in order to picture training with respect to individual and collective projects, it is necessary to plan in a more open and flexible way for all the aspects of the training process.

For this reason the design of a training policy needs to create shared spaces for reflection on the part of staff members in general and teaching staff in particular. This training should be both methodological and didactic and should also expose staff to the new competencies required for such a role. Among other things, this requires group learning and work on the project both in terms of specialised areas and the educational centre. These spaces for the exchange of ideas is what allows for the enrichment of the conceptual bases and the methodological proposals involved and, in particular, for feedback and the joint building up of knowledge inside the institution by the different groups involved.

In this sense the communication strategy becomes a fundamental tool for managing transformation and consolidating appropriation and institutional commitment. Usually communication is thought of in its outward function; however, in a policy such as the one introduced here, the identification and generation of conditions for transformation will not be achieved unless there is internal communication that defines as its target the institution itself and its programs (FORMUJER, 2003b)

Striking a Balance

Now, five years after it began, the FORMUJER programme has succeeded in getting its executing agents to institutionalise the gender perspective, incorporating it in their policies. They have made its main lines of action their own. The results of the systematisation process, and the evaluations done, show that the developed methodological proposal:

1) Validates the systematic incorporation of the gender perspective as a condition for improving the quality, relevance and equality of training. The methods and strategies implemented have substantially enriched the processes of methodological and organisational innovation in training policies and practices. They have also contributed to the democratisation of knowledge and to social inclusion by incorporating competencies and content into training, leading to improved labour insertion possibilities for individuals and to the strengthening of their performance as citizens.

Beyond the particular emphasis placed on this by each country, it is through technical soundness that institutions have visualised what gender intervention implies.

2) It is relevant and efficient enough to be applied by heterogeneous and diverse institutional environments. It has turned out to be functional and has been applied and validated by: public instances of the definition and orientation of training and employment policies (Ministries of Labour of Argentina and Uruguay); training institutions with national scope, whether financed and administered by the productive sector (INFOCAL, National Institute for Labour Training) or of a public nature but with private funding (INA, National Training Institute); local and sector training entities which execute the action financed by ministries; and international organisations committed to the design, promotion and funding of training and employment policies (Cinterfor/ILO and IADB).

3) Strengthens social dialogue over training. The participants in the proposal, each performing different roles, have included: the business sector, NGOs, research centres, public, private, social and community organisations, micro-entrepreneurial instances of production or promotion and other related programs.

4) Promotes and fosters the decentralisation and localisation of interventions. The programme has worked through pilot and demonstrative experiences both in the capital city and other towns or cities in each country, with good co-ordination with the local productive and social environment, and adapting its strategies to their realities and needs.[7]

5) Becomes applicable and powerful for the design of national policies on training and the fight against poverty, as well as for dealing with other populations affected by vulnerabilities or discrimination, particularly for the training of those who act in the different modalities of the informal economy (self-employment, micro-entrepreneurial activities, co-operatives, etc.). This conceptual and strategic development has been welcomed and accepted as input in national policy ambits, international forums and especially in the technical and gender divisions of organisations such as the ILO, the IADB, the UNDP and UNESCO. In this sense the most important examples are the transference and/or adoption of the guidelines and methodologies developed by: (i) the 'Vocational Training Component of the National Programme for Heads of Households' implemented by the Argentinean Ministry of Labour in the framework of its policy of poverty reduction and employment, and by the National Board of Orientation and Vocational Training, as reference points for its policy of strengthening quality; (ii) the Technical and Technological Training Strengthening Programme of the Bolivian Ministry of Education, co-financed by the IADB; (iii) the University for Work Programme promoted by the government of Costa Rica and by INA's foresight in promoting the realisation of a demonstrative training project in the framework of 'New Life', the national programme to combat poverty; and (iv) the second stage of the PROIMUJER programme in Uruguay which is the fourth country in Latin America to apply the intervening approach model.

Finally, and by way of an example, we note that, through the application of the methodological package prepared in pilot or demonstrative training action, in the first quarter of 2003 more than 3,000 women in conditions of poverty and social vulnerability have received training through the FORMUJER programme, and 560 through PROIMUJER, in more than 50 occupational profiles, both traditional and innovative, and revised and/or updated in collaboration with the productive sector. The number of indirect beneficiaries cannot be reckoned since there has been intervention in all dimensions of the policy. Besides, dissemination and transference of approaches, methodologies and instruments has been permanent and continuous throughout the region. Evaluations show an increase in employability competencies and in the preparation of occupational projects which enabled participants, men and women, to implement productive initiatives both individually and collectively. These initiatives have become a reality through wide-ranging co-ordination with local government, the community, other IADB programs, etc.

LESSONS LEARNED

In view of the foregoing, it can be said that the possibilities of men and women obtaining decent work increase when they strengthen their abilities to design and carry out their professional and life projects. From that perspective, the following lessons and suggestions may be identified and should be taken into account by any policy of training for work that has this goal. This would contribute to combating the conditions of vulnerability, precariousness and poverty which affect a large number of workers in the informal sector in the Latin American economies.

1) Incorporate the gender perspective as a conceptual framework which facilitates a double impact, on the social context and on individuals, thus improving the quality of intervention.

2) Adopt an integrating and systematic approach to deal in a global and joint way with the different spaces and dimensions where exclusion and inequality operate and regenerate, namely the objective and subjective profiles of the population, the economic and business-economic environment, the socio-cultural sphere, the family, the community environment and the characteristic dimensions of the training system.

3) Define and implement an active interaction strategy with the socio-economic environment in order to identify existing activities and/or employment niches, or those which could be created in co-ordination with projects of local, sub-regional and regional development, the new quality of life parameters and the needs of the population. The development of such a strategy should also promote the systematic consideration of the different possibilities and competencies of men and women. This strategy should also help in the implementation of exchange and co-operation networks with different actors in the context so as to develop a pro-active policy to generate insertion alternatives aimed at supporting the occupational projects of the participants and to feed an orientation and information system of labour supply. This strategy must make use of a number of resources (personal and institutional links, sensitisation and training actions, methodological transfer, support for the management of human resources, etc.) and remain in place throughout the training process.

4) Create strategic alliances on thematic, organisational and territorial levels. This means networking and the co-ordination of resources and potentialities of all the agents involved in the development process: government, workers, employers, public and private institutions, local and regional governments, community agents,

international bodies, non-governmental organisations, etc. The basic instruments required to manage these alliances are co-ordination and concentration, which may be:

(a) Horizontal: with other programs conducted by the executing body, directed to the same target population or similar ones, for the transfer of methodologies and instruments; with other institutions for complementing the execution of different components of the training plan as a strategy for obtaining support and recognition but also as another aspect of training oriented to promotion (e.g. with NGOs to work on occupational and vocational orientation or training in gender for participants and teachers, with credit institutions or PYMES promotion programs for access to capital and accompaniment tutorials).

(b) Vertical: with other programs or institutions with a wider scope at a national, regional or international level to obtain or develop the compensatory strategies required by the target population to overcome their initial disadvantages (support services for the care of children, transport, access to practices, work experience or any other way of connecting with the productive sector that may enable people to reinforce their practical knowledge, improve the quality of the service, etc.); within the educational continuum so as to strengthen employability competencies and make lifelong education possible

5) Prepare a sound diagnosis of participants, taking into account both the objective profile (educational levels, poverty levels, family and housing conditions, work experience) and the subjective profile (self-perception and self-worth, awareness or abilities, employment and training expectations, social and economic acknowledgement, awareness about gender roles).

6) Include in the intervention the relationship with the participant's family and community, since the family situation defines the possibilities and availability of work for women. In the case of women from disadvantaged groups, this problem is exacerbated because birth rates, intra-family violence or the condition of being the head of the household have a big impact on training and employment opportunities. Likewise, the community may favour or discourage individual efforts to improve employment or to develop it in the case of informal activities. This factor is particularly important for individuals who are impoverished or excluded.

7) Conceive of occupational orientation, competency training for employability and specific technical training as dimensions within the training process which receive feedback and reinforcement from one another.

8) Support and strengthen the design, development and management of individual and/or collective occupational projects, which enable men and women to become managers of their own employability strategies.

9) Include the design, development and management of the self-managing project as an objective of training for which it is necessary to develop specific competencies. Among them, an important role is played by those competencies that help people to learn how to start an enterprise. i) Competencies for enterprises should provide participants with functional knowledge (marketing, finance, management courses, etc.) that are co-ordinated with their project. It is necessary to work from the logic of the configuration of a project (the creation or improvement of their own enterprise), which begins with the phase of dynamic action and self-diagnosis (from being nothing to becoming an entrepreneur with an idea), then it continues with a

pedagogical phase (from the idea to the project), it consolidates with a pedagogical-logistic phase (from the project to the enterprise), and it concludes with a co-operation phase (from the single-owner enterprise or the micro-enterprise to the network). ii) They should always have a double dimension, the individual and the society, because starting an enterprise is an individual reality and project with an indispensable collective dimension. iii) It is necessary to agree on supplementary support with other bodies. Such support should be both technical and financial and should facilitate the process (preferred credits or subsidies at the beginning of the activity, enterprise promotion centres, etc.). But it is just as essential to work on the creation of networks and meeting points between participants and, in the case of women, with other women with successful business initiatives.

10) A participatory methodological approach is essential to achieve positive results in any training process, especially when the personal and affective dimensions of learning are being worked on and when a strategy for the collective building up of knowledge is defined. The active participation of actors not only facilitates their adaptation but also, from the didactic point of view, it is a sign of coherence, since one of the goals of training is precisely to strengthen active subjects who are the creators of opportunities.

11) Long-lasting experience and modular organisation, together with flexible didactic methodologies, are also requirements. This means co-ordinating in-house and distance education, self-learning and accompanying tutorials, and also developing educational and pre-entrepreneurial levelling for populations with greater deficiencies, thus allowing diversity and flexibility of content and incorporating vitality into the experiences, etc.

12) Implement a systematic and permanent monitoring and assessment regime (with a strong component of actor participation) to guarantee feedback and correction along the way. This should include an assessment model of employability with qualitative indicators of the process (including gender marks) and facilitate the measurement of the acquisition of identified competencies and changes in terms of insertion availability, planning ability and the execution of the occupational project, which becomes an outstanding indicator for assessment.

NOTES

[1] As understood by the ILO, 'productive work' is work which enables men and women not only to support their families financially but also to do this under conditions of freedom, equality, security and respect for their dignity and with opportunities of personal development.

[2] This article partially revises and updates information presented in a document of the ILO's In Focus Program on Skills, Knowledge and Employability (IFP/SKILLS) entitled 'Starting points and orientations for a labour training policy concentrated on the improvement of employability and gender equality in Latin America', as part of an action research project, 'Gender dimensions in labour training: With an emphasis on the informal sector, poor populations and social exclusion'. Its publication is another expression of cooperation and joint work between IFP/SKILLS, Cinterfor/ILO and UNESCO.

[3] The word 'employment' is used here in a broad sense, involving all the modalities of income generation within the goods production and services system.

[4] Extract of *Cartilla sobre Proyecto Ocupacional* by Cooperativa Punha and from a document currently in preparation, *Proyecto Ocupacional, material de apoyo para formadoras y formadores*, FORMUJER/Argentina.

[5] Programa de Fortalecimiento del Liderazgo Femenino Rural en Panamá, in operation from July 1997 to March 2001.

[6] The systematisation of results and elaborate didactic materials is now under way and will be published in FORMUJER (forthcoming-b), and in the aforementioned document *Proyecto Ocupacional*, FORMUJER/Argentina, as well as in various other documents by the co-executors.

[7] Argentina executed different actions in Great Buenos Aires, Cordoba, Mendoza and Jujuy; Bolivia did so in La Paz, Santa Cruz, Cochabamba, Sucre and Tarija; Costa Rica in San José Central, Alajuela, Alajuelita, etc.; and Uruguay in Montevideo, Cerro Largo, Río Negro and Rocha.

REFERENCES

Abramo, L., & Valenzuela, M. E. (2001). *El panorama laboral femenino en América Latina en los 90.* Santiago de Chile: ILO

Aguirre, R. (2003). *Género, ciudadanía social y trabajo: resultados de investigación.* Montevideo: Universidad de la República, Facultad de Ciencias Sociales, Departamento de Sociología.

Coto, J., et al. (2003). Manual con Actividades para Estimular la Empleabilidad desde el Aula. San José de Costa Rica: FORMUJER National Training Institute/IADB, Costa Rica.

CIOSL/ORIT. (2002). *Mujer y Trabajo. Diagnóstico sociolaboral y sindical de América Latina y el Carib.* San José de Costa Rica: Confederación Internacional de Organizaciones Sindicales Libres/ Organización Regional Interamericana de Trabajadores.

Ducci, M. A. (1998). La formación al servicio de la empleabilidad. *Boletín Técnico Interamericano de Formación Profesional* (Montevideo: CINTERFOR/ILO), *142*, 7–24. http://www.cinterfor.org.uy /public/spanish/region/ampro/cinterfor/publ/boletin/index.htm

ECLAC. (2002–2003). *Panorama social de América Latina 2002-2003.* Santiago de Chile: ECLAC

FORMUJER. (2001). *Incorporación de la perspectiva de género en la formación profesional.* Montevideo: Cinterfor/ILO.

FORMUJER (2003a). *Género y formación por competencias. Aportes conceptuales, herramientas y aplicaciones.* Montevideo: Cinterfor/ILO.

FORMUJER. (2003b). *Estrategia de comunicación: una herramienta para la gestión de políticas de formación y equidad de género.* Montevideo: Cinterfor/ILO.

FORMUJER. (forthcoming-a). *Un modelo de política de formación para el mejoramiento de la empleabilidad y la equidad de género: el Programa FORMUJER.* Montevideo: Cinterfor/ILO.

FORMUJER. (forthcoming-b). *Orientación Laboral y Proyecto Ocupacional: un componente y una metodología para una política de formación pertinente y equitativa.* Montevideo: Cinterfor/ILO.

FORMUJER/Argentina. (2001). *El Proyecto Ocupacional – Aportes conceptuales y metodológicos para el desarrollo del proyecto ocupacional como estrategia de articulación de la orientación laboural y la formación profesional.* Buenos Aires: FORMUJER – Ministerio de Trabajo, Empleo y Formación de Recursos Humanos/Secretaría de Empleo/Dirección Nacional de Capacitación Laboral y Formación de Recursos Humanos.

FORMUJER/Costa Rica. (2002). *Talleres Integrados de Orientación Ocupacional.* San José de Costa Rica: FORMUJER/Costa Rica—National Training Agency/Inter-American Development Bank.

Gehriger, A., Romer, D., & Stetter, H. (1999). *Gender-approach in small enterprise development.* PAI/ PPE Issue Papers 1. Bern: Swiss Agency for Development and Cooperation.

INFOCAL. (2000). *Cuadernos de Orientación para las Participantes.* Bolivia: INFOCAL.

InfoSud-Belgique. (2002). *Informe anual sobre los derechos de los trabajadores, 2002 Trabajar en el sector informal: una oportunidad, un riesgo, un reto.* Dossier prepared for CMT by the agency InfoSud-Belgique.

ILO. (2002a). *Panorama laboral 2002.* Lima: ILO.

ILO. (2002b). *Globalización y Trabajo Decente en las Américas. XV Reunión Regional Americana.* Lima: ILO.

Irigoin, M. E., & Guzmán, V. (2000). *Módulos de Formación para la Empleabilidad y la Ciudadanía.* FORMUJER. 4 vols. Montevideo: Cinterfor/ILO.

Sallé, M. Á. (2000). *Género y Formación Profesional.* Paper presented at the first Latin-American seminar on gender and training. Panama.

Sallé, M. Á. (2001). *Presentación del Programa Veranera, Seminario de Evaluación.* Panama: Enred Consultores.

Silveira, S. (2001). La dimensión de género y sus implicancias en la relación entre juventud, trabajo y formación. In E. Pieck (ed.), *Los jóvenes y el trabajo: La educación frente a la exclusión social.* Mexico City: Universidad Iberoamericana, UNICEF, IMJ, CINTERFOR/OIT, CONALEP, RET.

TRADE UNIONS AND ADULT LEARNING FOR WOMEN CONSTRUCTION WORKERS IN THE INFORMAL SECTOR

Christine Nathan

The informal economy is an extremely broad and diluted concept. Informal workers, in particular in the developing world, are workers who are unrecognised, unprotected and unorganised. We find this type of worker in practically all sectors of the economy, be it in agriculture, construction, public services, textile manufacturing or the building industry. Some governments continue to see the informal economy as an option. They consider it natural that people seek employment in the informal economy in order to survive. But this paper argues that workers are not there just to survive: they must be granted basic rights and protection through legislation and they must be given social security and education. The growth of the informal economy can often be traced to inappropriate, ineffective, misguided or badly implemented macroeconomic and social policies, which are often developed without tripartite consultations. Even at the international level, the role played by international financial institutions must be deplored insofar as they have actually promoted the informal economy through ill-devised programmes of liberalisation, which were often based on the blind faith that markets will fix everything.

In the first section of this paper we examine the situation of women construction workers in India and suggest what trade unions can do for them in the field of adult education. In the second section, proposals for education and training are discussed. Basically, it is argued that education and training should provide for training and retraining. Two forms of training are highlighted: (1) the acquisition of a different skill set and (2) the upgrading and improvement of existing skills. The design of learning and training programmes has to allow for such processes of readjustment. However, it is necessary to ask what the connection is between employment and skills, as well as between skills and income? What is the importance of education and training in the informal sector? How does technological change affect the need for education, training, retraining and further training?

The success of training largely depends upon a broad foundation of basic education. It is possible, of course, to become a skilled worker without being able to read or write, but limitations of such skilled workers are painfully obvious.

Madhu Singh, (ed.), Meeting Basic Learning Needs in the informal Sector, 119-129.

WORKING AND LIVING CONDITIONS AND SKILLS

In a developing country such as India construction activities take place in every corner of the country. Next to agriculture, the construction industry employs the largest number of workers, both in cities and in rural areas. This includes a large number of workers employed in construction and its allied industries, such as brick kilns, stone quarrying, tile-making, sand dredging, railway construction, construction of public works and erecting heavy electric stations.

There are an estimated 22 million workers in the construction industry, of which 35 percent are women. The forest and wood sector is yet another major source of employment for about 30 million people living in the forest and rural areas. Thus the two sectors, construction and forest/wood, together employ probably the largest workforce in India. However, it is unfortunate that although workers employed in these two industries are the front ranking 'nation builders', their own lives and working conditions are miserable and shameful. By and large these workers are employed on a casual basis by contractors, sub-contractors and petty contractors. They are paid low wages and, due to large-scale unemployment, they have difficulties getting jobs and holding them throughout the year.

As a result construction workers are totally unorganised, except in about 20–30 districts around the country. These workers do not have any security of service, and in the absence of the power to strike they cannot even bargain for a minimum living wage and standard of life. In addition, for centuries the landlord and construction companies have suppressed them, and in several cases they continue to be bonded labour.

It is common among smaller construction firms to employ a family unit, headed by the husband. In these cases the work done by women is simply not reflected in the wage register, since wage payments are made directly to male employees. Secondly, there is a tendency for unscrupulous employers to disguise wage payments to women workers to escape additional statutory responsibilities and costs under various labour laws.

A Major Area of Concern: The Barriers to Career Progress and the Acquisition of Skills

Opportunities for practical training in the building trades are a jealously guarded preserve of male employees. Yet many of these women are more committed to the industry than their male counterparts. They want to build, and build well. One such woman, whose ambition is to learn plastering, said the following in a discussion at a training programme: 'I would be able to do better work, easier work and earn more money. I could teach other women and we women would come up with better skills, practical knowledge and of course long-term employment. Why be assistants to men always?'

The skilled male workers, who refuse to transfer skills, are motivated by a wish to protect their own and their families' livelihoods.

The construction site is not just their place of work. It is also their home. A shed on a construction site can be an undesirable residence in a city where it is not even possible to sleep on the pavement without paying an unofficial 'rental'. For many of them, their work and their room on the construction site represent a chance to escape from the trap of rural poverty. They are prepared to undergo current hardships in the hope of achieving a better life for their families and better prospects for their children.

The building industry is one of the major employers of women workers in India. Reliable data on the strength of women workers in this industry is not available for four main reasons: (1) Payment is most often made on the basis of measuring work done by the family as a unit. (2) Employment figures released by the designated authorities are based on reports furnished by contractors, and only a handful of large contractors file employment reports. Medium- and small-sized contractors and sub-contractors are not required to, or do not, submit any reports. (3) In the building industry, work is casual, employment is temporary and labour is migratory. Employment data is difficult to compile and report. (4) Unscrupulous contractors may engage women workers but do not show them on pay rolls in order to escape additional statutory responsibilities and costs under various labour laws. Only the male head of the family receives the payment, is recorded in account books and is reported in statistics.

Most women construction workers are carriers of head loads and helpers to male workers at building sites. They are paid lower wages than male workers, while doing similar work. The unskilled male workers are able to designate themselves as skilled persons within a short span of two years and also command a higher price in the labour market. Such a progression is usually not possible for women workers. Women masons, brick-layers, plumbers, electricians, bar benders and carpenters simply do not exist. The patriarchal relations at work has denied women access to training, isolated them from high paying occupations and created wage discrimination. The following are quotations from a meeting at the construction site:

> I would like to learn tile work or plastering but there is no one who is prepared to teach it to me. I have to learn from men. The contractors will not let a tile-fitter teach me and waste his time. The *Mucadam* (Supervisor) gets angry if I try to learn any skill. There are more skilled persons today than unskilled workers. If women begin to learn skills, these contractors will never get unskilled workers. Even if I do learn some skills, I will have to face the competition from men. It is unlikely that they will allow me to get good work. Therefore, it is better to continue as an unskilled worker. I was eager to learn more but no one taught me. The skilled workers did not allow me to even lay a single tile or handle tools. They rebuke me and say that if women start doing skilled jobs, men would have to be helpers. They are very firm and do not allow women to learn any skill. I tried this on two occasions and won't try it anymore. I could get kicked out of my job and no one will give me work again.

Building Trades: An Exclusive Male Preserve

Women are kept out. Trade skills, such as those in carpentry and masonry, are traditionally passed on from father to son or between male members of a kinship group. Skill transfers to women is something that men do not think about. Male construction workers who continue doing unskilled work are those who lack access to such a network or are not part of any kinship group. This also strengthens the inaccessibility of skills to their female members. 'Learning building skills will only lead to problems at home and enmity at workplace. My husband is unskilled. He will think I have become big and superior.'

Despite the fact that much legislation has been made applicable to the construction and forest sector, the working conditions of workers in this industry are highly deplorable, and women construction workers are the worst sufferers since their employment is regarded as secondary to male workers. Since women do not have any construction skills, they are mostly employed as unskilled and casual labour. Women are considered incapable of understanding new technologies and hence construction remains a male-dominated profession, even though women make up 30 percent of the workforce.

How do the construction workers perceive their situation? How do they feel about the discrimination practised against them? Which restraining forces marginalise workers in development? What are the driving forces that enable women construction workers to perform their multiple roles, face discrimination and cope with their trying living and working conditions? How can women be encouraged to take up training? How can they be reintegrated into the labour market? How can women be given the confidence to take up jobs in responsible positions or certain male dominated jobs? How can change be anticipated through training in the event of industrial restructuring? What support measures should be put in place? These question address crucial issues of basic discrimination in the workplace, whether in hiring or promotion, and of understanding that women have always been undervalued in whatever they do, be it at home or in the job market. The world of work is changing dramatically. It is imperative that education, technical training and lifelong learning are considered as integral parts of a continuum.

TARGET GROUPS WITHIN TRADE UNION ACTIVITY

Women

While it is correct to regard women workers as a normal part of the workforce, special attention must be paid to the elimination of discrimination to which the vast majority of women are subject. Only some trade unions in the past have been part of the struggle for the equal treatment of women or have demanded their equality in schools. Yet not all trade unions have adopted this policy and some still do not accept that women can and should make an equal contribution to the economy. Today the situation has changed, however, since an increasing number of jobs in engineering, transport, construction and even coal mining are held by women.

On the other hand, very few women are on the staff of vocational training centres. Women's representation in trades such as secretarial work and dressmaking is higher than in other trades. Very few training centres with traditional trades have women instructors or principals. Unless trade unions take up this struggle, work, education and vocational training will continue to be instruments for the promotion of social injustice.

Rural Workers

Training facilities for rural workers are far worse than those for urban workers and yet trade union work, in most countries, tends to be concentrated in cities rather than in rural areas. Thus there is an urgent need to improve the situation of rural people through vocational training, especially as rural workers—in addition to the natural hazards associated with bad weather, uncertain harvests, poor social facilities—tend to be the victims of various kinds of oppression.

The Disabled Worker

Industry needs to include another group of workers who are victims of industrial accidents. Trade unions have to adopt a wide range of measures aimed at helping disabled persons to secure and retain suitable employment and thereby further their integration or reintegration into society.

Child Labour

Another group of workers to which trade unions have a very special obligation is that of child labourers. It is in the humanitarian tradition of the trade union movement to insist that the ill-treatment of one worker is a challenge to all workers. Working children are citizens of today and trade union members of tomorrow. However, the question for trade unions is: Should child labour be prohibited, or should children receive training in order to work?

TRADE UNIONS AND LIFELONG LEARNING OF WOMEN WORKERS

Learning by Doing and Income-Generating Projects for Women

This method has been used in the rural areas since theoretical teaching is of limited value in the absence of practical experience. It has been an essential element in initiating an income-generating project on bee-keeping for women workers in West Bengal. As the honey produced by the Indian bees was insufficient and the income was lower than the desired level, women started exploring ways to overcome this problem. After holding meetings with different agencies and projects, they were informed that the Italian bee known as the Malifera bee triples production of honey. It was tried and tested, and the project was successful. The method of learning-by-doing is more interesting for the worker, and it encourages initiative and imagination.

As the Indian government has few resources to undertake a large-scale training programme for local artisans, it remains necessary to take a bold and drastic step in this direction.

Safety and Health for Women Construction Workers

Construction workers report a variety of health problems and ascribe them to their work. The women suffer from menstrual disorders, cases of prolapsed uterus and backaches. Miscarriages are frequent. Lifting weight is the primary cause of these problems. Almost all workers complain of muscular pain in their limbs. A few show wounds on their lower legs and hands caused by handling bricks and gravel. Hard work, long working hours and poor health make them feel so tired that they take days off work to rest. Safety equipment (such as hard hats, safety boots, gloves, goggles and other prescribed safety gear) is reportedly not provided. Many even lack awareness of the value of safety equipment and remark that such gear could interfere with their movements. When anyone of the women suffers injury or a cut, she simply puts something on it and continues to work. First-aid boxes are rarely seen on building sites.

Many things are best learned by experience but safety is not one of them. Safety needs to be seen as an integral part of every lesson. For every work activity—whether it be cutting sheet metal or climbing a ladder—there is only one acceptable procedure: the safe one. Training should ensure that before workers start a job—whether it be starting a machine or using inflammable liquids—it is safe.

New Technology for Women

It is generally true, at least in most developing countries, that higher technology tends to marginalise the economic role of women and reduce their social status. Higher technology requires new and sophisticated skills which women rarely possess. While training and retraining offers are first taken by men, it is only the residual employment, if any, that goes to women. The building trade is a field which is becoming increasingly sophisticated with regard to the use of technology. In cities, high-rise buildings, complex designs based on communication technology, air conditioning and the use of new building materials, as well as mechanised construction, are becoming common. Where do women fit in this emerging scenario? Since most women are unskilled workers, the introduction of new technologies is more likely to make them redundant and push them back into destitution and dependency. Therefore, access to a higher order of technology is essential for the economic betterment and social uplifting of women construction workers. In the context of the building industry, this implies the use of a greater variety of building materials, the use of tools and machines and labour-saving and safe methods of work.

Women workers are usually aware of the changing scenario at their sites and those nearby. They see the coming of new technology and wish to be a part of it. Many express the desire to learn trades such as tile fitting, plastering and painting. They would also like to learn building trades, which are not as physically exacting as carrying head loads, and those that do not cause them physical injury. Many also express the need for functional literacy and numerical ability to enter new trades.

New skills, technologies and organisations are necessary to increase the productivity of the industry as a whole. But the development of the industry based on new technologies should be gender-neutral.

Development is a continuous and cumulative process. It necessitates setting up institutions that impart new skills. It requires new organisations that value those skills, as well as the willingness to put effort into learning them. Development is a process that implies changes in the very structure of society. Many organisations have a role to play in the development of women workers in the building industry.

TRAINING WOMEN CONSTRUCTION WORKERS

In most countries today, training in industrial training institutes is given to the young educated new entrants on the basis of the requirements of the industry. The industrial training institutes in Bombay, for example, with 2,000 seats in various trades, receive applications from nearly 100,000 young people. While those with influence and perhaps good marks are lucky to get selected, the others have to suffer disappointment. Most villages are devoid of any training institutes. As a result, artisans living in villages have to rely on traditional apprenticeship training or learn the trade from their fathers.

Women construction workers rarely utilise training places in industrial training institutes. This is attributed to a variety of constraints: the burden of domestic and childcare responsibilities; prevailing social values and stereotyping of certain occupations; fewer training facilities for women; and lack of awareness among planners, employers and women themselves about alternative opportunities and different training options available to them.

Training must take into account the following: Policy planners need to be sensitised to the gender dimension of construction work and skills training; training organisations need to be geared to meet the needs of women trainees before women construction workers can make the best use of skills training; they need entrepreneurial skills and an awareness of the rights of women as workers; infrastructure support for training activities for women workers needs to include childcare facilities; there needs to be flexibility in choice of training inputs, financial incentives and perhaps even a place to stay for the duration of the programme, or the option that training be provided on-site; the provision of training should entail placement or marketing services; the certification of skills for building trades would go a long way towards improving the access of women workers to the labour market; improving the conditions and performance of workers in this industry is not a matter of social justice alone but also a question of how to enable them to make a more worthwhile and effective contribution to the performance of the industry.

Special services should be provided for workers in the informal sector through: outreach; job development and job placement services; personal counselling; assessment and testing; career counselling and planning; support services, such as childcare; pre-employment preparation; books and materials, loans, tuition and assistance; referrals to relevant social services; occupational safety and health.

Women workers need to be regarded as equal partners in the building process. They want to learn, perform better, earn more and be a part of the industrial ethos in their own right. This should be seen as an opportunity for the building industry and its associations, government and training institutes, trade unions and non-government organisations to play their roles and introduce practical programmes so as to lead the workforce onto the path of modernisation and economic betterment.

Needed is: the technical upgrading of the building process, the introduction of cost-effective building programmes, improved working conditions, a decent living environment and payment of wages at the going market rates—all without any gender discrimination.

REFORMING THE EDUCATION SYSTEM AS A WHOLE

Emphasising investment in human resources is vital for an effective employment policy. But priority must be given to the development of the entire educational and training system.

Education and training is expected to contribute to the strengthening of democratic social structures. A society which emphasises education and training for all is in fact laying the social foundation for active citizenship and social stability, and thereby preventing social exclusion. This view of education is not shared by employers, however. For some, education is primarily an investment for increasing productivity.

The state's main responsibility is to secure basic education. At the same time, it should be in the interest of the state to improve the competencies of its citizens. While employers emphasise competencies, they treat the issue of equal opportunity as being less important and as a last resort issue for the disadvantaged. Their proposals focus primarily on supporting those who are already privileged.

It is important that the state and social partners co-operate in securing lifelong learning in an expedient manner. Tripartite co-operation at all levels is necessary. It is also important to assure equal opportunity for men and women in all forms of education.

Education and training is not only a social investment to make people more productive. The purpose of education and training is also to support the personal and cultural development of each individual, to increase his opportunities and further his or her participation in society.

Initial Education for Young People

Initial education—both theoretical and practical—should be designed to help young people to develop both personally and intellectually. The goal should be to create active citizens, who are capable of participating in the social life of the community. It is only when an individual's capacity for co-operation, communication, creativity, initiative and flexibility has been strengthened that he or she is also prepared for working life.

All young people should have the right to several years of broad-based education. This education should at the same time lay the necessary foundation for further education and training and also be available for older people in need of a new and broadened knowledge.

Resources are needed to enable enterprises and employees to make use of university courses as a recurrent form of education and to meet the needs of the labour market. It is also important to create a lively interaction between vocational training and university education.

People who are unemployed should have access to education and training which increases their competencies. It should be designed according to individual needs and result in better possibilities for entry into the labour market through improved general knowledge, higher vocational competence or a completely new professional direction. Work practice or similar measures need to be offered either during or after the education. Education and training—rather than cash allowances—should be provided to the unemployed. In the case of the long-term unemployed, it is necessary to offer rehabilitative measures before offering education or training.

The Responsibility of Employers

At a time of rapid change and constant rise in the level of qualifications in working life, it is not acceptable from a social point of view that enterprises force older people with obsolete knowledge to leave and be replaced by younger job applicants with more up-to-date knowledge. If all enterprises adopt this method of renewal and upgrading of its workforce, none can succeed.

Thus both society and employees, represented by their trade unions, have a legitimate reason for demanding efforts by enterprises to improve the competencies of their staff through education and training. All employees should be given on-the-job training and other forms of professional development in order to be able at least to maintain a position in the work process and to adjust to changing assignments and qualification requirements.

Enterprises should investigate future competency needs together with their employees and their representatives and make plans to provide the required education and training. Both enterprises and their employees are responsible for filling potential gaps in competencies.

Personal development and participation in the wider context of work should be given the same importance as skills training. Different measures of cost equalisation could be used in order to guarantee the possibility of enterprises to finance the retraining of its workforce.
The employer should be made responsible for on-the-job training and its financing, which is why on-the-job training should be carried out during paid time. It should have a wider content than that is required for the immediate assignment.

Competence Development and Work Organisation

Learning at work should be arranged to include employees who have traditionally been considered to lack both the need and the capacity to acquire new knowledge.
A number of studies, both European and American, show that the main characteristics of successful enterprises are the delegation of responsibility and authority, access to information for the staff and efforts to maintain good management support. The organisation of work should be changed in order to combine it with developing competencies. This has proved to be the most effective means of increasing productivity.

Lifelong Learning

Rapid changes in working life require confident and mature employees. People who feel threatened by changing work conditions often actively oppose change. Trade union organisations want to work for employment security, as well as to make it possible for employees to improve their occupational competencies in such a way that all employees have the possibility of choosing their employers and tasks and are not tied to a given employer or type of work.
This entails certain quality requirements with regard to the organisation, content and purpose of all education. It should always borne in mind that since certain knowledge and skills become quickly obsolete, it is necessary to offer basic knowledge and skills that broaden knowledge and contribute to the ability to learn continuously. General basic education and broad vocational training are therefore an important part of lifelong learning. From a trade union point of view it is essential that all education and training have a broad perspective.

Education and Training: A Trade Union Concern

We in trade unions are naturally interested in the survival and success of both the private and the public sectors of business life. The security of our members can be heightened by strengthening their position on the labour market. Trade union organisations want to play an active role in this connection, both on their own and in co-operation with others.

CONCLUSIONS

Society today is undergoing a transformation of unprecedented magnitude and speed, affecting all spheres of economic and social life. Knowledge, skills and competencies of all men and women have become the cornerstone of personal growth and employability, enterprises' competitiveness, and society's economic and social sustainability. In a competitive environment the comparative advantages of every individual, enterprise and country will increasingly depend on the asset of intelligent workers, based on knowledge, practical skills, innovation and technology. Investment in education, training and the development of human resources has become more crucial than ever. Education today must see clearly two objectives: education for living and education for making a living.

Education is a lifelong-process, which begins with basic education and does not end until the worker retires at the end of his or her working life.

Trade unions are instruments for protecting and promoting the interest of workers. One of its most important functions is to bargain with employers in order to raise wages and to improve conditions of work. But the leaders of trade unions usually recognise that the power to get more wages is limited by several factors. The main point is the relationship between productivity and skill: the higher we raise the productivity, the higher we can raise the wage. In other words, as trade unionists we should be just as interested in education and training as in wages.

What is urgently needed is mass education and awareness raising programmes involving a large number of workers. The educational programme should convince workers to organise themselves, create awareness, develop leadership qualities and, above all, help to build a strong physical and moral force in order to enable these workers to throw off their yoke of oppression and exploitation.

The planning of vocational training should include general education. The two activities must be fully co-ordinated. A good education from this point of view is one which results in broad rather than narrow skills.

In the context of the ever-emerging new skills, traditional training is of little help, and workers are finding it increasingly difficult to depend upon one set of skills to provide a lifetime of employment. That is why vocational training should now be seen as a continuous process, which needs to be adopted in every phase of their working lives.

SECTION 2:

COUNTRY STUDIES

SKILLS FORMATION FOR THE INFORMAL SECTOR IN BANGLADESH: A STRATEGIC FRAMEWORK

Rashed Al Mahmud Titumir

The formal work environment in Bangladesh is undergoing a process of rapid transformation due to globalisation and technological change, a process which is leaving behind the majority of the workforce in the informal sector, composed of non-farm or off-farm rural subsistence activities and work in family-run, urban micro-enterprises. The rapid expansion of the informal sector is a result of the inability of the formal sector to generate adequate employment opportunities.[1] The inability of the formal economy to generate employment is further aggravated due to the changes in the concept of employability and the organisation of work, which is characterised by labour market flexibilisation including non-standard forms of employment and shorter product cycles. This means that those who are unable to acquire the new skills for employability will find it difficult to find jobs. The process of skills formation for the informal sector is further challenged by the inadequate capacity of formal sector institutions and the non-affordability of formal training for those who want to acquire skills, as well as by the demand for skill shifts in response to changes in economic regimes and management the world over. The traditional system is further constrained by its inability to reach the disadvantaged, who mostly fall in the informal sector, and to reduce discrimination in access to training and education, thus reducing their chances of entering the competitive labour markets in the new economic order.

The present strategic policy paper seeks to provide an understanding of the issues and options involved in education, training and skill development for decent work in the informal sector in Bangladesh. The paper suggests a policy framework for improving the skills of the workforce, thereby enhancing worker employability, enterprise competitiveness and national growth, and strengthening collaboration among stakeholders (government, workers, private sector, NGOs). By analysing formal and non-formal training programmes offered by various agencies, this paper seeks to identify weaknesses and emerging needs of skills formation in the informal sector.

THE INFORMAL LABOUR MARKET IN BANGLADESH

One of the principal developmental challenges for Bangladesh is the creation of employment for new entrants into the labour force, a great many of whom are currently under-employed. The labour force[2] is growing at almost twice the rate of population

Madhu Singh, (ed.), Meeting Basic Learning Needs in the informal Sector, 133-154.

growth. This relationship is likely to persist over the next two decades or longer (World Bank, 2000). The decrease in population growth is more than offset by increased participation rates. The Bangladesh Bureau of Statistics (BBS) forecast a 42.6 percent increase in the labour force between 1991 and 2005 for the entire population, with an increase of 31.7 percent for males and 126.5 percent for females. To meet the country's employment needs by 2020 (from the current 56 million to a projected need of 100 million), Bangladesh will have to create 2.25 million jobs every year (Mahmud, 1999).

The Labour Force Surveys since 1983–84 have shown open employment in the range of 1–3 percent. However, the unemployment rate rises to 16.5 percent if those who worked less than 15 hours per week are included (BBS, 1996). The rate of underemployment for those aged 10 years and over, defined to include those who are working less than 35 hours per week, is 34.6 percent. The rate is higher for rural areas (37.9%) than urban areas. At the same time, female unemployment (70.7%) is much more evident than its counterparts (12.4%). Unemployment and underemployment rates of population aged 15 years and over are nearly 40 percent of the reference labour force (Mahmud, 1999).

The labour market in Bangladesh comprises three types of market: *formal*, *rural informal* and *urban informal*. The informal sector is made up of unregistered small, cottage, and micro-enterprises in rural and urban areas which employ less than 10 persons, who may be family members or hired workers. Activities in the informal sector enterprises include: non-farm activities (poultry, fisheries, livestock); industrial activities (manufacturing, processing, repairing); trading; services; construction; and transport. About 98 percent of the workforce in 'agriculture, forestry and fisheries' was in the informal sector in 1996. In the three sectors of 'construction', 'transport, storage and communication' and 'trade, hotel and restaurant', informal sector workers constituted more than 80 percent of the workforce. The corresponding shares of the 'manufacturing sector' and the 'household sector' are more than 50 percent. The informal sector accounted for 34 percent or less of the workforce in only two sectors: 'finance and business services' and 'electricity, gas and water'. According to the BBS (1996), the main occupations of informal sector workers are in: agriculture, forest and fisheries (71%); sales (11%); production and transport (3%); service (2%); and professional and technical areas (1%) (BBS, 1996).

The occupation of around 10 percent of the informal sector workers is 'not adequately' defined (Bhattacharya, Faiz & Zohir, 2000). In the total workforce of the country, self-employed or self-employed workers accounted for 32 percent, while the share of unpaid family workers and day-labourers was 37 percent and 18 percent, respectively. These three categories together accounted for 87 percent of the total labour force. Most of these workers belong to the informal sector, which shows that this sector is the largest source of employment in Bangladesh. With increasing rural-to-urban migration and the inability of agriculture and the formal sector to absorb the ever-increasing aspirants to the job market each year, the share of the informal sector in employment has been increasing.

PUBLIC SECTOR INVOLVEMENT IN SKILLS DEVELOPMENT IN BANGLADESH

Two ministries which mainly administer public sector training are the Ministry of Education (MOE) and the Ministry of Labour and Employment (MOLE). The MOE establishes curricula, standards and examinations for vocational and technical education through the Technical Education Board. The Directorate of Technical Education (DTE) is responsible for planning, development co-ordination and supervision of technical and vocational education and training (TVET) under the Ministry of Education. The MOLE provides skill training through its technical training centres. Altogether, the output of the formal system for skills has increased from about 5,000 to 10,000 students per annum. TVET absorbs about 2 percent of the MOE budget, and less than 10 percent of the much smaller MOLE budget. Attempts to shorten courses, merge TVET under a single ministry and establish a high level national body on skill development failed in the 1980s.

The Ministries of Youth and Sports and Women's Welfare provide non-formal training, delivering organised courses outside the regular school system.

Under the MOLE, vocational training is provided by eleven Technical Training Centres located in large urban areas and the Bangladesh Institute of Marine Technology. Under the MOE, vocational training is provided at 51 Vocational Training Institutes (VTIs), mostly located at various district and sub-district levels, under the direct supervision of the DTE. Of these, four VTIs are of larger size (with an enrolment of about 200 students each) located in larger district towns and the reminder are located in semi-urban areas and have an enrolment of about 80 students each.

Government initiatives in recent years include the establishment of 13 new modern equipped VTIs to cover all 64 districts in the country. Seven new institutions have been in operation since 2000. They offer Secondary School Certificate (Vocational) and Higher Secondary Certificate (Vocational) courses under the MOE.

Under the Ministries of Youth and Sports, there exist 45 centres mostly located in urban and semi-urban areas throughout the country which provide training in livestock, poultry and fisheries, as well as basic computer courses. Each year in each institute, approximately 1000 students enrol in and complete a training programme lasting 3–4 months.

TVET programmes are diverse in terms of the levels and subjects of skills taught and the varying lengths of training. It is difficult to make accurate generalisations about such a heterogeneous field. TVET is provided by formal, non-formal and informal means. Formal TVET is provided within the school system at the certificate level (Grade 8 + 2 years), diploma level (SSC + 3 years), and degree level (HSC + 3–4 years).

Bangladesh Technical Education Board (BTEB)

Under BTEB-affiliated institutions, there are 132 education and training centres. The BTEB has two levels of instruction. Successful completion of the first year leads to National Skill Standard (NSS) III certificate. Students may then choose to enter the second year of instruction, which leads to an NSS-II certificate. Each year is divided into nine months of laboratory and classroom instruction and three months of industry attachment.

Enrolment in each of the trades offered in VTIs remained quite low in previous years. This is also evident in the subjects offered since many of the trade courses did not match the local demand, and consequently enrolment remained low. This discrepancy is even greater when the training performance of the institutions is compared with their intake capacity.

Information on the gender composition of trainees in VTIs shows low participation of women. Female students have been admitted in these programmes since the mid-1980s. In January 1990, 2,827 students were enrolled in Part I of the programme. Among them, 71 were female, constituting only 2.5 percent of all students. Only two VTIs (out of 51 VTIs) provide dormitory facilities for women, though women hardly use them. Moreover, the dropout rate is high among female students. Of the 71 female students admitted in January 1990, 18 dropped out by December.

The centralised process of curriculum development does not readily allow for integrating elements which are relevant to women. A standardised curriculum reduces the initiative of teachers and causes them to ignore linkages with local labour markets.

Directorate of Technical Education (DTE)

The Directorate of Technical Education oversees several degree programmes: the Technical Teacher Training College (TTTC), polytechnics and monotechnic institutes, the Vocational Teacher Training Institute (VTTI) and Vocational Training Institutes (VTIs). An overview of present programmes follows:

The DTE plans to increase the proportion of students in secondary and post-secondary education enrolled in vocational technical subjects from 3.5 percent at present to 10 percent by the year 2000, and then 50 percent by the year 2015. To help achieve these ambitious goals, the DTE has planned new development projects (Planning Commission, 1998).

The Bureau of Manpower, Education and Training

The Bureau of Manpower, Employment and Training (BMET), the training arm of the MOLE, provides skills training and retraining in the Technical Training Centres (TTCs). The first year's course contents meet the requirements of National Skill Standard Grade-3 (semi-skilled), while the second year's course contents meet of those of National Skill

Standard Grade-2 (skilled). Although the main component of training activity of each TTCs is its regular institutional programmes, each also participates extensively in in-plant, apprenticeship and other types of industry-based on-the-job training and also conducts specially tailored upgrading courses for industrial employees on request.

The training performance of BMET during the Fourth Five-Year Plan and during fiscal years 1995–96 to 1998–99 reveals that apprenticeship training has been minimal and has not increased at the same rate although there has been sustained increase in institutional training over the plan periods. The number of trainees per year varied widely and the maximum number was 555 in 1983. Since then the number has gone down considerably, and in 1997–98 there were only 60 trainees attached to various establishments. In 1998–99 only 65 trainees were attached, whereas the target was set at 1000. Initially the public sector parastatal organisations were able to accommodate a number of trainees in apprenticeships. However, with gradual privatisation and a slowdown in public sector initiatives, the possible places for trainees are hard to find.

Table 1: Performance of Skill Development Programme under MOLE

Types of Training	1997–98		1998–99	
	Target	Actual	Target	Actual
Institutional Training	7,000	13,258	10,000	10,738
Apprenticeship Training	5,00	60	1,000	65
Language Training for Nurses	305	89	350	90
Total	7,805	13,407	11,350	10,893

Source: Mid-term review of the fifth five-year plan (1997–2002), Planning Commission, December 2000

Among the total students admitted from 1988–89 to 1993–94, about 7 percent were females. The male-female ratio of students has improved slightly over the years. A survey of TTC trainees (NVTRP, 1995) reveals that most female TTC students had relatives in the BMET or who were TTC staff members (Rahman, 2000), pointing to the fact that TTCs have not been able to expand their reach.

The capacity of TTCs and VTIs is small relative to the overall magnitude of labour demand, regardless of whether their facilities are utilised efficiently. Even if all efficiency concerns were resolved, informally trained workers would still, out of necessity, fill the vast majority of skilled and semi-skilled jobs.

Training programmes within TTCs have not been designed on the basis of industrial surveys, nor have they kept step with the latest technologies. Much of the equipment tends to be outdated. More modern equipment such as computers is in insufficient supply. There has also been a lack of an overall training policy, combined with an adequate legal basis, to influence employers to participate in vocational training. The institutions tend to work in relative isolation from labour markets. No industrial advisory committees exist, either at local, district or national levels.

Ministry of Women Affairs

From 1997 to 1999 two organisations under the Ministry of Women Affairs have provided women skill development programmes in tailoring, embroidery, blocked boutique, painting, *nakshi khata*, food processing, jute works, leather crafts and typing. The Jatiyo Mohila Sangstha has attained 87.70 percent of its target, and the Department of Women Affairs has reached 96.17 percent of its target group.

Table 2. Skills Development Programmes for Women (1997–1999)

Organisation	Duration of Training	Target	Actual	Actual as percentage of Target
Jatiyo Mohila Sangstha	7 days	105	105	
	3 to 4 months	6000	5600	
	6 months	3000	2280	
Subtotal		9105	7985	87.70
Department of Women's Affairs	7 days	572	1,813	
	15 days	160,988	156,169	
	2 months	1071	1,071	
	3 months	18,600	15,312	
	4 months	4850	4,845	
	6 months	2113	1,772	
Subtotal		188,687	181,456	96.17
Grand Total		197,792	189,441	95.78

Source: Mid-term review of the fifth five year plan (1997-2002), Planning Commission, December 2000

Ministry of Youth and Sports

The Department of Youth within the Ministry of Youth and Sports provides training leading to self-employment for people aged 15–30 years. Up to June 1997 about 630,000 youth had received training in different trades. Of those trained, nearly 60 percent took up self-employment projects, the majority with financial assistance provided by the Ministry.

At present the Ministry has 208 training centres distributed as described in Table 3.

Table 3. Training Programmes of the Ministry of Youth and Sports

	Duration	Number of Centres*
Youth Training Centres (livestock, poultry and pisciculture)	3 months	21
Pisciculture Training Cultures	1 month	64
Technical Training Centres	4 months	5
Secretarial Training Centres	1 year	5
Zonal Resources Training Centre	Various	4
Stenographic Training Centre	6 months	32
Block Batik Printing Training Centre.	3 months	9
Dressmaking Training Centre	4 months	68

*Note: Some premises encompass more than one training centre. For example, outside Rajshahi one house is occupied by both a Garments and Dressmaking Training Centre and a Stenographic Training Centre.
Source: Department of Youth Development, 'The Programmes of the Department of Youth Development at a Glance', no date.

In addition the Department provides mobile training courses lasting up to one month in which the instructor organises courses at the local level in borrowed premises (*madrasah*, school, house) with the help of extension agents and other resource persons. Entry requirements for mobile training are Class V.

The head office of the Department of Youth is organised around three main projects. The *Thana* Resource Development and Employment Programme (TRDEP) aims at poverty alleviation through the provision of training and micro-credit in rural areas of 32 *thanas*. The Youth Training and Self-Employment Project covers 470 *thanas* throughout the country, including 10 *thanas* in metropolitan areas. The project is based on the Commonwealth Youth Forum in India and is entirely government financed; it has two aspects. First, training is given to youth for 3–4 months in such subjects as typewriting and computer training. Second, small loans are arranged for trainees to engage in self-employment. Since its inception, 210,000 youth have been trained under the project, including 92,000 in 1996–97. About 40 percent of the youth (35,000) obtained credit following the training, and reportedly a total of 60 percent of the youth (64,000) became self-employed after the training in 1997. The main objective of the Youth Training Centre Project is to train youth in livestock, poultry and pisciculture as a means of entry into self-employment. Non-formal training is provided for three months in 21 residential youth training centres (each with a capacity of 100 trainees, or 400 per annum based on four courses) on the practical aspects of animal and fish rearing.

The 45 centres under the Ministry of Youth and Sports have sought to provide skills development training in the area of livestock, poultry, fisheries and basic computer to

466,071 persons during 1997–99. It is claimed that the centres have achieved 93 percent of their target.

Table 4. Skill Development Programme under the Ministry of Youth (1997–1999)

Organisation	Target	Implementation	Achievement
Ministry of Youth	466,071	432,142	93%

Source: Mid-term review of the fifth five-year plan (1997–2002), Planning Commission, December 2000

STRENGTHS AND WEAKNESSES OF PUBLIC SECTOR VOCATIONAL TRAINING SYSTEM

There exists a great mismatch between the demand for and supply of skill formation. The macro-level performance of the formal system within Bangladesh is minimal. The outcome of technical/vocational education at the certificate level amounts to only 1.8 percent of the similar level graduates at Secondary School Certificate (SSC) level, and the number of diploma technicians is only 1.4 percent of the High School Certificate (HSC) level graduates. Moreover, formal provision of training and vocational education is minuscule in relation to the informal ways in which the people actually become skilled. Only 0.4 percent of those in the labour force had any vocational, technical or commercial training. The formal training system accounts for only a small fraction of the occupational skills needed to be acquired each year.

Lack of Linkage with Job Market

The central shortcoming of public sector technical and vocational education is a lack of sufficient linkages with employers and the labour market. The main problem seems to be a lack of clear labour market connections. TTCs and VTIs cannot be converted into good investments unless more of the graduates find employment in the fields in which they were trained (World Bank, 1990). Training institutions lack linkages with the local labour market surrounding the institution due to excessive centralisation and rigidity in the system. Financial controls are also inflexible and institutional since managers can not give incentives and rewards for teacher performance. In short, there is a lack of delegation of authority to the heads of training centres.

Employers complain that public sector organisations are not quick enough to update curricula on short notice (that is, they are unable to introduce new courses, expand those in demand or reduce or close those for which demand has slackened) in order to compete with technological changes in enterprises (for example, TEB updates curricula every five years). Polytechnics, in particular, were slow to integrate computers and instrumentation as integral parts of training in all fields.

Training institutions do not have the capacity to carry out occupational analyses of the skills in demand in the local area. There is no institutional flexibility for priority training to upgrade skills for those who are already employed in occupations, including skills in the non-formal sector.

Underfinancing

Technical and vocational education and training is costlier than general education because it requires more instructors per student and for practice in workshops. TVET requires money for equipment, in-service training and consumable supplies. Most of these necessary inputs are insufficient in public institutions at present.

Most VTIs, polytechnics and specialised degree programmes are equipped with outdated, obsolete and worn out equipment. The share of total revenue spending allocated to TVET has declined by about 17 percent, from 2.4 percent in 1990–91 to 2.0 percent in 1996–97. It declined further to 1.5 percent in 1997–98. Capital investment in TVET virtually dried up in the 1990s (World Bank, 2000). Within the institutions students receive group rather than individual training. Lesson plans and job sheets are rarely used in training. Consequently, institutions cannot properly impart the intended practical training.

The success of the public sector vocational training system cannot be judged through the achievement of quantitative targets: the number of organisations in operation or the number of students who graduated. The success of such training has to be feeding a growing informal sector with appropriate skills. Currently, the public sector institutions are providing training only for the formal economy.

The formal training system suffers from system rigidity and inadequate flexibility in the courses or for lack of continuous revision of curriculum, which is mostly in demand for the informal sector. Such rigidity results in a mismatch between skill generation and skill utilisation. Removal of such rigidities will require appropriate linkages with the other sectors. There is no institutional process of dialogue with stakeholders—the employees and the employers. Moreover, the informal sector is not organised to engage in such dialogue. There is also no effective system in place to ensure the participation of employers and labour representatives in policy formulation and planning for skill generation.

Excessive centralisation: Most administrative decisions (admission numbers, curricula, etc.) are made at the centre. Since the administrators and staffs of institutes do not belong to the institutes themselves but to the central administration, there is little room for institutional ownership to develop.

Absence of institutional structure for dialogue with local enterprises and industries: The centralised system of curriculum development leaves no room for flexibility to reflect the enterprise and contextual reality, and employers have little or no say about the content of teaching programmes and operation of the institutes. However, in some courses industrial attachments are placed for most students.

Entrepreneurship: The education and training system does not provide entrepreneurship training as part of the course structure, which could pave the way for self-employment. Institutions are needed which focus on marketing surveys, preparation of business plans, applications for credit from available sources (such as the new employment bank), accounting and other practical issues in the start-up of micro-enterprises. This would be advantageous for those who have a natural inclination for small-business creation.

PRIVATE SECTOR

A large number of profit-motivated private trade schools exist. In the early 1990s it was estimated that over 200 such trade schools existed. However, no estimates have been made of the capacity of the institutions. According to another estimate, there are about 159 private institutions offering various vocational training courses in the country (Asian Development Bank, 1995).

The main objective of these private trade schools is to earn a profit without emphasising standards. The growth of private trade schools in the country is primarily connected to the large-scale export of skilled and semi-skilled manpower across the region but primarily to the Middle East.

These types of schools offer non-formal and non-standard training of short duration, and in most cases they have no standard facilities or qualified instructors. It is difficult to obtain accurate data on the number of trade schools or the type and quality of training. They are not required to register or affiliate with any training agency. They design their own training programmes and materials.

Table 5. Private Vocational Training Centres Offering Courses

Name of Trade	Duration of Courses	Students Enrolled in 1995
Electrical	2 years/1 year/6 months	854
Welding	3 years/18 months/6 months	100
Radio/TV	1 year/6 months	108
Refrigeration	6 months/3 months	113
Carpentry	4 years/2 years/18 months/6 months	162
Embroidering	2 years/1 year/6 months	576
Bamboo and cane works	2 years/1 year/6 months	482
Tailoring and sewing	4 years/3 years/2 years/1 year/6 months	780

Electronics	3 months	45
Printing	1 year	28
Painting	3 years	10
Tinsmith	3 months	40
Motorcycle	6 months	26
Watch repair	6 months	24
Lath operator	2 years	31
Auto	1 year	10
Mechanic	6 months/3 months	32
Shallow pump	6 months	30
Civil drafting	6 months	7
Computer	6 months	20
Preparation of sanitary latrines	1 year	25
Cycle/Rickshaw repair	1 year	10
Tape recorder repair	6 months	28
Photography	1 year	15
Commercial art	1 year	11

Source: ADB (1995)

The training capacity is also difficult to determine. The training curricula varied widely from the traditional industrial subjects, from mechanics training and welding to driving. Trainees are charged a fee for training, and it is not uncommon to see trainees paying from Tk. 3,000 to Tk. 8,000 per month for private training courses. Although most training lasts a few months, the length of training varies widely from a few weeks to more than a year.

The Directorate of Technical Education (DTE), through its Office of the Director of Vocational Education, provides some financial support to small private vocational training institutes, which numbered around 157 in 1995 in the country. These vocational training institutes offer training in various trades. The most popular trades appear to be tailoring/sewing, embroidering and bamboo/cane works (for women) and electrical, welding, radio/television, refrigeration and carpentry (for men). The entry requirements to such courses vary widely. Total enrolment in these 157 institutes in 1995 was 3,600 students.

The private sector has made little effort to institutionalise education, training and skill development. The BTEB has 26 affiliated institutions in the private sector, such as Institutions Offering Diploma in Commerce as well as secondary schools and two Women Career Training Institutes.

NGO TRAINING ACTIVITIES

The World Bank estimated that about 30 non-governmental institutions were involved in providing school-based occupational skill training in the early 1990s, but that total enrolments were only about 2,000 students (World Bank, 1990, p. xii). The Department of Technical Education of the MOE recognises about 160 non-profit vocational schools. Several non-governmental institutions also provide non-formal skill training. The schools are small, averaging only 25 trainees each (total capacity is 3,600). Courses typically last from four to six months, and the most popular trades were reportedly tailoring/sewing, embroidery, and bamboo/cane works for women, and electrical, welding, radio/tv, refrigeration, and carpentry for men. According to an ILO study, NGOs run 107 institutions, which have provided training to 16,039 persons from 1991 to 1995. In addition to the training NGO, many of the large multi-input NGOs provide micro-credit as well as various types of training.

Two types of NGOs are involved in imparting skill training: one specialises in training functions and regards the provision of other inputs such as credit as secondary; the other type includes NGOs whose major function is to provide credit and who regard training as secondary. Within the first category, over 100 NGOs have taken initiatives in vocational training. Given the nature and intent of the NGOs, such programmes are directed at the poor.

An ILO commissioned study (World Bank, 2000; Mahmud, 1999) lauded the performance of two NGO training organisations: Underprivileged Children's Educational Programme (UCEP) and Mirpur Agricultural Workshop and Training Programmes (MAWTS). They operate in training centres located in three main cities which are characterised by high industrial concentration. UCEP offers training courses in 14 different trades. However, it provides training only to children aged 10–14. The World Bank, however, favours UCEP-administered vocational training over public training institutions. Separate cells of the UCEP conduct regular surveys of the labour market; UCEP maintains intensive linkage with industry (including the Industrial Advisory Committee), sectoral committees and frequent contacts with employers through mandatory shop-floor assignments organised by a separate UCEP office; entrance into the programme is set at a Class 7 or 8 equivalent of non-formal education, and virtually all want to enter blue-collar occupations. Their students complete 3–12 months of training, which is done systematically, and the practical work occupies 80 percent of the total hours. Furthermore, students are assessed continuously. The focus of teaching is on practical competencies and attitudes to work, which results in highly structured daily lesson plans and job sheets. The exit examination also places emphasis on Basic Skills Test I & II and permits commercial work contracts (e.g. auto repair) for supplemental income and practice. The operating costs per student per annum is TK 12,000, and the internal success rate is 95 percent. Compared to this, MAWTS has limited capacity.

Within the second type of NGOs, the primary goal is to provide training on agricultural production, eco-agriculture, legal aid, gender awareness, handicrafts, etc. Most training is of a general nature and does not address skills development adequately.

Training programmes of the credit NGOs are usually directed at rural areas and concentrate primarily on their borrowers. Most training is conducted with poor materials. The course contents do not include all the essential ingredients. Inadequate physical facilities and lack of equipment, along with poor quality of trainers with poor salary and job prospects, result in a poor quality of training. The duration of the course is short, ranging from a few days to 2–3 weeks, and results in a shortage of skills needed to sustain and compete in the labour market. Fundamentally, training is often conducted without a proper assessment of the skills provided which often results in frustration not only among the trainees but also among the training providers.

THE TRADITIONAL SYSTEM

The traditional system in Bangladesh has served as a means of skill transfer to informal sector workers. The vast majority of people have acquired occupational skills (such as welding, turning, carpentry, and bicycle and small engine repair) through informal apprenticeships or other on-the-job training. The traditional apprenticeships, or the informal guild system, is responsible for teaching most of the skills imparted in the country. The trainee learns the skills by observing and assisting the 'master' (or *ostad* in the Bangladesh informal sector context). By observing the actual operation of the enterprise at close quarters and helping *ostad* in all kinds of work, the trainees learn how to produce a particular product and service.

The relationship between the trainer and trainee, which is quite different from that in the formal educational system, can be potentially exploitative. Nevertheless, in Bangladesh it is an institution that has successfully transferred skills over the years. It is an on-the-job, workplace-based, hands-on instructional system. Its unstructured and improvised character makes it flexible and adaptable to immediate needs of the employers.

After the completion of training, the graduate usually stays on at the workshop as a skilled worker until he or she eventually starts his or her own business. Informal apprenticeships therefore usually lead to self-employment, whereas formal apprenticeships are usually for wage employment in formal sector firms and may not always lead to immediate employment.

The major disadvantage of informal apprenticeships is that they impart a very narrow range of skills of variable quality with, in most cases, no defined standards and usually no access to supporting technical and social knowledge and skills.

SKILLS DEVELOPMENT IN BANGLADESH: THE LESSONS LEARNED

The kind of vocational training currently available from government, private sector and NGO-sponsored institutions falls short of what is needed to meet the growing demand. It also appears not to be very relevant not only with regard to curriculum and linkages with the enterprise but also to the beneficiaries of the training themselves. The training fails to reflect on the realities of the labour market and thus has not adequately matched the needs of the trainees. At the same time, most training institutions do not have the capacity or the mandate to reach out to people who work in the informal sector.

There is neither a master plan nor a comprehensive programme for skill formation catering to the needs of the informal sector. In most cases the training institutes have not been able to establish precisely who should be targeted in the informal sector. A balance between training for school dropouts, who are prone to end up in the informal sector, and training for people who already work in micro-enterprises has yet to be struck in Bangladesh.

Still lacking is a training strategy for the informal sector which is based on a need analysis of the national labour market with a focus on informal sector workers. Considering the lack of a clear overview of both the demand and the supply side of the training system, such a training strategy is necessary if one is to formulate precise reasons for intervening, if one is to set priorities, take into account equity considerations, quantify objectives and specify resource implications. There is a strong need and urgency for investigation based on data collected through primary sources.

RECONCEPTUALISING THE ROLE OF EDUCATION, SKILLS DEVELOPMENT AND TRAINING

Modes of Skill Formation

In Bangladesh three modes of the delivery of skills training can be identified. First, the school mode provides a wide range of general, technical and vocational courses on a full-time basis in vocational schools. Second, the dual mode encompasses apprenticeship programmes offering initial vocational training under the formal school system and part-time training in enterprise or industry. Third, there is the mixed mode, which resembles the dual mode but places greater emphasis on non-formal training.

The present system of delivery reflects the colonial legacy (see Singh, 2001). Skill formation in Bangladesh followed an elitist approach, which overlooked the need of those who needed most. The only skills which were promoted were craft-related skills such as carpentry. One of the most damaging effects of colonial involvement had been the destruction of indigenous education patterns, which had close links to technical and vocational learning and cultural practices of local people. To this day, the lack of emphasis on technical and industrial education can be seen in the Western paradigms represented in the ideas of multilateral and bilateral donor agencies decisively dictating policy options in countries like Bangladesh. Most of the policies of bilateral and multilateral donors follow the top-down model, which largely ignores the local context and felt needs.

The prevailing delivery—the age old and traditional school-based teacher-centred approach—has not been replaced by the learner-centred approach. The system has not been adapted to accept learning as a free exchange of ideas within a wider frame of flexible curriculum, and trainees are not given the opportunity to decide on either their own learning needs or the time and medium of learning.

Towards a New Framework for Skill Development

If vocational training and education is to cater to informal labour markets, along with the formal one, it needs to capture the traditions and values of the sector and the society within which it operates. First, the provision of training has to be *need-based*: that is, it has to be based on an understanding of the kinds of competencies people in the informal sector want in order to optimise their potential. Second, the training has to be *context-specific*: that is, it has to capture the socio-economic and cultural contexts within which people in the informal sector work. Often vocational education and training is conceived from a narrow perspective of human capital; the individualistic approach ignores the wider social context within which much learning takes place, as well as the relationships—personal and institutional—which actually constitute the vehicles or channels through which learning takes place. Third, the provision of skill formation needs to be embedded in the people's *coping strategy*: that is, how people in the informal sector cope in order to sustain their livelihood strategies. The concern is not only one of employment but also of securing a decent livelihood and the right to work for all.

In a rapidly changing world, modes of education, training and skill development must integrate the process of technological change, required levels of skills and changes in the organisation of work. There is little room for fragmented strategies. Emphasis must be on conceptual learning, technological literacy, cross-disciplinary relationships, worker flexibility and a smooth transfer of skills.

The present relationship between skill formation and the labour market indicates that training has to be planned and monitored closely, since it does not necessarily lead to related jobs for which the training is intended. It is imperative that training institutions and enterprises work together and complement each other's efforts. The relationship between training institutions and jobs is complex and problematic. It cannot be assumed that training programmes will prepare one to meet the requirements of jobs with specialised skills. Thus the main issue is not one of diversification and vocationalisation, nor is the issue only an economic one (earning opportunities, better jobs), but how to integrate science, technology and socio-technical reality of working life into the curriculum, and how to combine education with productive work (Corvalan, 1988).

What is urgently needed now is a broader view of education and training which would link schooling with work, that is, the system has to evolve to provide people with opportunities for continuing acquisition of knowledge and skills. There has been much debate focused on the comparison of the short-term and narrow skills development approach of non-formal education and training and those of the long-term general skills development of the formal system. Lifelong continuing education now emerges as the main component of the broader view of education, training and skill development. The broader view is based on the premise that a system of skill formation is difficult, if not impossible, to institute without a solid educational base at basic levels.

General and vocational competencies are regarded as interrelated dimensions of vocational learning. Equally important are personal and social competencies. In addition to cognitive competencies, there is a need for acquiring 'learning to learn' competencies. Of course, specialised skills and knowledge are needed; however, at issue is the balance between them and wider forms of knowledge (Krug, 1999).

The broader view advocated by the present paper departs from the school, dual and mixed modes and instead presents a co-operation-based integrative system, since learning is provided by a host of institutions at different levels—societal, formal and enterprise. Competencies are acquired and utilised in relation to societal institutions—family and community—in addition to educational-training institutes and enterprises. Modes of learning therefore need to be developed through improved co-operation between learning sites. Education and training institutions have to evolve to become client-oriented centres of open learning for empowering trainees by playing the role of facilitators.

The educational and training system must guarantee sufficient flexibility in the organisation of the curriculum. In view of the increase in occupational and geographical mobility, it is also necessary to promote the acquisition of language skills. There is also a need to introduce elements of modularization in learning. The system must be structured so as to allow transparency, diversity and flexibility.

Inter-linking Formal, Non-formal and Informal Learning

The system of skill formation should be designed to recognise formal, non-formal and informal learning as equally valuable means in the overall vocational learning process. While basic and primary-school education is necessary for promoting cognitive competencies, non-formal basic education can be an alternative instrument for the transmission competencies linked to economic activities. Studies have indicated that non-formal training programmes for the informal sector, including trade courses, survival training, apprentice training and other training measures within the framework of community development might be useful in the informal economy. Non-formal training programmes, nevertheless, should contain modules of basic general education. It is important to recognise informal learning experiences in the family and community and relate with learning domains.

Diversification of Training Systems

With the expansion of the informal economy, it is necessary that vocational training institutions reflect economic opportunities and respond to the competency requirements of the majority of the labour force, as well as undergo diversification to suit the needs of the expanded clientele. This requires restructuring in terms of subject matter and redesigning learning processes. Diversification also implies the promotion of self-employment by tying learning processes to opportunities that help individuals to gain competencies and income benefit for self-employment.

An inverse relationship between employment potential and competency levels is found in the informal sector, and a growing amount of self-employment is losing out in competition due to a lack of facilities needed in order to prevail. Since the informal and the formal labour markets are linked through forward and backward linkages, curriculum should be diversified to promote work-based learning in both the formal and the informal economies.

INSTITUTIONAL DESIGN AND CAPACITY BUILDING

Role of the Public Sector: The Constitution of Bangladesh provides for education as a basic right for all citizens and calls for 'relating education to the needs of the society and producing properly trained and motivated citizens to serve those needs'. The World Declaration of Education for All promoted 'an expanded vision' which goes beyond literacy and numeracy.

In addition to the pledges in the Constitution and World Declarations, there is a need for the state to play an effective role in terms of engagement and action. Public intervention is necessary in light of the reality of 'market failure' which is pronounced in developing countries due to a lack of control over the distribution of the costs and benefits of training. Individuals often lack the finances to invest in an asset over which they have little control. In countries like Bangladesh, there is a strong case for government financing of skill formation, especially in the case of the informal sector, since employers in that sector are rarely in a position to finance the large fixed costs associated with training.

Upgrading Teaching Staff: There is a strong need to improve and upgrade the skills of teaching staff in the new emerging trades in order to use the existing training institutions effectively and efficiently. This will ensure the quality of occupational competency, and Bangladesh will benefit from the sustainable availability of a qualified labour force.

There is no standard recipe for improving conditions in the informal sector. However, appropriate programmes may be designed by drawing general lessons from experience in a variety of countries, in particular looking at best practices.

Social Accord: Before developing a training strategy for informal sector enterprises, it is important to reach a consensus among the stakeholders about the share of responsibility, priorities, targeting, use of resources and partnership.

Equity-Oriented Targeting: The system of targeting has to be based on equity, favouring measures aimed at 'picking a few winners', offering training courses to those who need most.

Participatory Governance: It is now widely recognised that ownership matters, as does the effectiveness of upgrading training when clients are involved in making decisions which affect them. It is equally important to explore the decentralisation of the public provision of training, including the transfer of control over budgets to training managers. It is also important that programme implementers are given room to manoeuvre and to carry out experiments, for example, as regards training contents and methodology.

Flexibilisation of the System: There is no denying the importance of attempting to make training systems and their products more flexible than what is usually the case, especially it is desirable to keep in mind the future skill requirements.

Gradualism: The basic approach to systemic reform should be crafted to pursue gradual changes in existing structures and procedures rather than wholesale change. There should be ample opportunity for evaluation and for making adjustments as they are deemed appropriate.

Area of Coverage: The present system has to be reoriented to go well beyond typical, government-sponsored, 2–3 year programmes to include, among others, school dropouts. Therefore, related concepts, notably those of trainee and trainer, should be defined accordingly.

Access to Complementarities: Training is by no means self-serving. For training to achieve its desired goals in the informal sector, training for work in micro-enterprises should be complemented by before- and after-training services, such as vocational guidance and troubleshooting in respect of access to credit, market or technology.

Role of the Private Sector: The private sector provides for traditional skill development without an institutional framework in many areas of the urban informal sector. These activities in the private sector can be institutionalised. The owners of the informal sector or their associations can establish training institutes for the skill development of workers which will play a prime role in enhancing productivity.

The private sector can seek support from the government, including credit facilities and logistics. Tax exemption for private sector investment in this regard can be considered. Capacity building includes the founding of new institutes to upgrade curriculum, intake capacity and the level of skills of the instructors and strengthen the industrial and market attachment.

REORIENTATION OF CURRICULUM

Vocationalising the School Curriculum

Currently the National Curriculum and Textbook Board (NCTB) offers general curriculum for SSC and HSC, which mainly serves as a foundation for higher-level studies in various disciplines. The school curriculum can include various vocational courses as compulsory or optional. In this way, the students can get some skills in various engineering or non-engineering trades. For many students of the country who have not been able to obtain higher-level studies in universities and colleges, vocationalising the school curriculum would be beneficial since it may create job opportunities for school dropouts. The NCTB should also consider the proposal of vocationalising school curriculum for the skill development of workers in the urban informal sector in Bangladesh. This will help formal and informal sector workers to get an education at a minimum cost since the existing school and college infrastructure can be used for this purpose. This will not only benefit school dropouts but also create good opportunities for enhancing job-related or market-oriented competencies of the labour forces.

Matching the Market Demand

There is a direct correlation between the quality of trained workers and the implementation of productivity improvement programmes. Relevant productivity-related subjects should be incorporated in the curricula of VTIs and TTCs. Efforts should be made to conduct productivity-based on-the-job training programmes. The course curricula of the training institutes should be designed in such a way that they are flexible enough to respond to the changes in the market. Practical and need-based training should be strengthened.

It is evident that achieving an occupational match will increase productivity and returns. Development of a comprehensive 'labour market information system' would be a positive step towards resolving the problem.

Use of Communication and Information Technology

Information and communication technology can play an important role in promoting the provision of training, education and skill development for decent work in the informal sector. Although information technology is considered a priority area, there is no clear policy on its development or its use in training and education.

Affirmative Action for Women Participation

Nearly 50 percent of the Bangladesh population are women. But women's participation in economic value addition is still very low. Their participation in engineering workshops is also negligible. During the last few years, the employment of 'sales workers' has grown more than 10 percent (a figure largely made up of female workers), though the number of professional and technical workers has grown by 5 percent (and here too female labour dominates the growth pattern). Although female workers have received some training for the TTCs and VTIs in the public sector, gender disparity is very high.

Female labour force participation underscores a significant need for the integration of females into formal skills training programmes which will enable them to make significant inroads into active and meaningful labour force participation. There is a need for effective intervention to support skill development for women workers in non-standard forms of works. Financial assistance, such as subsidised loans as well as the opening of specialised training institutes for women, can enable them to overcome the problems of gender segregation. There is a need for affirmative and equal opportunity programmes, as well as for passing anti-discrimination legislation for overcoming employer practices that exclude women from equal access to training.

FORGING STRATEGIC PARTNERSHIPS

Partnership and co-operation among the key stakeholders are the pre-requisite for the qualitative and quantitative development of education, training and skills for decent work in the informal sector. Although the informal sector enterprises exist outside government regulations and are not registered with authorities, they have important linkages with the formal sector. The government has to play the central role to increase the economic potentiality of informal sector enterprise by providing sufficient education, training and skill development for decent work.

The government can play an effective role in the field of resource mobilisation by creating funds to provide sufficient credit facilities for the development of education and training in the informal sector. Interest-free loans or nominal interest bearing credit can be allocated by the government for the purpose of education, training and skill development, which can encourage informal sector entrepreneurs to invest in skill formation. Financial institutes like the Employment Bank can serve the demand in this regard, especially where governments have resource constraints. In this regard development partners can play an important role.

Such strategic partnerships have several important advantages. First, they relate to incentives which employers' associations, trade unions and NGOs can provide. Secondly, such multi-stakeholder involvement constitutes a powerful counter-force to market failure in training. Since employers in the informal sector are rarely in a position to finance the large fixed costs associated with training, NGOs including community-based organitions can play a pivotal role in such alliances. The influence of employers' associations and trade unions on multi-stakeholder arrangements could also serve as a way to increase commitment, particularly among employers, to take training goals more seriously. Another advantage is the support which employers' associations and trade unions can provide by means of valuable training-related services, including apprenticeship arrangements.

NOTES

[1] Formal sector employment has hardly grown in recent years. Most of the additional jobs have been in the informal sector. As much as 87 percent of the country's workforce (employed persons aged 15 years or more) are engaged in the private informal sector. The shares of the 'private formal sector' and the 'public autonomous sector' in employment are 8.8 percent and 4.2 percent, respectively (BBS, 1996).

[2] The country has a workforce of nearly 56 million people, of which 34.7 million (62%) are male and 21.3 million (38%) are female (BBS, 1996).

[3] The formal market is operated under the legal framework which follows the presence of contractual employment relationships, labour laws and regulations and trade unions.

[4] Statistical information regarding such programmes (school-based or otherwise) is not available from any single authority. The Association of Development Agencies in Bangladesh (ADAB), which co-ordinates the activities of international and national NGOs, and the Association of Private Non-Profit Trade Schools (APNTS), which promotes the programmes of private trade schools (many owned by NGOs), also do not keep statistics needed.

[5] MAWTS trains less than 100 workers each year.

REFERENCES

ADB. (1995). *Vocational training project for the People's Republic of Bangladesh*. Manila: Asian Development Bank.

BBS. (1996). *Labour force survey*. Dhaka: Bangladesh Bureau of Statistics.

Bhattacharya, D., Faiz, N. & Zohir, S. (2000). *Policy for employment generation in the informal sector of Bangladesh*. Dhaka: Centre for Policy Dialogue.

Corvalan, V. (1988). Trends in technical-vocational and secondary education in Latin America. *International Journal of Educational Development*, *8*, 73–88.

GOB. (1998). *Fifth five-year plan 1990–1995*. Dhaka: Government of Bangladesh.

GOB. *Fifth five-year plan 1997–2002*. Dhaka: Government of Bangladesh, March, 1998.

GOB. (2000). *Mid-term review of the fifth five-year plan 1997–2002*. Dhaka: Planning Commission, Government of Bangladesh.

ILO. (1999). *World employment report 1998–99*. Geneva: ILO.

ILO. (2000). National workshop on the strategic approach to job creation in the urban informal sector in India. February 17–19, 2000, Surajkund, Haryana. Sectoral studies and background papers.

Krug, P. (1999). The new role of adult education institutions. In M. Singh (ed.), *Poverty alleviation, work and adult learning* (pp. 25–29). Hamburg: UIE.

Mahmud, I. (1999). *Vocational education and training system for employment in Bangladesh*. Dhaka: ILO Area Office Planning Commission.

Rahman, R. I. (2000). *Skill development in Bangladesh: Responses to globalisation*. Dhaka: BIDS.

Singh, M. (2001). Reflection on colonial legacy and dependency in Indian Vocational Education and Training (VET): A societal and cultural perspective. *Journal of Education and Work, 14*, 209–25.

World Bank. (1990). *Bangladesh: Vocational and Technical Education Review*. Washington, DC: World Bank.

World Bank. (2000). *Bangladesh Education Sector Review, I–III*. Dhaka: UPL.

TRAINING AND SKILLS DEVELOPMENT FOR DECENT WORK IN THE INFORMAL SECTOR: CASE STUDIES FROM SOUTH INDIA

Amit Mitra

While various conceptualisations of the informal sector have been debated ever since it was formulated in the early 1970s (Bangasser, 2000; Hart, 1973), the fact remains that globally nearly 500 million people are employed in the informal sector/economy today (ILO, 1998). It is increasingly recognised now that the phenomenon has come to stay and that government policies for economic and social development, including education and training policies, should target those who work in this sector. Despite the international attention over the last two decades to informal sector analyses, training, skill formation and education for workers in this sector have received much less attention than they deserves from researchers as well as policymakers.

The present study, based on case studies of NGOs from South India, seeks to understand the ways in which the learning needs of young people and adults are developed in this sector and how the workers are trained and educated, if at all. Attempts are made to map interesting cases of skill transfer which combine social and technical learning processes and to draw relevant lessons from case studies for the formulation and design policies and programmes.

A central argument of the study, based on the case studies, is that the very notions of skills development, capacity enhancement and training may need to be reformulated, departing from the concept of vocational training and education, if the notion of decent work is to be actualised. As will be discussed, at least in the Indian case some of the contemporary notions of skill-building and training, as well as practices derived from the same, seem to be incompatible with the notion of decent work. At the same time, however, decent work, as a principle, can be attained only by including in it the notion of skill/capacity enhancement. Obviously, much depends on how the informal sector and training/skill building are conceptualised.

The study deals with training/skill/capacity building in the informal sector, especially in South India in order to analyse the nature of the training/capacity building interventions. The present paper compares different kinds of training inputs, bearing in mind the distinction between training for employment and training for empowerment. It also compares the various training delivery systems and learning mechanisms and interventions, both formal and informal, of the government as well as of development

Madhu Singh, (ed.), Meeting Basic Learning Needs in the informal Sector, 155-182.

NGOs. In each of the three sub-sectors of the informal economy—services, production and trade—a distinction is made between 'traditional' and 'contemporary'. Traditional production includes traditional techniques of production as well as traditional forms of skills acquisition that occurs in traditional apprenticeships or the family. The category 'contemporary' includes those traditional production processes and techniques that have been modernised, as well as the trade in and servicing of contemporary products, such as air-conditioners and computers. As a rule, a certain level of education and training characterises this segment.

It has been possible to identify several examples that could be taken up as case studies. Five examples, all from the NGO sector in South India were selected. These were Skills for Progress (SKIP), Goodwill International Association, Management Enterprise and Development of Women (MYRADA-MEADOWS), MAYA and the DHAN Foundation.

CONCEPTUALISING THE INFORMAL SECTOR IN INDIA

The Informal Sector Concept

Contemporary conceptualisations of the informal sector tend to address themselves to the characteristics of an informal sector unit. While Hart (1973, p. 68) emphasised that 'the distinction between formal and informal income opportunities is based essentially on that between wage-earning and self-employment', today's definitions go beyond manufacturing activity to include construction, trade and services.

Typically, three categories are distinguished in the informal sector (ILO, 1998, p. 168): (1) The *small or micro-enterprise sub-sector* is considered the economically stronger and more dynamic element. Typically regarded as an extension of the formal sector, it is held that a significant part of it is usually connected with the formal sector through various sub-contracting arrangements. A majority of such enterprises, however, are independent and cater to markets at the lower end of the economic scale. (2) The *household-based sub-sector*, where most of the activities are carried out by family members (largely unpaid female labour). This sub-sector extends to many different markets, activities, seasons and locations. Most households cannot break out of low incomes and poverty, but some households catering to strong markets may evolve into more specialised enterprises. (3) The *independent service sector*, comprising domestic helpers, street-vendors, cleaners, street barbers, shoe-shiners and so on, as well as those referred to as casual labour. Female labour is highly represented in many of these occupations. In terms of size, it constitutes the bulk of the informal sector. The exact nature of the occupation is often changing and seasonal in nature, though the change is normally within the bounds of the sub-sector itself. The skills required by these occupations are the lowest in the informal skill hierarchy.

INDIA'S INFORMAL SECTOR

In 1995 the informal sector accounted for nearly 92.5 percent of India's workforce (Subrahmanya & Jhabvala, 2000, p. 2). In 1999 organised sector employment was only 28.11 million, roughly seven percent of the total employment of over 397 million in the country. As much as 19.41 million, or over two-thirds of the total organised sector employment, were in the public sector (GOI, 2001, 2.24). For the economy as a whole, thus taking rural and urban areas together and including agriculture, 52.9 percent of the workers were self-employed in 1999–2000. For the urban sector, the self-employed comprised 42.1 percent, 40.1 percent were regular salaried while 17.8 percent were casual workers (GOI, 2001, 2.30).

The major component of the informal sector comprises what Breman (1994) calls the world of 'wage hunters and gatherers', who are usually but not always uneducated, have little or no chance of earning a living wage and no security. They look for what they can salvage on the margins of the industrial economy—and this is literally the case for rag pickers and recyclers. These people lack assets completely, and only a small portion of them find employment, which is often all too temporary, while the larger portion has no choice but to 'go out hunting and gathering a wage' (Breman, 1996, p. 225). Survival takes precedence over everything else (Pathy, 1993). In these groups, notions of human capital investment, or even savings and investments in the ordinary sense of the term, are rarely known. The only investment is in building up relationships in the community, where caste, kinship and place of origin plays an important role (Das, 1994). This is a complex social system, which cannot be reduced to a unilinear labour hierarchy.

Nearly 44 percent of India's labour force is illiterate and only 33 percent of it has had schooling up to the secondary level or above (GOI, 2001, 1.10); the skill and technology base is rarely sufficient to allow to move up the economic and social ladder, something that is accentuated by lack of access to micro-finance, new technologies or information.

Acute poverty marks the informal sector. Nearly 40 percent of the Indian population is below the poverty line, and it is reasonable to assume that a major part of the people below that line are in the informal sector, too. Particularly women are confined to informal sector employment, with 96 percent of all female workers being in this sector (Subrahmanya & Jhabvala, 2000). These women constitute the 'ultimate army of reserve labour' (Omvedt, 1990, p. 70).

Research shows that most informal sector workers belong to socially depressed groups, also known as the Dalits or the scheduled castes (the ex-untouchables of India), and scheduled tribes, or persons belonging to tribal communities (Das, 2001, p. 186; Anand, 2001, p. 278).

Creating a solid educational base for the majority of the workers in the Indian informal sector remains a distant dream. In 1999–2000 only 56 percent of the country's workforce was literate and just 22.7 percent had schooling up to the primary level. If the minimum level of education necessary to function in a modern economy were defined as schooling up to the middle level, then only 33.2 percent of the labour force would meet or exceed this minimum. Of the latter group, 57.4 percent were from the urban labour force but only 25.4 percent from rural areas (GOI, 2000, 6.1). Only five percent of the labour force aged 20–24 years had any vocational training obtained through formal institutions, as compared to developed countries where the figure ranges from 60 to 80 percent. In 1998 Columbia and Mexico had corresponding figures of 28 percent (GOI, 2000, 6.7).

As India debates the introduction of a policy of compulsory education for all, it should be noted that such a policy, while desirable and necessary, will not solve the problem of the illiterate adults and out-of-school young people who are already in the workforce. Education for these people will not necessarily lead to employment of higher quality even if they do find the time to acquire it. For them competitiveness, equity or growth have entirely different meanings: the sheer need for survival dictates every action. Skill formation for these people cannot await the attainment of education. Some of them may have indigenous skills, but such skills often become obsolete due to migration, which uproots the workers and cuts them off from their social and cultural skills and thus can restrict their employment mobility, which is high horizontally but low vertically. They lack access to skills upgrading opportunities or facilities to acquire new skills since they do not have access to technologies and training. A large majority of the workforce thus comes to be seen as having no 'marketable' skills, that is, skills which would get them regular employment. This is shown by the results of the National Sample Survey 50th round (1993–94) on Employment and Unemployment. The results, from a list of some 30 marketable skills ranging from typing to nursing, are given in Table 1.

Table 1. Distribution of Persons with Marketable Skills, 1993–94

Possessing	Rural Men	Rural Women	Urban Men	Urban Women
No Skill (%)	89.9	93.7	80.4	88.8
Some Skill (%)	10.1	6.3	19.6	11.2
Total (%)	100.0	100.0	100.0	100.0
Sample size	183464	172835	109067	99283

Source: GOI, 2000, 6.5

Despite various problems associated with the NSS data, the above table shows that irrespective of the kind of indigenous skills or knowledge (even in the sample), these are not marketable in this sense the majority of workers cannot secure regular employment or incomes from their skill base.

Questions relating to training and skills development become all the more important in the contemporary context of globalisation and structural adjustment policies. As changes due to globalisation accelerate, the risk of exclusion of low skilled informal sector entrepreneurs and workers from more remunerative occupations and jobs increases (Mamgain & Awasthi, 2001, p. 264). Enhanced competitiveness in the informal sector labour market due to trade liberalisation requires a faster rate of adjustment to the changes. Herein lies a major contradiction. To modernise, India needs a highly skilled and qualified labour force. Since the formal sector is shrinking due to globalisation, many people are being dismissed from the formal economy and forced to join the informal sector. In this sector, the vast majority of less trained people, who have next to no access to training, will hardly find the markets they found hitherto. For the wage hunters and gathers, this will increase the struggle to survive.

Conventional training today in India typically places a great deal of emphasis on higher education, though it is of a general kind and thus is not linked to jobs or employment. Formal vocational training and apprenticeships also exist, but these require some prior education and do not cater to the illiterate and the poorest of the poor. Access to formal training remains confined to a minority of educated people. For the vast majority of the workforce, training if any is often hereditary, acquired through informal apprenticeships and learning on the job—though on-the-job learning is also found to a large extent in the formal sector. A recent Government of India study makes a significant observation in this context:

> The actual number of persons expected to enter the labour force is about 12.3 million persons per year. Allowing for under-utilisation of seats in training institutions and some overlaps, the percentage of those entering the labour force with some degree of formal training is probable around 1.5 million. While *a significant number of the new entrants will be absorbed in various types of unskilled labour in agricultural and non-agricultural occupations, where skills are not needed,* the level of skill endowment of new entrants to the labour force revealed by these numbers is clearly not consistent with triggering a process of rapid economic growth and high quality employment generation. (GOI, 2001, 6.11; emphasis added)

Obviously, 'modernisation' is the major concern of the state, but this excerpt glosses over the fact that of the 10.8 million persons who enter the labour force without any formal skills each year, not all will be absorbed in agriculture. Many will become part of the informal sector's wage hunters and gatherers, very much in need of skills, even those basic skills which are necessary to survive.

RE-DEFINING TRAINING AND SKILLS DEVELOPMENT IN THE INDIAN CONTEXT

The Present Paradigm and Approach to Training and Skills Development

Contemporary approaches to training in India, as well as in many developing countries, have been geared to meet the needs of the manufacturing sector. There has been strong resistance to the introduction of training for non-manufacturing sectors, including trade and the services sector.

Vocational training is often equated with technical training/education, which itself is geared towards the formal sector. There is a strong rural-urban bias, and the training system is highly centralised. As Singh (1999) points out, one reason for this is the colonial legacy, which prevented vocational education from developing local approaches. Another reason is a carryover of the basic approach to development itself taken in the 1950s and 1960s (Bangasser, 2000).

Generally, the issues of diversification and vocationalisation of secondary education are dealt with purely in economic terms (earning opportunities, better jobs and higher technical fields). Public technical and vocational training in India does not have a good track record in efficiency and flexibility; such training is far removed from local, cultural, social and market realities. Many students pursuing technical/vocational training are unlikely get the full-time wage employment they seek. Unemployment rates for educated youth were 14.7 percent for those educated up to the secondary level and above and 23.7 percent (24.5 percent for urban areas) for those with any kind of technical education (GOI, 2001, 2.18).

At the same time, the technically educated, as well as graduates from mainstream general education, are out of touch with the working conditions and technical possibilities in small and micro-enterprises. There is little or no attempt to cater to the needs of those who wish to continue living and working in rural areas but who, as a result of their lack of skills, are compelled to join the urban informal sector (Singh, 1999, p. 171). In most rural areas, facilities for even elementary education, to say nothing of those for vocational education, are severely lacking. Some development efforts are being made, but not with much success to date, isolated examples notwithstanding.

The informal sector generally comprises small entrepreneurs, paid and unpaid establishment workers, independent workers and casual workers. For the small entrepreneurs, the need is for managerial and marketing skills, in addition to technical skills, as well as for the regular upgrading of skills and access to knowledge and information.

The majority of young people and adults in the informal sector learn their skills on the job, something that is common to both the formal and the informal sectors. In the formal sector, training usually begins with apprenticeships, which is replaced by learning from a master craftsperson in the informal sector. However, as Singh (1992, p. 126) points out, while apprenticeships (formal and informal) or informal on-the-job training may provide basic skills, they not familiarise the workers with new technologies or managerial skills. Constraints of both time and money often prevent workers in the formal and informal sectors from acquiring further training, even when such facilities exist. In the manufacturing sector, indigenous forms of training may be sufficient for adapting technology to simple production and labour-intensive activity, but that does not necessarily mean more efficient production or market competitiveness. Modern technical training probably needs to complement, rather than replace indigenous work techniques.

Outside the manufacturing sector, the issue remains as to how independent workers, rickshaw-pullers, hawkers and the like can be trained. They are often highly unorganised and may not operate from fixed locations. Besides, these workers have irregular working hours. In addition, they have limited resources and little time to engage in training. Many are so poor that they may be unable to afford even minimal extra expenses. Finding the time to attend training programmes or courses is a major difficulty, since the same time that would be used for training would otherwise be spent earning a living. Rampant illiteracy also restricts the potential of some to acquire retraining and upgrading.

Casual workers, a most disadvantaged group, rely heavily on manual labour. These jobs need little training and they usually pay low wages, although some may pay more than their counterparts in the formal sector. Work skills can usually be learned incidentally on the job.

Due to the high level of horizontal mobility among these not so exclusive categories, many individuals end up with multiple skills, since they often have moved through different jobs in the course of their working life. Such occupational mobility complicates the formulation of approaches to training (Singh, 1992, p. 126).

But if vocational training and education are to cater to both the formal and the informal sectors, it is essential to take into account the traditions and values of the system of vocational learning in working life. Such learning needs to fulfil the requirements of local development and be based on an understanding of the kinds of competencies people in the informal sector want, need and utilise, as well as the socio-economic and cultural contexts within which they work, how they cope and the skills, capabilities, attitudes and values that are required to sustain their livelihood strategies (Singh, 1999, p. 171). The very concept of learning needs to address capabilities to change professions, as well as to learn and adapt quickly to changing environments. Indeed, the understanding of livelihood strategies in specific social and cultural settings (according to caste, ethnic, class and gender background), as well as the labour market conditions, is of paramount importance if a meaningful re-orientation of existing approaches to training/skill building is to be achieved.

It should be noted that in the literature on the informal sector, issues like education, skill development, modes of learning in apprenticeship, building capabilities and learning needs are treated rather sparsely (Raghunandan, 2000) and consequently that literature does not help us much in reformulating the ways of understanding the issue of training and skill formation. As such, training materials and the documentation of vocational training and skill building efforts in India are hard to come by. The little work that does exist on training and skill building in the informal sector assumes the existence of some kind of basic education. There is a clear emphasis on vocational training. The need for training or skill building of other kinds, that is, the bigger picture, which would be relevant to the Indian informal sector workforce, as well as the need for rights, gender equity, access to credit or markets and so on, generally gets ignored. Furthermore, there is hardly any mention of the fact that caste and ethnicity, both very important issues in the Indian context given that the majority of the wage hunters and gatherers, the illiterate or those below the poverty line, belong to the disadvantaged castes, such as the scheduled castes and the scheduled tribes. (These are disadvantaged castes and tribesmen who receive benefits and concessions and protective measures and legislation from the government. For example, a certain percentage of places in educational and public service institutions are reserved for them.)

Gender relations in the context of work in the informal sector or how the gender divide can be bridged through training or skill building are rarely addressed in the literature on training in the informal sector. It is well known that men and women are treated differently in the informal labour market, but the bulk of the burden of working for survival, as well as that of formulating and actualising livelihood strategies, falls on the women.

The literature is also largely silent about the needs of children in the informal sector. While the debate on working children remains restricted to whether or not to ban child labour, neither side seems to be concerned about what can be done for the millions of children who are presently in this sector, working and living under abominable conditions (Breman, 1996, p. 171). While compulsory primary education—about which there are also debates—would in large part ensure the prevention of future recruitment of children into the workforce, it is imperative that thought be given to those who are already part of it. It is obvious that child labour should be eradicated, but what happens to the children who are already part of the labour force once they are withdrawn from it? While their skills would need to be built up, it would likely be rather difficult to have them join the mainstream educational system for a wide variety of reasons. Educational and vocational training need to be tailored to their needs so as to equip them with skills that will see them through a lifetime.

Training schemes, some of which are quite useful and relevant, are to be found in the literature on training and skill development, but even these do not speak of how to actualise their theoretical formulations into concrete realities, especially for the Indian context. Thus, while useful as a categorisation, Lenhart's (1997) typology of non-formal training programmes for the informal sector does not answer some basic questions about who is going to impart the training, how are the trainees going to be selected, what will be the follow-up and so on.[1] The diversity of the informal sector is reflected somewhat in the typology, but not the different training processes that would be needed to meet the diverse learning needs of young people and adults.

Broadly the term 'training' applies to any transfer of knowledge, skills or attitudes which is organised to prepare people for productive activities, or to change their working behaviour. It concerns first-time learners as well as people who have worked all their lives, and it covers efforts both in and out of school. It also encompasses vocational, technical, managerial, entrepreneurial, societal and other useful skills (Singh, 1992, p. 129 n. 2). It is a question of determining what is needed, by whom and at what point in time, as well as the methodology not only of delivery but also of determining how these basic questions are to be answered.

Towards Redefining Training and Skill Development

In light of the realities of the informal sector, a paradigm shift is needed towards the basic approach to training and skill development. Most workers in the informal sector lack skills, or have skills that are outdated or of little relevance to the present conditions, and have little more than their own physical strength to depend on. 'Learning by doing' is a common practice from an early age. As Breman (1996, p. 113) points out, non-specialisation—so as to avoid concentrating on a single-trade—is the most fruitful strategy for those who exist on the broad underside of the labour hierarchy. Progress in the art of survival is determined by success in the constant search for new sources of income. Survival depends on the will and ability to be as flexible as possible. One's family, household, neighbours and community are of central importance for securing basic survival needs through diverse and often complex livelihood strategies. Indeed, the critical purpose of any training/skill building effort has to be to turn the social capital the informal sector workers possess to their economic advantage.

It is important to re-conceptualise training and move away from its narrow mechanical and mere employment connotations. Training will need to be seen as an input for empowerment, and not just for employment. Thus, in the context of self-help organisations and networks, for instance, such training would imply that learning is not only generated in the process of production, but also that it takes place through other external mechanisms, such as 'learning by negotiating' and 'searching for openings'. Learning would imply both a process of becoming aware of the potential of a network or cluster of enterprises to solve problems and the acquisition of the competencies that are needed to implement solutions (Singh, 1999). Additionally, the training would need to build up capabilities to shift from one profession to another, to obtain the freedom to make choices without loosing status. Essentially, what is required is the freedom to choose a career and develop it. In this context we note that the paradigm shift from training for employment to training for empowerment is closely linked to the notion of decent work.

At different points in life, people have broad and complex goals that they see in an integrated way, goals which almost always have work and income security as central elements (Rodgers, 2000). In 1999 Juan Somavia, ILO's Director General, summed up this set of goals with the term 'decent work', but the term denotes more than just an economic-centred notion of development. While the word 'decent' is meant to capture the combination of sufficiency and desirability, the meaning of 'work' goes beyond employment or a specific job. Work includes not only wage employment but also self-employment and work at and in the home. It includes a wide range of activities in the informal economy. It also extends to domestic activities, such as cooking and cleaning, which most people regard as work. In other words, 'decent work' does not refer only to wage employment in large firms, but reflects a broader notion of participation in the economy and the community.

Decent work has four main dimensions: work and employment itself, rights at work, security, and representation and dialogue. In *Development as Freedom* Sen (1999) argues for a conception of development which consists in the expansion of freedoms which embrace political, social and economic goals. Development also involves the removal of 'unfreedoms' such as poverty, lack of access to public infrastructure or the denial of civil rights. In essence it involves the expansion of people's capabilities to achieve their valued goals. These freedoms, on Sen's view, have a threefold relationship with development: (1) as goals in their own right (constitutive); (2) because they contribute to the achievement of other valued goals, such as security or social integration (instrumental); and (3) in the definition and building of consensus around social needs, values and priorities (constructive). The interaction between freedoms and development is an important aspect of the rationale for decent work as a development goal. Decent work brings together different types of freedoms, which Sen (1999, p. 75) identifies as: worker's rights, income security and employment opportunities. These are goals in their own right, but taken together they are more than the sum of the parts. Both social and economic factors are involved, and the decent work approach attempts to bring them together and to set them within a coherent framework (Rodgers, 2000).

Seen in the framework of decent work, training and skill building takes on a totally new meaning. Such training would have to encompass the constitutive, instrumental and constructive aspects of work. Empowerment has to be an outcome of the training and skill building, since the attainment of decent work entails empowerment.

What, then, are the requirements for the training methodologies for the majority of young people and adults in the informal sector? How should it be packaged and delivered? Should it be piecemeal or comprehensive or a mix, depending on situational exigencies? Obviously, any such strategy would need to build up multiple skills in the workers in a broad way, enabling them to take up multiple trades, as well as to negotiate a wide range of issues, which are not only trade-specific but also relate to issues such as how to deal with the oppression of local strongmen and criminals. Such strategies, for both the formal and the informal sectors, need to be holistic.

The skill-building package would have to be different for producers, traders and service-providers, and developed on the assumption of near total illiteracy. This would include issues such as accessing credit, mobilising micro-finance through self-help groups, marketing, accessing information, knowledge of markets, gender and other forms of social inequity. The role of various interventionists, including the government, is critical in all this. Training will have to be both formal and informal, but systematised. An attempt will be made to address some of these issues in this study.

METHODOLOGY OF THE STUDY

The choice of the cases considered here was guided by the diversity of the training and skill building requirements of the informal sector. Some have certified formalised courses, that is, course affiliated with vocational learning courses, though not necessarily recognised by the government. Others are examples of training for employment. Still other examples are chosen as instances of co-operation between private sector industry and a development initiative for self-employment. Some are examples that deal with training for empowerment and critical citizenship with person-to-person learning and basic foundation courses for training community leaders and the creation of self-help groups. Given the large size of the informal sector, working with a model can provide at least some solutions to the problems of training in the informal sector.

GOVERNMENT EFFORTS IN BUILDING CAPACITIES OF INFORMAL SECTOR WORKERS IN INDIA[2]

In India there is a plethora of schemes under various development programmes of different ministries. However, in spite of the large network of state-run vocational education and training programmes, the informal sector hardly seems to be benefiting from it. In this section, some opportunities for training and skill building in such programmes are examined. These opportunities are geared towards providing training for employment.

Formal vocational education and training: There are three systems of vocational education prevalent in India today: the lower school stage, the class 10+2 stage and the first-degree level.

The vocational training programme for women started in 1977, with the assistance of ILO/SIDA. It is implemented through a network of one national and 10 regional vocational training institutes set up exclusively for women. In an attempt to promote the participation of women in training programmes, separate women's Institutes for Technical Training (ITIs) have been set up. Under the World Bank assisted Vocational Training Project, schemes for setting up 100 new ITI-wings exclusively for women are being implemented.

The Department of Education has initiated a scheme of non-formal, adult and continuing education for the urban community through the *Shramik Vidyapeeths*. During 1997–98, 58 such institutes were set up. The thrust of the scheme is to provide multidimensional or polyvalent training and education to the urban community through specially tailored programmes which aim at imparting knowledge and skills in an integrated manner. Under the scheme, courses of varying duration for developing vocational and technical skills and for developing and upgradint skills in income generation activities are conducted.

Continuing education and distance learning: The Indira Gandhi National Open University (IGNOU) and the National Open School (NOS) have jointly launched distance vocational education programmes for the benefit of the youth. The NGOs offer vocational course in agriculture, industry, trade and commerce for any person above the age of 14, who does not have a formal school certificate.

In India *formal apprenticeship* was introduced through the Apprenticeships Act in 1961, which requires employers in certain industries to engage apprentices in specified numbers in proportion to the workforce.

Assessment

The Government admits (GOI, 2001, 6.11) that the quality of the vocational training institutions is not very high. Evaluations of the ITIs have shown that there is a great deal of variation in the quality of different ITIs, which reflects differences across states and also partly characteristics of individual ITIs. Many states have encouraged the creation of new ITIs to cover new areas, but without adequate preparatory work, resource input or effective follow up action. The following deficiencies have been noted:

(1) Much of the training provided in the ITIs is in skills for which there is little current demand. The curriculum has not been revised for many years and therefore is not attuned to current market requirements. Some revision has taken place recently, but much remains to be done. One reason for the lack of attention to market requirements is the lack of industry involvement in the management of the ITIs. (2) The transfer of skills also needs improvement and the testing process at the end needs to be made more reliable. All government and private ITIs affiliated with the NCVT, as well as the private training institutes running DOEACC-accredited courses, rely on formal trade or certification by an independent authority. However, there is widespread perception among employers that students obtain certificates even though the actual skills they have absorbed are very poor. (3) The facilities and infrastructure in most ITIs are inadequate, with obsolete equipment in laboratories and workshops. Maintenance is also poor. These deficiencies reflect the scarcity of state government resources, which is exacerbated by the tendency to create new institutions in places where they do not exist, even though existing institutions are under-funded and under-utilised. (4) There is a shortage of suitably trained faculty in most ITIs. (5) There is hardly any follow-up on trainees, since the courses remain rather obsolete and piecemeal affairs. Placement is not a certainty. (6) The apprenticeship scheme also has its share of problems. The major problem seems to be that of quality, which varies according to the nature of the firm. The bulk of the apprenticeship seats are in public sector organisations, since private sector firms generally do not comply with requirements. One of the problems that has arisen is that apprentices view apprenticeships primarily as an avenue for subsequent employment rather than as a mode of training. Although the law clearly does not entitle them to employment, the courts have interpreted the law to mean that apprentices must be given preference and this in turn discourages employers from fulfilling their obligations under the Apprenticeships Act.

By and large, the government training and skill building efforts are not directed at the informal sector, or at least at the wage hunters and gatherers. As noted in the World Employment Report (ILO, 1998–99, p. 70), training systems in India are a typical example of central-government-driven, supply-led systems, where the government takes on the prime responsibility for formal sector training in training institutions. There is little or no pressure on employers to train. The Government of India has done little to change the present supply-driven and governmental-led training system (GOI, 2001, 6.23).

A significant proportion of the educational and training resources—including the material and financial resources—of the formal institutional structure are geared to formalised industry sectors and the 'upper end' of medium and small-scale enterprises. There is a strong emphasis on the 'technical aspects' of the trade and a very marked gender division in training and curricula. Women and girls are most likely to join beautician's courses, whereas boys usually take up trades, for instance, as fitters and motor mechanics. The upper castes and classes benefit mostly, since quite often there are strong economic and extra-economic barriers to entry into some of the courses.

Issues of the kind just delineated are almost unheard of so long as the notion of decent work remains a distant dream. In most of the ITIs, the syllabi are long outdated, structurally defined and centralised, teachers are bored and without much sense of market conditions, let alone how to impart multi-skills or a lifelong learning process. Not much interaction takes place, since questions are not encouraged, for 'courses have to be finished'. Marketing, accessing credit, or even simple labour or environmental laws, which are applicable to a particular trade or profession, are not taught.

NGO INTERVENTIONS FOR YOUNG PEOPLE AND ADULTS IN THE INFORMAL SECTOR

Five NGO interventions were chosen from the southern states to give a sense of the broad spectrum of the kinds of training being provided to young people and adults in the informal sector.

Presentation of the Cases

Skills For Progress (SKIP) was formed in 1968 as an association of member organisations which provide technical training to economically and socially deprived youth. Headquartered in Bangalore, today it has 195 members all over the country. SKIP seeks to act as a resource support organisation in the field of vocational skills.

Goodwill International Association, also based in Bangalore, was established in 1971 and registered under the Societies Act in 1982. Started by industrial workers from various workers' movements and trade unions, *Goodwill International* imparts earning skills to unemployed youth and school dropouts. The programmes range from functional literacy to vocational training in 16 Bangalore slums.

MEADOW (Management Enterprise and Development of Women)/The Myrada/Plan International Dharampuri Project, Hosur. This is essentially a collaboration between the watchmakers Titan and Myrada. It began in 1995by organising various women's groups to assemble watchstraps for the company. By 1998 the women formed themselves into a company with a board of directors.

MAYA (Movement for Alternatives and Youth Awareness) is a Bangalore-based development and training organisation which was initiated in 1989. It works to address children's rights with a specific focus on the eradication of child labour. Adopting a holistic approach to the issue of child labour eradication, an approach to which involves vocational training is integral, the organisation has initiated several community-based initiatives in the 52 slums in which it works. The activities differ from one area to the next, depending on the socio-economic conditions of the families, the employment patterns, the availability of basic amenities and the organisation of the people in the area as a community.

DHAN (Development for Humane Action) Foundation, headquartered in Madurai, is a non-profit organisation which is a spin-off of PRADAN (Professional Assistance for Development Action). Registered as a public trust in 1997 to cater to the needs of the southern states, it engages in multi-faceted developmental activities, but is based on the conviction that it is necessary to empower the poor by forming community organisations and upgrading their skills with the aid of development professionals. Its Community Banking Programme, *Kalanjiam*, which is geared towards gender and development, seeks to train for empowerment by promoting alternative banking efforts through locally formed self-help groups of poor women in the informal sector, in both rural and urban areas. The self-help groups are federated at the appropriate levels. A major part of the intervention involves establishing linkages with local and apex banks, as well as government schemes to promote employment generation. Another ain of the programme is to stabilise the income of the *Kalanjiam* members by strengthening the existing activity base and skills by providing appropriate training inputs when needed.

Basic Approaches

The case studies are of organisations from different areas in South India. All of them seek to uplift the poorest of the poor and in that sense can be said to have a similar vision. All deal with Dalits (ex-untouchables), tribesmen and other lower castes, which are very much discriminated against in all spheres of Indian life. Caste, however, does not enter the discourse of any of the organisations.

Yet there is a marked diversity in the approaches taken by the organisations, which stems from their basic philosophies. SKIP and Goodwill focus on the individual and are supply-driven. Training is equated with providing skills in a particular vocation only, but there is no market sensitivity or any way of gauging the market. No effort is made to identify the capabilities of the individuals or to link the training to overall employability. Instruction in additional life-supporting skills is rather weak. From time to time, statements are made concerning educational programmes, but that does not mean that every trainee is provided with basic education. Training is a one-time affair rather than a continuous process; the trainees have no choice in what they are taught. Consequently, given the high rate of obsolescence of most of the manufacturing skills taught, the trainees often fail to find a job or have to devise other means of learning appropriate skills. The intervention of these organisations is essentially a welfare delivery system in which the community plays no role. Empowerment certainly does not rank among their objectives. Concerns of gender equality mostly imply ensuring access to training programmes, but even here women's enrolment is negligible and there is a marked difference between the courses boys and girls are encouraged to take.

MAYA's efforts at building vocational skills along with education are aimed at developing the overall personality of the child, as well as at empowering the community to make its own informed decisions and its own choices. Constant monitoring of the trainees, which takes the form of formal instruction, learning by doing, learning from peers and apprenticeships, marks the pedagogy. Follow-up and employability are very strong. The word 'training' takes on new meaning in this context, and is not restricted to technical vocational skills. The attempt is to impart an all-round education, including technical skills, so that the youth are prepared for life. For women, the skills imparted include negotiation skills. Effectively, this can happen when the interventionist takes a rights-based approach in order to enable the community to make its own decisions, thereby build up its skills to improve the quality of life and standard of living in the community. Dependencies are not generated. Training becomes enabling and facilitation. Gender equity is a major concern. MAYA is more concerned with the processes than with the scale of its operations.

DHAN operates totally in an enabling and facilitating mode. Vocational or technical training is not an overt priority. The objective is to empower the community, especially the women, and then to upgrade their existing skill base so as to improve their economic opportunities. The intervention is certainly not welfare-based, but seeks to enable workers at the lowest level of the informal sector to attain their rights. Here again training takes on the meaning of building lifelong skills, a continuous process in which women build up their self-image and confidence, develop their social skills and—more often than not—learn from each other more than from external persons. DHAN functionaries create the necessary enabling environment and gradually withdraw completely. The community is the sole owner of the process.

The example of MEADOW is one of successful, NGO-mediated collaboration between private industry and the people. Today MEADOW is set on becoming self-sustaining and will become so soon. But the training here is only for a particular objective. While empowerment is sought, the collective is not so important. It is akin to working in a large factory: Individuals are empowered as long as they are on the job and get a salary. The group is cohesive, disciplined and follows high standards. The women earn fairly good wages in an occupationally safe workplace. The freedom to associate, in the sense of forming unions, does not exist. The dependency on Titan is high. If the demand for Titan watchstraps were to fall tomorrow or the firm were to decide to pull out of the contract, the women would be left high and dry. They do not have marketing skills, since by contract Titan obtains whatever they make. Some diversification, such as in the assembly of alarm clocks, is taking place, but that too is dependent on Titan. MEADOW seems to be aware of this problem. As a consequence, it is thinking of working with some firms in order to assemble personal computers. Since the personal computer market is currently in a major slump internationally, it is uncertain how successful this effort is will be.

The scale of this training intervention is also limited and not geared to the informal sector. Moreover, the process needs to be scrutinised in the face of globalisation and liberalisation, since the paradigm is that of big industry acquiring cheap labour of high standards, in this case that of women (which adds another gender dimension) without giving the workers their basic rights.

SECTORAL INTERVENTIONS

The interventions of the NGOs in the various sectors are analysed in this section. Table 2 indicates the organisations working in each sector.

Table 2. Sectoral Intervention

Sector	Traditional	Contemporary
Service	MAYA, DHAN	SKIP, Goodwill, MAYA
Production	MAYA, DHAN	SKIP, Goodwill, MEADOW, MAYA
Trade	MAYA, DHAN	MAYA

Traditional Services

Three of the case studies selected here (SKIP, Goodwill and MEADOW) do not deal with the traditional services sector at all. In MAYA's intervention, this sector is indirectly covered, that is, through the women's associations which are formed. On the other hand, DHAN's intervention in both rural and urban areas does provide much support—including that for skill building in the sense described above—to people in this sector, the 'underbelly of the informal labour sector market', many of whom are women. While it may be difficult to organise training and skills development for this large army of causal labour, street vendors, construction workers and so on, nevertheless, as DHAN's example shows, a lot depends on how training and skill building are conceived and delivered.

In fact the early work of Myrada, which gave birth to MEADOW, was geared to training and skill building in this sector. In the early 1990s, before launching the MEADOW/Titan collaboration, Myrada experimented with organising washerwomen into self-help groups, who then took up laundry contracts with Titan in its Hosur factory. While formal training sessions on laundering were not organised, the women, on the basis of day-to-day interactions with the Titan and Myrada staff, as well as with their peers, soon learned the finer aspects of doing an industrial house's laundry. Some aspects of laundering had to be taught to the women, such as the importance of timely deliveries and how to keep money away from alcoholic husbands. When the women saved enough money, they took out a loan matching their own contributions and bought a van to reduce their drudgery in carrying the laundry to and fro between the factory and their village. A driver had to be hired initially, but the women themselves soon learned to drive. Bidding for tenders was something else they had to learn. The effort still continues. But no formal training sessions are held.

SKIP has tried off and on to upgrade the skills of domestic help, but the effort has not been very helpful. The major reason for this is that domestic help (conventionally considered a 'woman's job') is treated as if it does not require any training or skill building. This meant that the women were not given the training opportunity or means to organise 'domestic help' in a better way so as to form an agency or hire out services—along the lines of what is happening across the country in security agencies, which are mushrooming.

MAYA's organics programme is structured to attain the aforementioned kind of objectives. The case study from SPMS (Shri Padmavathy Mahila Abudaya Sangam) based in the urban slums of the pilgrim city of Triputi, Tamil Nadu, provides many examples of this. The formation of groups of women has not only empowered them in numerous ways, but has even led to skill enhancement. Recently, for instance, some of the women wanted to purchase handcarts and take up street vending. A discussion within the group led to a design modification of the cart, after numerous arguments with male cart manufacturers: the carts for the women were made lower in height. Survival in this sector, as discussed earlier, depends on multi-skilling and group solidarity, where, instead of having external agents guide skill building, the group members themselves learn from each other. The SPMS demonstrates this amply, since each new proposal and each new activity is hotly debated in the weekly meetings and the members review the present state of the 'market'. When necessary they seek expert advice, be it from DHAN professionals or bank or government officials. Since the workers own the process of skill building and training, they decide on the curricula; as a consequence, the impact is much better in that it is much more empowering and enabling. As in the case of the bakeries (owned and managed by women) and the toy making units that erstwhile 'casual labourers' have founded after the formation of the SPMS, there has already been a great deal of capacity building, even in terms of obtaining, for example, market information and knowledge of sales techniques. Certainly, there has been a tremendous boost in the workers' self-esteem, something that comes when one belongs to a group and knows that as a result basic social security is assured.

The important principle, as evident from the examples, is that in this segment, the best means of training and skill building is to form a collective which owns the processes involved. Even when such a collective seeks expert help, it does so on its own terms.

Traditional Production

Again the SKIP/Goodwill/MEADOW interventions do not deal with this sector specifically. SKIP has done some work in goateries, poultry raising, fish cultivation and so on, but the results and the impact of the work are not clearly known. Since there did not seem to be any major departure from the usual practice of focusing on individuals, the SKIP partners gave some loans or grants to women to raise goats, poultry and so on, but did not try to work out market linkages.

DHAN does deal with this sector a lot, even in the SPMS intervention in Tirupati. Here the papier-mâché toy makers, traditional artisans who migrated from Tamilnadu decades ago, have formed groups and today are thriving because as groups they have modernised the traditional forms of the trade, including the usual informal apprenticeships that mark this sector. Skill building is on the job, but innovations, including the use of new techniques of production and implements, are possible because of the group operation. Technologies and tools that would be very difficult for an individual to acquire have now become accessible to the group. In some cases, DHAN has helped the women to get loans in order to buy milk animals, but only when there is a potential market. Similarly, traditional vegetable production is encouraged, but only if the group wants to engage in it and there is a market potential.

Traditional Trade

SKIP, Goodwill and MEADOW do not deal with this sector at all. MAYA has made major interventions in the traditional craft of lacquer work, as a part of its organic programme, which seeks to improve production methods and enable artisans to get a better deal, in terms of marketing their products and producing them better. Both MAYA and DHAN work with traditional vendors and petty traders, many of whom are petty producers, too. Skills to build up the capacity for collective negotiation when dealing with big traders or for loans is emphasised. Some of these examples, such that of the vendors and toy makers, have already been discussed in the previous section.

Contemporary Services, Production and Trade

SKIP, Goodwill and MAYA all provide training and skills in both contemporary services and production, but not in trade.

SKIP in many ways replicates the government institutions. It places strong emphasis on vocational training, and entry to systematised courses is restricted to those who have prior qualifications. The curricula are based on the ITIs and, as the SKIP personnel themselves admit, do not often match current industry demands. While individual courses—depending on the faculty—may be interactive, the students do not have much say in what they are to be trained in. Although elementary exposure is given to worker's rights as they exist in statutes, strategies to actualise them are not imparted. Business management, marketing or other skills are not imparted. The training is oriented towards individual job-seeking, and not so much towards setting up self-owned enterprises. Individuals do not leave the training as multi-skilled works, nor have they gained much knowledge about how to access information or credit or about the market. Gender and other social concerns likewise need to be strengthened greatly. In fact it can be said that SKIP practices a form of vocational training that is found in state training institutions, with the exception that care is taken to 'do whatever is done sincerely' and efforts are made to find jobs for the students who graduate from the training courses.

The Goodwill models itself on SKIP but improves on the model. Thus it offers both formal and non-formal courses for fitters, turners, electricians, plumbers, welding, tailors and so on. The range is wide but again much emphasis is placed on attention to students' individual needs. While technical skills are built up and while the Goodwill faculty has earned a reputation in South India as technical trainers par excellence, there is not much emphasis on building up other necessary skills, such as marketing and access to finance. The institution does not stress the promotion of group enterprise nor is there much emphasis on building up the educational capacities of students. In terms of quality, however, the technical skills imparted are better than those learned at the ITIs; indeed, many dropouts from the latter join the Goodwill programme, do well and find jobs. This is perhaps due to the individual attention given to the students.

By contrast, MAYA has a holistic approach to vocational training and building skills. While, on the one hand, the technical training imparted, be it in carpentry or motor maintenance and repairs, is fairly rigorous and is based on some of the latest knowledge in the respective fields, much emphasis is placed on education, personality development, dealing with customers, teamwork and so on. Upon entering the programme, the youth trainees are mostly illiterate, and even if they had been to school, they often have forgotten what they learned there. First, a baseline assessment is made, in which the students' aptitude is tested; special classes are offered for slow learners. Those who have been trained, for instance, in the *motorfiks* find jobs in regular service centres of TVS, Honda and so on. One can see the elements of decent work training being imparted to the trainees. Much emphasis is placed on quality management and control, which sometimes does create problems, since the market often does not want good quality. Stipends are provided to the trainees.

Presently, MAYA faces two major challenges: that of expanding its production and labelling its products, in addition to marketing some of its services. This is partly because it depends more on individual orders and supplies. This raises the question of how competitive it will remain if it does not enter the market soon. Marketing seems to be rather difficult for the organisation at this stage. According to MAYA functionaries, although the organisation gives an introduction to its trainees, it does not believe that it is possible to impart marketing skills in addition to vocational skills in a way that would sufficiently guarantee that the trainees could do their own marketing in such a competitive environment. ORGANICs was formed for this purpose, that is, to provide marketing support to producing groups in the area of product and service development, to groups initiated by MAYA or to other groups in the region. It has been rather successful in marketing some of its carpentry products, but it has yet to advance beyond small-small projects.

MEADOW likewise trains women in the manufacture of watchstraps. While this is dependent on the nature of the demand, MEADOW itself is aware of the associated problems. A multi-skilling process has been developed in which the watchstrap makers are also taught skills ranging from those involved in assembling computers to managing accounts. Titan initially trained some of the women in office management and accounts. Now that the women have registered their own firm and are competently doing this job, so much so in fact that senior workers who show some interest are imparted office management skills. The idea of assembling computers for some brand name manufacturer is in a nascent stage, but is seen as one of the solutions to being too dependent on Titan.

DHAN does not focus much on the contemporary services, production or trade sector. But there is nothing to prevent the women from venturing into such areas. The choice is theirs. The organisation's express emphasis has hitherto been on the absolutely marginalised women, and it may take quite some time still before it gets involved in contemporary services, production or trade. It has made a small beginning, however, in a federation in the Madurai District, where women are seeking to manage computerised information centres. Another successful contemporary service that many of the federation members provide in almost every district in which DHAN works is that of resource person: they have turned out to be very good resource persons for training sessions organised by many NGOs.

The approaches to training and skill formation for each of the sectors differ for each of the organisations. On the basis of the foregoing discussion, we summarise our findings in Table 5.2.

Note that this table seeks to present diagrammatically the approaches to training followed by the NGOs. It is highly stylised and summarised. To sum up, two of the case studies selected, SKIP and Goodwill, follow a traditional approach to training, concentrating more on vocational training or training for employment. These interventions have problems similar to the governmental or formal training systems, including that of obsolescence and treating training as a one-time affair. One of the interventions, MEADOWS, represents a collaboration of women with a private sector enterprise, but here too training takes the form of training for employment. This intervention has its limitations, especially that of being over-dependent on one firm. Efforts though are underway to break out of these constraints. MAYA combines training for employment (i.e. vocational training) with training for empowerment. DHAN's training, on the other hand, concentrates on empowerment. The lessons from these case studies are discussed in the next section.

Table 3. Approaches to Training and Skills Development

Issues	SKIP	Goodwill	MEADOW	MAYA	DHAN
Qualifications of trainees	Minimum basic education (10+2).	Minimum basic education (at least 10th class).	Minimum basic education (at least 10th class).	Education not a must.	Majority illiterate; few with some primary education.
Age group and sex	Youth, mostly men, not yet part of the workforce.	Youth, men and women, not part of the workforce.	Youth, women part of the workforce.	Youth and children, both sexes not part of the workforce.	Adults, women, part of the workforce.
Orientation of the Programme	Vocational trainees choose a course according to their perception; focus on technical aspects based on the ITI model. Does not include education.	Vocational trainees choose a course according to their perception; focus on technical aspects based on the ITI model. Does not include education.	Various aspects of manufacturing watchstraps, no room for exercising choice. Education is not included. On-the-job learning component high.	Multifaceted, basic vocational training followed by specialisation. Includes education. Focus on building life skills, including social skills.	Multifaceted training for livelihoods, including self-image/ confidence building skills, social skills, esp. those related to negotiation, basic technical skills imparted on demand. Self-chosen skill upgrading; individual given space by the collective.
Training thrust and meaning	Individual, training implies one-time acquisition of some skills.	Individual, training implies one-time acquisition of some skills.	Individual, training implies one-time acquisition of some skills.	Individual to some extent, but focus on community. Training defined as enabling, a continuous process.	Community, individual training only if group wants and needs it. Training is seen as enabling, for empowerment. Continuous process, virtually lifelong.
Pedagogy	Individualistic, piecemeal, process owned by teacher/instructor, not very interactive.	Individualistic, piecemeal, process owned by teacher/instructor, not very interactive.	Learning from instructor, followed by learning from peers and by doing.	Combination of teaching by instructor, learning from peers, by doing and from community. Interactive.	Learning from peers, resource persons; processes owned by community; highly interactive.
Quality of Training	Supply driven, high obsolescence level classroom-oriented.	Supply driven high obsolescence level, classroom.	Narrow demand-based, classroom and workshop oriented. No flexibility.	Need-based, with some supply driven aspects included. Classroom, workshop as well as community.	Need-based, Community spaces, with need based. Very flexible, caused by situational, contextual.
Follow-up	Practically non-existent, some find placement in industry as apprentices.	Minimal follow-up, but attempt made to find placements in industry as apprentices.	Not applicable.	Continuous follow-up placements and post-apprenticeship follow-ups.	Continuous follow-up, interaction on a day-to-day basis.
Trainers knowledge base/openness	Fixed syllabi orientation, government modelled.	Fixed syllabi orientation, government modelled.	Specific task-oriented.	Knowledge base high, trainers reoriented frequently, high degree of openness. Trainers flexible in terms of changing sylla-	Knowledge base high, trainers reoriented frequently; high degree of openness as well as practicality.

				bus.	
Trainers Accountable to:	Organisation.	Organisation.	Titan mostly.	The students and the community.	The community.
Sustainability of Training Process	Will last as long as funds exist.	Will last as long as funds exist.	Depends on market demand and industrial partner.	Dependent on external funding.	DHAN itself is dependent on external funding, but many community organisations have become self-sustainable. The intervention seeks to make them self-reliant. Many community organisations provide employment to professionals.
Gender Sensitivity	Needs strengthening.	Needs strengthening.	Though it involves women only, virtually non-existent insofar as gender in wider society is concerned.	Gender equity is an implicit concern.	Intervention-oriented to attain gender equity in society.
Decent Work Components/Rights Issues	Trainees given exposure to workers' rights.	Trainees given some exposure to workers' rights.	Some decent work components, such as occupational safety. Basic principle, empowerment of freedom to choose missing.	Orientation to practice, decent work, empowerment, freedom to choose, multi-skilling a future goal.	Orientation to practice, decent work, empowerment, freedom to choose, multi-skilling, intervention rights-based.
Employment Effect of Training/Intervention	Attempt made to place trainees as apprentices but net employment effect of intervention difficult to ascertain in the absence of adequate data.	Attempt made to place trainees as apprentices, but net employment effect of intervention difficult to ascertain in the absence of adequate data.	All employees.	Attempt to place vocational trainees in jobs; for others creation of enabling environment to build livelihood security.	Creation of livelihood security by creating enabling environment and empowerment.
Creation of economic spaces	Nil.	Nil.	Niche due to linkage.	High Potential.	Intervention seeks to create spaces.
Capacities to create markets and linkages	Doubtful.	Doubtful.	Doubtful.	High.	High.
Access to Information	Low.	Low.	Low.	High.	High.
Access to Micro credit	Nil.	Nil.	Nil.	High Potential of some.	Based on micro-finance.
Potential for enterprise development / formation of co-operatives	Little.	Little.	Little.	High.	High.

LESSONS LEARNED FROM THE CASE STUDIES

Given the complexities and the heterogeneity of the concept of the informal sector, it is difficult to make very general arguments in favour of adequate training. There is a wide variance in the training needs of the informal sector, needs which must be contextualised and for which appropriate strategies must be formulated. To do so would require a lot more research on the nature and character of the informal sector, survival strategies, mobility and available choices in each sector—service, production, trade—and within each sector according whether the activity is traditional or contemporary. These studies also have to be local. However, some important lessons can be derived from the foregoing case studies regarding basic processes. These become all the more important given the present conditions of globalisation and liberalisation and the sheer magnitude of the informal sector. It becomes imperative to think of issues of scale in considering any model of intervention. The major lessons are as follows.

Training for Employment

If the size of the informal sector is to be addressed, it is necessary to redefine training as training for empowerment and not just for employment or vocational training. This is one way of addressing the issue of the 'wage-hunters and gatherers'. Here a major challenge for researchers, policy makers, trainers and other interventionists is to build up a more realistic picture of the informal sector, the diversity in it, and map the diverse survival strategies inherent in it sub-sectorally. Formulation of training packages and approaches will have to be based on such understanding and go beyond narrow definitions of technical training only and be treated much more holistically than at present.

Creating an Enabling Environment

Training for empowerment necessitates the creation of an enabling environment, which is a big challenge in itself. This has many facets, but begins with building up the self-image and confidence of workers. As the experiences of DHAN and MAYA show, training for empowerment, building social and negotiating skills, as well as skills to enhance productivity cannot be a one-time affair.

Pedagogy of Training for Empowerment.

In training for empowerment and creating an enabling environment, external inputs, in the form of trainers, are needed, but they have to play a facilitative process if they are to enable the community to learn on its own and from each other. Highly skilled resource persons who constantly upgrade their own skills are required, but these people have to be accountable to the community. The pedagogy of this training process stresses co-learning and sharing with peers, which brings about crucial linkages and contacts with markets and the supply chain. The process places more emphasis on creating spaces, so that workers can exercise all the necessary freedoms and choices entailed in the notion of decent work. The upgrading of skills also takes place in this context insofar as the collective gives the individual space to grow. In fact a major part of the capacity building, training and so on for these groups takes place on a day-to-day basis, where the members themselves set the agenda according to their needs. The creation of the necessary social spaces and the enabling the workers to develop their own models of social security and support have to be a part of the capacity building process.

The Role of Change Agents

The interventionist has a critical role to play in this process. The success of the intervention crucially depends on the interventionist's perception of both the problem and the solution, and what is required in a particular context. This in itself has to be based on a thorough understanding of and respect for the culture of the workers, their belief systems and their dignity and self-respect. The latter may need to be built up so that the informal sector workers can freely choose their future.

The Intervention Package

The intervention package has to be worked out in a rights framework, including gender and child rights, where the community organisations are of paramount importance as the implementers, monitors and evaluators of the skill building packages. The aspects of human resource, especially of basic human skills, are of critical importance.

The Non-negotiables

While the contents and the pedagogy of the intervention packages will need to be worked out according to the specifics of each situation, the non-negotiables of such packages will bear on decent work, which will have to be seen as a strategy to attain the worker's sustainability in the labour market. The focus, in a rights framework, has to be on empowerment, building up survival capacities so as to ensure: (1) the basic security of incomes and other social securities; (2) the ability to choose when not to work, more so if the conditions of work are degrading and dehumanising (cf. the thousands of manual scavengers in the country); (3) labour market mobility irrespective of caste, gender and ethnicity; (4) occupational safety and health, that is, if the workers have to work in hazardous jobs, they should be provided at least with basic minimum protection; and (5) adequate and appropriate, timely remuneration, on the basis of equal pay for equal work for both men and women, fair wages for adults so that they are not forced to take their children out of school and put them to work.

Essentially, training and skill building in the informal sector needs to be seen as an enabling device, to which the components of decent work are integral. In terms of rights—which includes the right to economic, social justice and rights, as well as the right to a livelihood—the enabling environment can best be created by forming community organisations which are supported if necessary by external professionals who do not appropriate the spaces of the community or the individual, but facilitate the building of skills and survival techniques among the group members. Techniques here also include simple intermediate technologies, as well as social and negotiating skills. Thus the women members of a savings and credit group need to know all about the opportunities and frontiers open to them, including knowledge about sources of cheap credit or the labour laws that apply to them. Similarly, for a street vendor it is most important to secure the necessary economic space and negotiation skills.

Such skills and training processes for empowerment need to be owned by the community, and over time the role of the external agent should become progressively marginal. As the community organisation takes over the empowerment training functions, the external facilitator should gradually withdraw. Life skills, education, flexibility of training and decent work components all must add up so as to fulfil one objective, the attainment of what is needed to survive while transcending the needs by restoring the workers' self-esteem and self assurance.

The interactive process under discussion here can be represented diagrammatically, as in Figure 1. (Note that this is a stylised representation and is not generalisable to all situations and contexts without modifications.)

Figure 1. The Empowerment Approach to Training

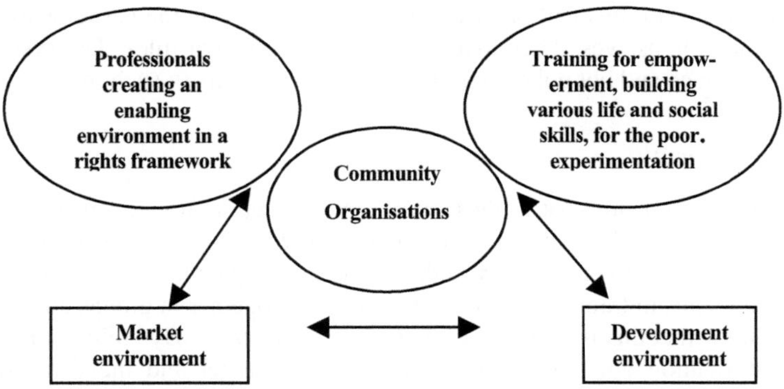

There is a three-way link between training for empowerment, community organisations and the market and development environment to promote successful income augmenting activities for the poor. The various skill building techniques used are not class- or gender-neutral; hence, it has to be adapted so that the poor can use it. Local organisations are needed as purveyors of these techniques. But it is necessary to make the benefits tangible which would be derived from the implementation of such techniques if viable and sustainable local organisations are to be built. It is critical that the third factor, the enabling environment, be effected by the other two factors. Note that the techniques refer here not only to the hard core technologies of production and so on, but also to the human skills, values and so on, as well as the basic knowledge required to survive in an increasingly competitive world. The overall purpose of training is to create that enabling environment in such ways that the community and hence its individual members are empowered and can exercise their rights, including the right to decent work. Gender and other forms of social equity (caste, ethnic equity) are a part of this.

The success of the training and skill building process depends on the best mix of these factors. Indeed, training and skill building have to be seen as processes, all the more so when the numbers of those involved is so high. Also the basic approach to processes—and, deriving from them, institutions, knowledge systems and styles of functioning on the part of the enabler, the external agent or the training provider—has to be very different if the intervention is to be sustainable. This is the enveloping function or approach to the above triad.

In this context the formation of self-help groups and micro-finance cannot be emphasised enough. But again, it is necessary to be cautious here. All over the country, NGOs are forming such groups, but very often their success is limited. The human investment in a group's formation is either insufficient or, at times, the very parameters are misplaced. The success of DHAN's endeavour rests on the fact that it has put into operation the continuous lessons learned by the people, it has been able to ignite the potential of the rural poor to save and help each other. This has been possible because DHAN has created institutions and processes which are owned by the participants, that is, the poor women themselves. They make and follow their own rules. The system is one of good governance and not policing, unlike what often occurs in such interventions.

Training for Employment

For the upper end of the sector, that is, those with some education, training also has to be oriented to empowerment. This means that along with technical and vocational skills (which need to be updated continuously) other important capacities must be built up. The first of these relates to training people in how to work together in groups and teams. Success stories show that this is often a means for upgrading skills. By building up ways of accessing information about the latest trends in the market and the demand for particular skills, the workers are further empowered. The MEADOW experience is illustrative of this process. The trainers need to be highly competent, while the community, and even the trainees themselves, must be an effective watchdog.

Finally, for all segments of the informal sector, training in marketing and the establishment of linkages is a must, because ultimately that is what determines the success of an endeavour. Yet within this sector, and even in its successes, there are two critical issues which, unless they are addressed from the very beginning, can more than anything else derail the efforts. These are the barriers of gender and caste inequity. Even DHAN has had to face problems on both scores. To redress them, it is necessary to gain a deeper understanding of gender and caste influences equations in the informal sector, but unfortunately there are still no relevant studies available that would help in this regard. In the final analysis, the government has the greatest role to play in promoting these concerns. This means it has to prioritise capacity building in the informal sector, taking into account the different cultural, social and economic contexts such as caste and gender differences, as well as the educational and economic levels, and play the role of prime enabler. At the same time the actualisation of decent work can also be set in motion by upholding the enabling functions of external agencies, so that the workers concerned become truly empowered to exercise their choices.

NOTES

[1] Lenhart's typology comprises the following:

- Training directed at trade-boosting programmes relevant more to who is already active in production in different types of units in the informal sector.
- Survival training in an anonymous market (labour, goods, services).
- Improving the vocational training performance of 'masters' in the informal sector.
- Training measures within the framework of community development, such as in neighbourhood, slums, schools, providing counselling, recreation, health, welfare, housing and care for the elderly.
- Training programmes within the framework of social work or special education projects, such as at juvenile homes, prisons, etc.

[2] This section is based mostly on Mamgain & Awasthi, 2001 and GOI, 2001.

REFERENCES

Anand, H. (2001). Linkages between informal and formal sectors: Some findings from micro-level studies. In Kundu & Sharma (eds.), *Informal sector in India*, 276–98.

Bangasser, P. E. (2000). *The ILO and the informal sector: An institutional history*. Employment Paper 2000/9. Geneva: ILO.

Breman, J. (1994). *Wage hunters and gatherers*. New Delhi: Oxford University Press.

Breman, J. (1996). *Footloose labour*. Cambridge: Cambridge University Press.

Das, B. (1994). *Socio-economic study of slums in Surat City*. Surat: Centre for Social Studies.

Das, K. (2001). Workers and earnings in informal manufacturing: Evidence and issues in estimation. In Kundu & Sharma (eds.), *Informal sector in India*, 179–95.

GOI. (2001). *Report of the task force on employment opportunities*. New Delhi: Government of India, Planning Commission, June 2001.

Hart, K. (1973). Informal income opportunities and urban employment in Ghana. *Journal of Modern African Studies*, *11*, 61–80.

ILO. (1998). *World employment report*. Geneva: ILO.

Jhavbala, R., & Subrahmnya, R. K. A. (2000). *The unorganised sector: Work security and social protection*. New Delhi: Sage Publications.

Kundu, A., & Sharma, A. N. (eds.). (2001). *Informal sector in India: Perspectives and policies*. New Delhi: Manohar Publishers.

Lenhart, V. (1997). Vocational training for the informal sector: A typology. *Education*, *55–56*, 25–34.

Mamgain, R. P, & Awasthi, I. C. (2001). Technology and training for informal sector: Need for new initiatives. In Kundu & Sharma (eds.), *Informal sector in India*, 363–81.

Omvedt, G. (1990). The 'unorganised sector' and women workers. Unpublished report on the proceedings of: Seminar on Women and Work, Centre for Social Studies, Surat, Gujrat, India.

Raghunandan, D. (2000). Best practices in technology dissemination for rural industries: National scenario in India. Paper presented at APCTT Workshop on Best Practice for Technology Delivery aimed at Promoting Rural and Small Industries, Bogor, Indonesia, 1–2 December.

Rodgers, G. (2000). Decent work as a development objective. V Giri Memorial Lecture given to the 42nd Annual Meeting of the Indian Society of Labour Economic. Jabalpur: Madhya Pradesh.

Sen, A. (1999). *Development as Freedom*. Oxford: Oxford University Press.

Singh, M. (1999). Social and cultural context of vocational learning in the informal sector: Implications for vocational education and training systems. In M. Singh (ed.), *Adult learning and the future of work* (pp. 166–88). Hamburg: UNESCO Institute for Education.

Singh, S. (1992). Training for employment: Some lessons from experience. *Journal of Educational Planning and Administration*, *6*, 119–32.

EDUCATION, TRAINING AND SKILLS FORMATION FOR DECENT WORK IN THE INFORMAL SECTOR: CASE STUDIES FROM NORTHERN INDIA

V. V. Krishna

INTRODUCTION

The last decade witnessed considerable attention by international and national agencies, national governments and researchers to informal sector analyses, trends in labour processes and employment opportunities and the role the informal sector continues to play in national economies. In light of different estimates from censuses and surveys, particularly those carried out by the International Labour Organisation (ILO), it is now clear that in terms of labour force the informal sector is on the increase while the jobs in the modern or formal economy is beginning to shrink in developing countries. The latest World Employment Report of the ILO (1998) puts the figure of people working in the informal sector at 500 million.

Most definitions of the informal sector characterise it as the work composed of rural subsistence activities and work in family-run, urban micro-enterprises. Three broad categories can be identified in the informal sector: (i) establishment-based units, local self-help organisations, (ii) foot-loose, that is, all kinds of vendors, from those selling vegetables or manufactured goods to door-to-door merchandise sellers—foot-loose labour in the informal sector is done by flexible people engaged in a variety of activities to make their livelihood—and (iii) home-based units engaged in preparing and selling various things and goods.

In large measure, not only the informal sector based units, individuals and groups in India are characterised by low wages and productivity, but their work environment is reported to be marked by exploitation, unhygienic working and living conditions, high rates of illiteracy and very low education levels, low efficiency, etc. Given these persisting conditions, much of the attention of research and institutional efforts of organisations such as ILO has been on developing in the informal sector what is known as 'decent work' (ILO, 1999). Apart from expressing concerns to eliminate hazardous and unhygienic environments and prevailing exploitative conditions, the converging focus of four objectives of establishing decent work underline (a) the promotion of rights at work, (b) employment and (c) social protection and social dialogue.

Madhu Singh, (ed.), Meeting Basic Learning Needs in the informal Sector, 183-214.

While much of the research literature on the informal sector is devoted to macro- and microeconomic aspects, ongoing government policies and schemes address the issues of poverty, employment and other structural features of this sector. Due to the importance of these issues on all counts, including policy-related issues, very little attention is given to studies on education, training and skill formation for decent work in the informal sector in India. In a situation of continuing poverty, very low formal education levels and illiteracy, low productivity and a quite distressing economic development situation in the informal sector, one may regard education, and particularly knowledge and skills, for poor people in the informal as key ingredients in anti-poverty strategies and programmes directed at social and economic development. Small technical changes which improve living and working conditions, technical and social skills which help to add value to micro-enterprises and their management, and the development of networks with a range of formal and government agencies—all these elements demand awareness, education, knowledge and, above all, training in skills.

In recent years a number of governmental and non-governmental organisations have initiated programmes or taken steps in education, training and skill development with a view to establishing decent work in the informal economy. Such initiatives have been scattered and not well documented. There is limited information about the extent and type of educational and training programmes, which either reach out to or arise within the informal sector. There is also limited information on the successful experiences of skill development initiatives and programmes which combine technology dissemination and training which leads to the improvement of socio-economic conditions, particularly for women.

BRIEF REVIEW OF STUDIES AND RESEARCHES ON THE INFORMAL SECTOR

A general survey of studies on the informal sector in recent years shows them to be dominated by economic and sociological issues, including urban informal activities in slum-based clusters. The literature draws attention to some basic issues involved in the characterisation of the informal sector. First, as reported in a recent study by Kundu (1999), the complexity of discourse on the informal sector has raised issues concerning indicators and statistical size. As Kundu's study shows, the size of the informal sector in India has become a subject of debate since there are at least four sources of indicators: the population census, National Sample Surveys, the Economic Census and the data and indicators given by the Development Commissioner of Small Scale Industries (DCSSI). This being the case at the macro-level, researchers have sought to identify informal sector workers at the micro-level as comprising household-based activities with family labour involved in micro-enterprises.

Secondly, studies spanning the informal sector draw attention to the issue of the sector's heterogeneity. Given the conventional divide between urban and rural India, studies have also by and large employed this categorisation in dealing with the informal sector.

In fact even the training policies and programmes and the skill development schemes initiated by various government departments legitimise this divide by basing programmes on the distinction between rural and urban sections of the informal sector (see Table 1, below). For instance, in a recent study of urban informal sector in India, Kundu (1999) identifies three categories of studies: (a) those pertaining to a specific industry, or occupation-based studies; (b) those covering informal work activities in the city, or locality-based studies; and (c) studies on the urban poor which emphasise their economic activities in the slums. These studies focus on employment statistics and the nature of employment, including capital requirements (Bhattacharya & Dey, 1991), earnings per day, labour supply and demand statistics and analyses, age-sex composition and migratory behaviour (Arunachalam & Azad, 1985; Das, 1994); dynamics related to skill and technology (Singhania, 1997); the nexus between the informal and formal sectors and the nature of exploitation (Bremen, 1996); and urban, slum-based issues of the informal sector (e.g. Banerjee, 1982; Kundu, 1993). The issue of heterogeneity becomes glaring when one explores the spectrum of the informal sector which ranges from rag pickers, roadside vendors selling all kinds of daily necessities and people involved in small house-based activities to the small enterprises of computer professionals.

Thirdly, the literature draws attention to the debate of the structural linkages between formal and informal sectors and the nature of exploitation within the latter. Dupont (1995), for instance, highlights the segmentation of labour markets based on the non-economic criteria for certain categories of workers in the town of Rajasthan. Similarly, a study by Nagraj (1984) focusses on the subcontracting operations between the formal and the informal sectors in the manufacture of various items and goods. In this process the studies have drawn attention to the fact that the informal sector supports the formal sector because of the availability of cheap labour in the informal sector. This is referred to in the sociological literature as undercutting wages and exploitation (see Bremen, 1996). While subcontracting in sectors such as the *beedi* industry, brass works, carpet manufacturing, etc., might validate the findings of these studies, the evidence from the high technology-based industries, such as computer and information technologies, the upper end of the small and medium enterprises in the manufacturing and industrial sectors is likely to throw light on the other side of the debate. In other words, there is some justification and rationale for suggesting that in the informal sector there are economic prospects of higher income generation and gradual 'economic prosperity' for workers. Educational levels of informal sector workers, levels of skill and technology training in the process of 'learning by doing' might be taken as factors responsible for contributing to the different scenarios in these segments of the informal sector, which is mostly urban-based compared to rural-based industries, such as in carpets, *beedi*, metal- and brass-based units.

In dealing with the transactions and linkages between the formal and informal sectors, policy-related reports from governmental sources do not pay adequate attention to this subject. There is indeed an underlying assumption in the governmental policy-related documents that the structure and problems of the informal sector are transitional and that they are likely to be gradually absorbed by the pace of both rural and urban industrialisation processes. While government documents and reports by and large deal with policies, programmes and schemes concerning informal sector activities, international agencies such as ILO have generally been concerned with employment-related aspects, including the nature of work elements in the informal sector (ILO, 2000). At the ILO national workshop on the 'Strategic Approach to Job Creation in the Urban Informal Sector in India', papers were presented on *khadi* textiles (Chadha, 2000), food processing (Dewan, 2000), leather (Damodaran, 2000), software services (Kumar, 2000) and tourism (Singh, 2000); they show the preoccupation with economic-related aspects in studies on the informal sector. On the other hand, a cursory look at some of the literature referred to above shows that in these studies education, skill development, modes of learning in apprenticeship, building capabilities and training needs in the informal sector are accorded little or no space; at best they have been dealt with only in a marginal way. Even the availability of training material and documentation for vocational and skill training in India is hard to find, both in the literature and in studies available on the informal sector and in government-related documents and reports.

Whereas institutes for formal education and vocational training have received considerable attention in the literature from education specialists and scholars, including social scientists dealing with educational policy and administration, the educational needs of the adult population has only recently begun to attract the attention of scholars and institutions (see Singh, 1997, 1999 and 2001). However, adult education and training which are geared to income generation, work and employment are the relevant areas of focus for the informal sector when the aim is the alleviation of poverty (Corvalan, 1997). Similarly, while the issue of skill development and the dissemination of technical knowledge to industry and organised sectors has received considerable research attention, little or only marginal attention has been given to the subject of training in upgrading the skills of workers in the informal sector, particularly in the rural context (see Raghunandan, 2000 and Singh, 2000). In the recent years two major initiatives have been advanced by international agencies which have attracted the attention of government policy makers and in the relevant literature: the attainment of suitable livelihoods and the right to work for all (ILO's core mandate in most of its programmes and objectives), and the ILO document which emphasises decent work. In the literature dealing with education in the informal sector, a good deal of attention is given to processes of training and skills acquisition. Here different processes of learning and types of competencies are seen as fundamental elements for workers in the informal sector. Singh (1997) draws attention to two ways of understanding learning in the informal sector: (i) learning is understood as the acquisition of technical skills and abilities on the level of enterprise and related in varying ways to the production process in an enterprise, and (ii) learning is understood as the acquisition of organisational, small-entrepreneurial and social competencies that are external to the production process in an enterprise. On social competencies Burckhardt (1997) also draws attention to personality components which are by and large moulded by the society or its agencies of socialisation and hence can be called 'social competencies'. Burckhardt divides these social competencies into two spheres: 'inwards, directed towards individual personality', and 'outwards, directed towards others'. The first is said to include self-awareness, the ability to learn, motivation, creativity, intellectual agility and the capacity for planning ahead. The second concerns the ability to communicate with others, tolerance and flexibility. In summary, while these authors underline learning processes relevant to workers in the informal sector, other authors have sought, from a somewhat different perspective, to draw our attention to the dimension of training which itself involves learning processes. For instance, Lenhart (1997), in tracing the 20 year study on vocational training for the informal sector, proposes a typology of interventions in the informal sector through training which include: (i) training directed at trade boosting programmes which is relevant more to those who are already active in production in the informal sector; (ii) survival training in an anonymous market (labour, goods, services, etc.) with a view to improving the vocational training performance of 'masters' in the informal sector; (iii) training measures within the framework of community development bearing on the neighbourhood, slums, schools, counselling, recreation, health, welfare, housing old age people, etc.; and (iv) training programmes within the framework of social work-special education projects, such as in juvenile homes and prisons.

The ongoing process of globalisation and market-oriented policies is bringing about a whole new set of demands in the technology and service-related economy; and this also has much to do with the expanding middle classes, which now possess more disposable income than in the previous two decades. With such expansion and growth of the economy, globalisation poses new challenges for the workers in the informal sector. From the positive side, the new challenges of globalisation will force the workers in the 'upper end' of small and micro-enterprises to confront and internalise new skills and business practices. This will certainly help them to enhance their income levels. Further, given the higher levels of education and skills of professionals in this segment of the informal sector, it can easily compete with the formal sector regarding the access to credit, the acquisition of new technology and skills, etc., and thereby derive certain economic advantages previously available only to the formal sector.

On the other hand, the current wave of globalisation is also penetrating the traditional sectors of operation (carpets, shoes, leather goods, ancillary industries in cycles, motor parts, metal works and locks industry, electrical equipment, etc), which were formerly the traditional preserve of the workers and units in the informal sector and are now facing new competition. Not only are the goods and services of the traditional informal sector subject to a new threat from globalisation, but the very survival of workers is threatened due to their inability to enhance their educational and skills in accordance with the demands of the 'new, global economy' (see Mamgain & Awasthi, 2001). Along with insecurity of income and employment, the growth of the global economy brings with it the demand that workers improve their skills and keep step with technological developments and that traditional apprenticeships be accordingly reoriented. Even though family ties, caste- and community-based social and cultural processes continue to shape the orientations and skill acquisitions of workers in the informal sector, their economic sustenance in the urban and metropolitan cities will demand that they continuously upgrade their skill base and their technical and social competencies (Singh, 1999; Corvalan, 1997).

An important problem that is noted increasingly in the literature is the relative stagnation of wage levels in the informal sector despite expansion and improvement in the economy. One key cause of this for informal sector workers is their lack of bargaining power. In an effort to address this problem, Singh (1997, p. 61) draws our attention to what is known as 'collective competencies', suggesting 'collective representation of interests in local organisations. An important source of learning is "learning by negotiating", particularly in the sphere of the expansion of markets, and in the search for markets in competition situation'.

Table 1. Overview of Case Studies from Northern India

Case Study	Successful Cases / Projects	Rural / Urban-based	Type of Competencies Developed	Education / Training Skill / Technology	Replication Status
SWRC Barefoot College	Barefoot Solar Engineers	Rural	Technical	Upgrading skill & training	yes
	Night Schools / Children's Parliament	Rural	Social	Education	yes
	Water harvest & hand-pumps	Rural	Technical	Training	-
Annapurna	Micro-credit	Urban	Social & Economic	Education	-
	Tiffin Supply	Urban	Social & Economic	Skill	yes
	Women Entrepreneurs	Urban	Social & Economic	Training & Skill	yes
CTD / STD	Leather & Food Processing	Rural	Technical	Technology & Training	yes
	Branding and Marketing of Rural Products	Rural	Economic	Training	-
PRADAN	Flayer Co-operatives	Rural	Social	Education	-
	Rural Enterprises	Rural	Social & Economic	Skill & Training	yes
SETU / Church	Domestic work	Urban	Social	Education & Training	-

Table 2. Training Programmes Offered in the Informal Sector

Institution	Location of Training	Duration in Months	On-job/ Exclusive	Areas / Fields / Subsectors
Barefoot College, Tilonia	Tilonia, Rajasthan.	3–6	Exclusive & on-job.	Solar energy repair & maintenance.
-do-	-do-	2–3	On-job.	Hand-pumps, water harvesting, construction, handicrafts, etc.
-do-	-do-	Not specified	Exclusive & on-job.	Night schools, health & environment.
CTD/STD New Delhi & Mandi, Himachal Pradesh	Not specified.	2–6 or as required.	Exclusive & on-job.	Establishing NGO based micro-enterprises in leather, food processing, etc.
Annapurna Mahila Mandal (AMM), Dadar, Mumbai.	Mumbai Region, Pune & Maharastra.	As required.	On-job.	Midday meals, local tiffins, company meals, catering, sweets for women entrepreneurs.
(AMM)	Shriwal, Shindewadi.	As required.	On-job.	Bakery and confectionery, goat rearing, chicken farming, mushroom cultivation, sewing, knitting, nursing.
PRADAN	Northern region.	3–24 or as required.	Exclusive & on-job.	Professional workers for grassroots development projects.
SETU, School of Social Work	Mumbai.	As required.	Exclusive.	Domestic workers.
AMM	Dadar, Mumbai.	As required.	On-job.	Micro-credit for women.

Source: *Northern India Case Study*, January 2000.

SOME SUCCESSFUL CASES IN THE INFORMAL SECTOR INVOLVED IN SKILL DEVELOPMENT, EMPLOYMENT GENERATION AND SOCIAL EMPOWERMENT

The main successful cases and projects executed by those NGOs in the informal sector in Northern India which have been selected for investigation in the present study (see Boxes 1–5) are shown in the Tables 1 and 2. At the outset it should be noted that all five case studies selected for the present study are NGOs which are connected and rather dependent for financial support on formal institutions, mostly government agencies such as the Ministry of Rural Development and CAPART. As shown in Table 1 above, while two case studies (Annapurna and SETU/Church) are urban-based (operating in the Delhi and Mumbai regions), the other three (SWRC, CTD/STD and PRADHAN) operate primarily in the rural states of Northern Indian. In what follows, we shall look into some crucial features of success in these cases.

Solar Devices and Barefoot Solar Engineers

During the last decade the SWRC's promotion of solar energy devices in the remotest parts of Ladhak, Sikkim, Kargil and Himachal Pradesh—where it is economically cheaper to install and use solar-based energy systems than grid systems; and areas of Ladhak are so remote that a normal electricity system is unthinkable and Kerosene is costly and difficult to obtain—clearly demonstrates its approach of community participation with skills and training. More importantly, the Barefoot College sought to 'demystify high technology' in rural areas through its innovative way of winning the confidence of village youth, women and men: it has done so by showing that with the right training even the uneducated and semi-literate can operate and manage solar devices, their repair and maintenance.

The entire campus in Tilonia of the Barefoot College, where an average of 200 people live and work, is solar electrified and maintained by its Barefoot Solar Engineers (BSEs). Between 1989 and 1996 the SWRC covered 35 villages and thereby 730 houses in the Kargil and Leh Districts alone. This also provided 850 units (840 for domestic lighting and 10 in Sonam Norbu Hospital and Bal Ashram at Leh) with electricity. In addition even 30 night schools were solar electrified in Leh. SWRC trained 25 BSEs in the hilly regions who in turn trained 180 semi-literate youth to install, repair and maintain solar lighting units all over the rest of India (Roy, 1996).

In training the BSEs to provide basic lighting in the mountainous regions, the SWRC adopted certain principles and methods. Fundamentally, the SWRC had tremendous faith and confidence in the common sense and innate ability of village people and youth specially to adapt the sophisticated technology to meet their own needs. The head of the SWRC, Bunker Roy, notes that the following decisions were made concerning the training of BSEs:

> No electronic engineer or anyone holding a formal professional degree would be involved. BSE would be trained from the same village to do the job.
>
> The BSE would be from the village, not from any nearby town or city, because the investment in training should not be lost. They should have roots in the village and want to go back and stay there.
>
> The BSE should have the minimum of educational qualifications. If they were semiliterate or even illiterate it did not matter. If it took longer to train then that did not matter either. The training of BSE covered the following elements: How to install the solar panel on the roof of the house; How to carry out the entire wiring of the house and the fixing of the individual solar tube lights at the agreed location in the house; How to fabricate and solder inverters and charge controllers in extremely primi-

tive rural conditions; How to carry out repairs and change defective parts in the village itself; and How to in turn become a trainer and a leader in the village, to teach others to maintain their solar energy system in other villages without depending on expertise from outside. (Roy, 1996, p. 47)

These features met with considerable support and confidence on the part of the villagers, especially the youth, in the dissemination of solar technology in the villages. While promoting the solar devices in the villages in collaboration with its sponsors, the SWRC sought to consider unemployed or unemployable youth in the villages selected by their community to be trained in the installation, fabrication, maintenance and repair of the solar photovoltaic devices. The minimum requirements of formal educational qualifications, the focus on training and the involvement of communities in choosing the BSE trainees is crucial for building capacities and the demystification of sophisticated solar energy devices. Emphasis was also placed on training women from the villages particularly in the dissemination and maintenance of the solar lamps used by the SWRC's night school programmes in villages in the Rajasthan and Leh Districts.

Another important reason for the success of BSE training and the programme of solar technology dissemination is the emphasis on informal processes and what is known as the 'learning by doing'. As Bunker Roy pointed out, 'all training is informal and non-formal—on the job. From the first day they arrive, they are under twenty-four hour training in the campus'. There are not many written manuals and books. Oral communication processes and primary group interaction are the dominant modes of transmission in training programmes. Rather than the traditional mode of learning, which is based on the interaction and relationship between '*ustad* and *chela*', process is very much respected in the SWRC training programmes. These informal and oral-based training programmes are generally based on the subjective experience, knowledge and abilities of the trainees rather any set method. The trainees spend three to six months in training and progress at their own pace in most of the programmes.

Rain Water Harvesting, Hand-pumps and Barefoot Mechanics

The SWRC's programmes in ground water, rural industrialisation and housing, and the growing need for upgrading the skill base of artisans and master craftsmen (*mistries*) working in the areas of construction, steel moulding, mechanical devices, agriculture implements, etc., led to its programme of training barefoot construction engineers, mechanics and communicators. Fundamental to the training in and upgrading of skills provided in most of these areas by the SWRC is that the latter regarded it as important to work with the village wisdom, local knowledge and practical skills in the rural areas in order to understand the problems and develop methods both to upgrade the available knowledge skills and to optimise their use. As in the case of BSEs, in most of these programmes community participation and participatory research and training are seen as crucial for the success of the SWRC's programmes in rainwater harvesting and in barefoot hand-pump mechanics for the implementation of groundwater development programmes.

The SWRC's one-tier system replaced the three-tier system of maintaining hand-pumps in Rajasthan. The old three-tier system consisted of one hand-pump caretaker selected by the government, one mechanic to oversee hand-pumps in 100 villages and one mobile team of engineers for every 500 hand-pumps to make any necessary repairs. This system proved to be costly and the people responsible did not belong to the respective villages. The SWRC sought to develop a one-tier system with the aid of the government's Training of Rural Youth for Self-Employment (TRYSEM) programme.

The SWRC set out to determine whether local youth could be trained as mechanics who would be responsible for both installation and maintenance. So far 750 barefoot mechanics and 40 women mistries have been trained to repair and maintain 45,000 India Mark II hand-pumps, mostly in the State of Rajasthan. The one-tier system involves: (i) the identification of rural youth from economically poor backgrounds who have mechanical aptitudes and whose skills can be upgraded through training; (ii) the mobilisation of government resources to pay stipends to the hand-pump mechanics for the three months during which they are trained; (iii) the placement of trained mechanics in villages where they are accountable to the community; and (iv) the provision of credit banks for the purchase of tools so that hand-pump mechanics can eventually be self-supporting.

Over a period of time village-based hand-pump mechanics have replaced the government's inefficient, three-tier system, saving considerable resources. In the one-tier system, each mechanic is responsible for 30 hand-pumps within 5 kilometres of his or her place of residence. The training for these mechanics is non-structured and informal, incorporating on-the-job learning while the mechanics earn a wage. Self-reliance and rural self-employment are the two main objectives which have been put into practice since the early 1980s. The SWRC's experience with the hand-pump mechanics has shown that villages and rural communities have tremendous potential for developmental work, which can be realised only when there are social intervention mechanisms which understand their problems in context.

Another important area of work involving training and the utilization of traditional knowledge systems is rainwater harvesting. The SWRC mobilised people for 165 roof-top rainwater harvesting tanks, constructed in 150 villages and collecting 12 million litres of water every year mostly in schools located in backwater areas in the Ajmer, Jaipur, Sikar and Barmer Districts. It is easy for rural communities to understand rainwater harvesting in terms of their own traditional knowledge base on water. Another SWRC programme seeks to train barefoot mechanics and engineers in the area of alternative housing, which uses local materials and scraped steel to fabricate geodesic domes. In large measure its water and hand-pump programmes were successful because individuals and communities in the villages participated and the SWRC catalysed the process of building up people's confidence in their ability to adapting to technologies and develop skills. An important feature of the success of SWRC programmes is its emphasis on the demystification of technology so as to remove a peculiar psychological barrier of 'fear' among poor people and thereby making it easier for them to understand that technology.

Upgrading Skills in Leather Processing and Flayer Co-operatives

Artisans and communities involved in flaying, leather processing and other related work such as cobbling make up one of the most backward and socially oppressed groups in India. Flayers who are sometimes tanners in Indian villages produce products of low value and consumed locally in villages. Often the flayers are exploited by middlemen, who pay very low prices for flayed hides. These hides are then collected and processed in urban markets, the products of which are then sold in these villages at high prices. Often the processed leather also finds its way back into the hands of village cobblers and petty leather product manufacturers at high costs. In this whole process the local village flayers are exploited.

There have a number of attempts by KVIC and other formal institutions to improve the social and economic conditions of flayers and village tanners through appropriate technologies developed by institutions like Central Leather Research Institute, Chennai, but those attempts did not meet with replicable success until NGOs such as CTD/STD (Centre for Technology and Society for Technology and Development) and PRADAN (Professional Assistance for Development Action) intervened—from mid-1980s and 1970s, respectively—and addressed the aforementioned problem at both the technical and the social levels.

The work of CTD/STD (the latter is the offshoot of CTD) began in Mandi, Himachal Pradesh, when it was found that 85 percent of the raw hides were leaving Mandi and the rest were being tanned in the backyards with traditional methods. The leathers produced had no commercial value and moreover the flayers were paid very low prices for their hides. Discussions by the CTD/STD with flayers and local tanners revealed that the household level of tanning yielded low quality leather, which could fetch only low prices. Moreover, the whole process of household-based tanning was drudgery-ridden due to old methods. It was at this stage of survey in the mid-1980s that CTD/STD, in consultation with flayers and tanners in Mandi, worked out an alternative scheme aimed at developing a network of flayers and tanners by establishing local facilities for tanning with technical input from formal institutions such as the Central Leather Research Institute, Chennai. The establishment of nodal tannery in Mandi by this informal network of tanners, flayers and CTD/STD, and later with the involvement of with DST, CAPART and CLRI institutions, led to social and economic gain for the local flayers and tanners. The work of CTD/STD in collaboration with formal institutions involved tailoring the available leather processing technology for a small unit which was linked to a network of flayers and tanners. This new process based on vegetable tanning involves a series of technical operations at different stages of processing, as well as very low pollution levels compared to chrome tanning. It also involves use methods for safely discharging pollutants inside the tannery premises through four or five pits.

The STD-based nodal tannery in Mandi has been in operation for the last 15 years and currently has a network of 160 flayers and 10–12 tanners. By eliminating middlemen and the individual flayers this NGO based network has obtained at least four times the price which they previously had obtained from the middlemen traders. Over the years, STD also began to process and finish the hides at the nodal tannery for leather grade material to make leather products and supply leather to local cobblers and small entrepreneurs at reasonable prices. STD began manufacturing and marketing leather products with 12–15 artisans and tailors (forward linkages). STD has been able to provide employment to the flayers' children after giving them training, which contributes to the social and economic mobility of flayers.

In the initial stages the intervention of CTD/STD was crucial in order to enlist the aid of formal institutions such as CAPART, CLRI and DST to address the problems of local flayers, leather workers and processing operations in Mandi. However, the crucial element of creating a nodal tannery with the network of flayers and tanners required that traditional methods and skills be upgraded and reoriented; to achieve this CTD/STD organised a series of training programmes at different stages. As in the case of the Barefoot College, the notions of 'learning by doing' and 'learning by interaction' proved to be of considerable importance to both the leading actors of CTD/STD and the artisans involved in processing and marketing the leather. The success of leather processing and marketing experienced at Mandi through the intervention of CTD/STD has since been replicated 12 other states, including Manipur and Tripura, 20 tanning units have been established on the model of Mandi with the co-operation of CAPART and DST.

Along lines somewhat similar to the approach taken to leather processing, CTD/STD have organised a food processing unit in the Kullu region of Himachal Pradesh for fruit and vegetable processing and marketing through the establishment of farmers network. The significance of CTD/STD as a successful NGO increases with regard to its efforts concerning the 'branding' and marketing of leather and food products. We shall explore this case along with the marketing and 'branding' strategies of the Barefoot College in another section below.

Flayer Co-operatives: Closely related to the work of CTD/STD in leather processing in order to improve the social and economic status of flayers through networking is the case of PRADAN, which has achieved considerable success in organising flayers into co-operatives in Uttar Pradesh since the late 1980s. Before PRADAN's intervention, the Uttar Pradesh government's Zilla Panchayat (District Authority) auctioned geographical areas to contractors, who then had the right to process the hides of fallen animals in the region. The license system resulted in a contractor-held monopoly on hide trade, reducing the self-employed flayers to the status of low paid wage-workers. After several court cases, the establishment of a policy of issuing licenses to flayer co-operative was meant to redress the problem of the flayers' low income; however, 'dummy' co-operatives run by contractors further complicated the system. It is at this stage that PRADAN entered in the late 1980s to form genuine co-operatives in the two dozen blocks of the Sitapur, Hardoi, Barabanki and Lucknow Districts in Uttar Pradesh to deal with the flayers' problems. According to recent estimates (Annual Report of PRADAN, 1997–98, p. 18), the output from co-operatives established through the intervention of PRADAN is rupees 50 lakhs per annum, which serves/supports 4000 families in the districts of Uttar Pradesh.

PRADAN's efforts to enhance the economic status of flayers had to go beyond the co-operatives and their proper operation. In order to organise co-operatives, the NGO had to educate the flayers and their representatives about the merits and functioning of co-operatives and their legal aspects. The NGO organises periodic training and education sessions focused on political and social knowledge and on the legal rights of flayers. In recent years PRADAN made efforts to consolidate co-operatives further with regard to economic sustenance and viability by initiating a hide market in Khairatabad in Sitapur, where a large number of co-operatives have been formed through the efforts of the local Zilla Panchayat. Furthermore, the project moved the Panchayat to hold the market on a regular basis. To assure that the flayers obtain competitive prices in the new market, PRADAN helped the federation of flayer co-operatives to fix a base price.

Tasar Silk Enterprise with Tribal Communities in Bihar

Over the last decade PRADAN has been involved in the development of rural enterprises in the non-farming sector with the aim of improving the livelihoods of people, generating employment and endowing what is known as 'decent work' with meaning in the tribal context. Its work on the Tasar silk enterprise, which involved tribal communities and developed a series of schemes ranging from setting up plantations and silk production to marketing, has been quite impressive for the last eight years. This case is important since it involved 2200 tribesmen and other workers and combined rural technology adaptation through skill training, education and peoples' participation.

Following a study by PRADAN in the late 1980s of the Tasar sub-sector, which is grown in the Santhal Pargana region of Bihar on Arjuna and Asana trees in forests by tribesmen, the NGO sought to improve livelihoods through a project promoting Tasar host trees. Shortage of rearing stock was identified as the key constraint. During the first five years PRADAN mobilised people to plant Tasar host trees on privately owned waste lands. These plantations were raised on 1000 acres owned by about 2000 people, mostly tribesmen, in the Godda, Dumka and Banka districts of Bihar. This stage involved the training of plantation owners in rearing since the declining stock of Tasar host trees was seen as a problem.

The other problem confronted by the NGO concerned the non-availability of disease-free eggs of the Tasar moth (DFLs), which was seen as even more critical element affecting the incomes from and viability of Tasar silk rearing. Thus the NGO simultaneously set up grainages as service enterprises to produce and sell DFLs by training and educating the local youth. Twenty such enterprises have been established thus far (seven in 1998–99 alone), and 30 are proposed by the end of 2001. In 1999 these grainages sold 53,000 DFLs to 370 rearers.

Thirdly, the availability of seed cocoons was the main constraint faced by grainage owners. There had been no tradition of rearing cocoons for seed purposes due to low productivity, since rearing is done during the monsoons and such markets for cocoons did not exist. Then the project team linked the grainage owners to rearers and promoted seed cocoon rearing. Grainage owners now pay attractive prices for seed cocoons, and each has a network of rearers who produce them. Some information on the families served through PRADAN's intervention is provided in Table 4.

Another important stage of the Tasar silk enterprise involved the Tasar spinning and reeling, which leads to fabric production and marketing involving a mix of technological innovation, organisational and institutional innovation and training and the links between them. PRADAN introduced Tasar spinning and reeling in response to the demands for livelihoods from members of women's savings and credit groups promoted by the Tasar project. More than 125 women were trained in spinning, and a locally adaptable reeling machine was introduced in 1998 on which 20 women worked. PRADAN'S project team evolved quality standards for yarn to ensure marketability and price returns. The project further mobilised women to organise in groups so that they can collectively procure cocoons from the rearers. This gives rearers better returns since the monopoly of middlemen traders on the cocoon trade is broken and the women are able to stock up on cocoons for an entire year. The project was further extended to fabric production using locally produced yarn, and it has been reported that three production consignments are slated for Indian and external markets.

Table 3. Non-Farm Livelihood Activities of PRADAN

Project/Activity	Output of Rupee Lakh	Families served
Poultry at Kesla	23.0	65
Mushroom cultivation at Kesla	1.35	80
Flayer co-operatives	50.00	4000
Tasar plantations	-	1200
Tasar gainages	1.34	20
Tasar cocoon rearing	2.50	378
Tasar spinning, reeling & weaving	2.00	150
Total	5.84	5893

Source: *Annual Report, PRADAN, 1997–98.*

Helping Women through Co-operatives and Micro-Enterprises: Tiffin Supply Network, Domestic Help and Micro-Credit

Three case studies are selected in this section: the development of women entrepreneurs through co-operatives and micro-credit society (Annapurna), and the social and legal aid cum general education project for domestic help (SETU project) in Mumbai and Navi Mumbai. Even though these projects did not particularly arise from demands generated by metropolitan urbanisation, these demands certainly reflect the social objectives of women's development through micro-enterprises and self-reliant co-operatives. Moreover, these case studies indicate the further potential of replication in the metropolitan centres undergoing rapid urbanisation.

Annapurna Tiffin Meals Supply Network: This is a network of 200 women initiated by Padma Purao in four districts of Mumbai, Dadar, Mumbai and Vashi Nagar, Navi Mumbai which runs a training centre and a kitchen to supply about 1500 Tiffin meals to workers in different parts of Navi Mumbai and 1000 meals daily at the Dadar unit. The Annapurna institution began with the social objective to give shelter to distressed and exploited women. The Vashi Kitchen unit cum training centre (24,000 sq. ft.) has a provision to house 120 women, and half this number, some with their children, live in the kitchen complex.

Annapurna also functions as a women's rehabilitation centre since several women approach the institution. When a woman or child in distress approaches the Annapurna, the person in question is counselled and many times the problem is solved by bringing about a compromise between parties in conflict. In problematic cases which are deemed beyond resolution, the woman or child is given shelter at the Vashi Centre, in consultation with local police. Once medical and legal aid is given, the person is trained in the kitchen along with other women. The kitchen supplies food to offices in Navi Mumbai, a railway station stall, 'Meals on Wheels' and a working women's hostel maintained by Annapurna. In addition to such regular everyday supply to businesses, the Annapurna Kitchen also makes all kinds of sweets and other dishes typical of local Maharastrian cuisine and sell them through its outlets at festivals, weddings, outdoor party catering, bakeries and confectioneries, conferences, etc.

The training in the Vashi Kitchen Centre complex is given in preparing different kinds of food, as well as in hygiene, sanitation, cleanliness, food nutrition, food flavouring, packaging, preservation, food transportation, etc.—in short, in central aspects of the business of food preparation and catering. The chefs and supervisory staff working in the main kitchen centres are given training in formal Hotel Management and Catering Institutes, and they in turn impart hands-on training to others in the kitchen complex. Since the entire kitchen unit functions as a society of which all the working women are members, the society takes care of the children of women in the kitchen and educates them. The 'Meals on Wheels' mobile canteen operates in Navi Mumbai and is also used for training small scale entrepreneurs. Over the last eight years, the Annapurna centre gave 24 training courses on food processing which involved 800 girls and women. The kitchen centre at Dadar, Mumbai, which is a smaller unit comprising about 30 women, runs department stores. The success achieved at the Annapurna kitchen complexes at Dadar and Vashi led to their replication at Belgam and Kolhapur in 1994, Pune in 1993 and Marathwada in 1996.

Micro-credit for Women Entrepreneurs: The Annapurna Mahila Mandal (AMM) began its micro-credit operations for women in 1975 with 14 members; currently the society has 200,000 women members all over Maharastra. Initially members stuck to cooking food and serving, but over a period of time the members also engaged in other activities, such as selling vegetables, fruits, bangles, flowers, fish, grain, papad, namkeen and local sweets, sari fall stitching, repairing bicycles, tailoring, making toy and tanning, in the urban and metropolitan context. The AMM plays an intermediary, facilitating role between formal financial institutions and poor women. Over the last 25 years it has distributed loans worth rupees 35 crores to 150,000 women.

Even though granting loans to individuals is in principle not ruled out, AMM has sought to develop the esteem for group, community and social cohesion, etc., through its micro-credit activities. The AMM guides the loan seekers to form groups of 10–20 women from the same area who are counselled on the credit society's norms, values and policies of accountability. Then the group selects a leader, and this is repeated each year for as long as the group continues to be a member of the credit society. The loan recipients are accountable individually, however, and every member of the group is also responsible for other repayments and settling of accounts. The leader normally addresses some of these problems and liases with AMM members. Leadership qualities and values become meaningful for the group inasmuch as each loan application by group members has to receive the leader's approval. The area leader also over sees loan utilisation and attends weekly meetings of the AMM.

The AMM has given top priority to the education and training of its members. This is intended to make the members aware of and conversant with the formal dealings, rules and regulation of the AMM organisation as a credit society. Training and education of women members is also intended to help them to understand the social role of the organisation and its objectives of empowering women, inculcating social responsibilities in area leaders, imparting values of credit, savings and accountability. The counselling and training is in large measure geared to child and adult education and social development.

The group leaders attend weekly workshops and act as intermediaries between the AMM and group members. The area leaders and co-ordinators of the AMM have assumed social roles apart from fulfilling the obligations of credit for mutual benefit. They play a crucial role in imparting entrepreneurial abilities and develop new business opportunities. They are also organise neighbourhood group meetings, discuss the problems confronted by the members and provide counselling at their level of understanding and effort.

More than anything else, the social and economic role is given importance by the AMM. Credit for illiterate, grassroots-level women is considered to be not just another commercial or financial institution, but rather is viewed in a broader social context. Socially oppressed, exploited and poor women without any state and formal support are mobilised into groups and communities for micro-level business opportunities. Micro-credit is seen as an important tool for generating sustainable social and economic development which empowers poor women, who otherwise have nowhere to go for help and food.

Training Domestic Helpers

Industrialisation and urbanisation processes over the last decade have given rise to very complex and busy life-world patterns in metropolitan towns such as Delhi and Mumbai and have generated considerable demand for domestic work and housekeeping, including cooking. Even though the tasks involved in domestic work are nothing new and can be traced back 100 years or so, the rise of a middle class with high levels of income (where increasingly the trend is for both spouses to work) has created a skill-based demand for domestic help both to prepare of delicious, varied dishes and to take care of housekeeping, as well as to provide childcare and deal with related tasks. While the demand for such domestic workers is increasing, unfortunately their wages and occupational and social entitlements have not seen any improvement. Workers in this sector continue to be both economically and socially exploited.

The SETU(*Ghar Kamgar Sanghatna)* project at the School of Social Work, Mumbai, initiated a field action programme in 1992 to address the situation of domestic workers. The chief aim of this programme is to empower powerless women workers and to develop their human potential through education and training. The project strives to establish a bridge between isolated and scattered domestic workers, between domestic workers and their employers and between domestic workers and society at large.

The domestic workers are often migrant workers from tribal and rural areas working in metropolitan centres. They suffer not only from loneliness and alienation but also from insecurity and vulnerability. They work in isolation with minimum communication outside their workplace. They have no job security and are vulnerable to physical and sexual abuse; in addition, they are deprived of education. The SETU project thus has the objective to educate and work with the domestic workers, building up their confidence by counselling them about their social and legal rights and about basic features of legal and normative procedures which exist in their context. The project also seeks to involve the community at large by asking them to volunteer to teach domestic workers in literacy classes and skill development sessions. The SETU project has also mobilised the public to urge the government to pass legislation so that domestic workers will be entitled to one day of holiday each week or one day's extra wage, 15 days paid holiday per year, one month's wage as a bonus during main festival periods, medical allowance and an annual rise in monthly wages.

Night Schools and Children's Parliament

Since its inception in 1975, one of the most important activities of the SWRC's Barefoot College is the provision of non-formal education and training programs for children and adults. Over the years innovative concepts and methods of adult education and knowledge dissemination developed by SWRC have been adopted by the Rajasthan government through their Shiksha Karmi and Lok Jumbish Programs. The Barefoot College monitors and maintains 40 day care centres for children from birth to five years of age. These centres are also used to educate parents about nutrition, health care, education and women's rights.

There are four day schools run by the Barefoot College, but much of the organisation's emphasis has been on night schools. It has established them in 89 villages to meet the needs of the children who work during the daytime in the fields, in homes and in various other activities and therefore are deprived of an education. The Barefoot College offers them an alternative. Girls' education is given special emphasis and 60 percent of the night school students (each school having 15–25 children) are girls. Each night school cuts across caste, creed, community and religious differences and promotes values of equality, community and village development, harmony and environmental protection. Children are generally educated with specially written material from class 1 to 5, and there are several cases where many children have joined formal education from the night schools. About 15,000 children have completed the Barefoot College, and there are many workers in the Barefoot College who are themselves products of the night schools. Night school teachers are local village residents who have generally completed eighth class minimum. The system has developed comprehensive teaching material and books specially designed for the night schools.

Village Education Committees (VEC) have been organised on village levels and are important components of the night school programme. They are constituted of men and women from the village who seek to mobilise support for the night school and get others involved in various activities, such as the selection of the site for the school, the monitoring of the educational programme, participation in the selection of teaching staff and the canvassing of village households to encourage their children to participate and complete the education offered in the night schools. Two members of each VEC hold a joint bank account, manage the expenses of the night school, including the payment of teacher salaries, and are accountable to the Barefoot College.

One of the Barefoot College's innovative programmes aimed at imparting political awareness and village self-government to children in the night and day schools is Children's Parliament. Children learn about and participate in the political system, as well as addressing the village's educational and developmental needs. They participate in the election process, which teaches them self-governance and about the *panchayat* (local government) system and the need to select the best candidate, regardless of caste, class or gender. Since children come from villages where money and liquor play a role in political elections, they are educated about these aspects and how to elect the right people regardless of these brides the role of money. In the elections in the Children's Parliament, the participants elect their representatives and ministers, including their Prime Minister. These ministers monitor village development and are also provided small budgets from the Barefoot College. Once familiar with the activities of the Barefoot College, many of these children choose to work in the area of their abilities or take up whatever positions are available to them and some of them also become teachers.

Table 4. Six Themes: The Different Activities and Tasks of Education, Training and Skill Formation for Decent Work in the Case Studies Explored in Northern India.

1. Content/Forms of Training Programmes Upgrading skills, new skills, technical competencies Social competencies, self-esteem, self-assurance Basic education, literacy Social, political and economic knowledge base relevant to the needs of workers in the relevant sector.	**4. Decent Work Components** Promotion of rights in the workplace Employment assurance Social dialogue Non-exploitative Hygienic Democratic values
2. Process of Delivery Pedagogy Learning by doing On-the-job training, reaching out directly to members Books, manuals, products, designs, etc. Classroom-based learning Traditional learning process (master-pupil), formal learning processes	**5. Gender issues** Women empowerment through social and economic competencies Building women's leadership abilities Resistance to discrimination against women Building values of equality
3. Other Training Elements Employment prospects Self-employment Quality of training Nature of training: flexible, need-based, multi-skilling Economic empowerment	**6. Market and Access to Economic Space** Capacities to create markets Micro-finance, credit facilities Creating markets Market information, advertising, branding

MATRIX OF DIFFERENT ACTIVITIES IN TRAINING, SKILLS AND LEARNING

The exploration of successful experiences as documented above demonstrates different types and forms of training and skill development imparted by NGOs; different modes of delivery of training, gender sensitivities, decent work components, various other training-related components and market and micro-finance systems were observed in the case studies. Table 4 above summarises the 'best practices' observed in the foregoing case studies as a whole, identifying six major themes and various elements within each theme observed in the cases explored. However, these 'best practices' should not be taken as exhaustive. On the other hand, the relevance of all these themes and elements does not correspond to, or is not reflected in, each of the cases reported above. For example, the case of 'Night Schools and Children's Parliament' reflects themes 1, 2, 3 and 4, but not necessarily themes 5 and 6. Furthermore, when we try to explore the relevance of various elements mentioned in each of these themes (1–4) to the latter case, not all the elements or components of the theme are relevant. For example, the elements of 'democratic values' and 'hygiene' under the theme 'Decent Work' are relevant for this case but not necessarily for the others. There are cases, however, such as the Annapurna Tiffin Meals Supply Network and its Micro-credit for Women Entrepreneurs, in which all the elements in the 'Decent Work', 'Gender Issue' themes are relevant, whereas only one or two of the elements from themes 1, 2 and 6 are relevant. The 'structure of relevance' of the themes and their elements in Table 4 to the case studies is shown in Table 5 below.

Table 5. The Relevance of Different Themes to Case Studies and their Outcomes

Cases (NGO, Organisation)	Relevance of Themes (Numbers Relate to Table 4)	Outcome
Solar Devices and Barefoot Solar Engineers (Barefoot College).	(1, 2, 3 and 5) New skills imparted and existing skills upgraded through on-the-job training. Directly related to decent work components; programme is gender sensitive in the development of economic competencies. Traditional form of learning emphasised.	Contributes to employment and self-employment.
Hand-pumps and Barefoot Mechanics (Barefoot College).	Same as above	Contributes to self-employment.
Leather/ Food Processing (CTD).	(1, 2, 3, 4 and 6) Upgrading skills through learning-by-doing and on-the-job training. Emphasis on skills formation is on designing and production processes. Main components in decent work: promotion of rights in the workplace and social dialogue. Nature of training is need-based and flexible. Training programme creates markets; emphasises quality.	Sustenance of traditional employment / self-employment.
Flayer Co-operatives (PRADHAN).	(1, 4 and 6) Directly relevant to developing social competencies and imparting political and economic knowledge relevant to flaying activities. Democratic values and social dialogue are given very high importance since the focus here is on mobilising the flayers to form co-operatives in order to resist exploitation.	Contributes to sustaining traditional self-employment by gaining access to market in changing economy.
Rural Enterprises in Silk (PRADHAN).	(1, 2, 4 and 5) Imparts new skills and develops technical competencies by directly involving members. Reflects most of the elements of decent work. Gender issues: the project contributes to women's empowerment by developing social and economic competencies.	Creating employment opportunities by gaining access to new market spaces.
Annapurna Tiffin Supply Network (AMM).	(1, 2, 4, 5 and 6) Upgrading poor women's skills and developing their social competencies through self-esteem and self-assurance. Skills imparted through on-the-job training programmes. All elements of decent work are reflected here, since this case deals with the skills and employment-related work involved in preparing meals in big kitchens for clients. Very high importance is given to gender-related sensitivities.	The main outcome is the creation of markets and the generation of employment for women.

Micro-Credit for Women (AMM).	(1, 3, 5 and 6) Technical and social competencies are imparted, as are multiple other skills through counselling . Building leadership qualities among women entrepreneurs and providing women with legal and economic knowledge. The training is need-based and very flexible.	Contributes to self-help group solidarity. Self-employment through micro-finance and credit.
Night School and Children's Parliament (Barefoot College).	(1, 2, 4 and 5) The focus is on basic education and literacy among rural children. Hygiene, values of democracy building leadership qualities in women are the main elements of gender and decent work.	Contributes to social competencies and political awareness.
Domestic Helpers (SETU/Church).	(1, 3 and 5) Upgrading skills and developing social competencies of domestic workers through group counselling. Trains women to resist discrimination and imparts values of equality. The training and counselling is more need-based.	Enhances income and contributes to gender sensitivities, particularly resistance to discrimination.

SUMMARY OF THEMES RELEVANT TO DIFFERENT CASES

(i) More than social competencies and basic education (including literacy), the elements of actual technical skills—both learning new skills and upgrading pre-existing conventional skills—dominate the training programmes of the cases explored above. The notions of 'new' and 'upgrading' do not necessarily refer to skills which are relevant to the modern sectors or the 'upper end' of the informal sector. When a person learns a traditional skill for the first time, it is deemed a 'new' skill. Similarly, when a pre-existing conventional skill is upgraded by making very minor modifications, it is regarded as having been 'upgraded'.

(ii) The learning processes of formal institutions which focus on books, codified knowledge, classroom-based teaching and learning seems to be less meaningful and relevant to the workers in the informal sector explored above. The traditional methods of learning common to the 'master–pupil' interaction and to on-the-job training and learning which entails learning-by-doing are considered more meaningful.

(iii) The concept of 'decent work' becomes relevant through some of its elements, such as hygiene and occupational safety, democratic values, promotion of rights, non-exploitation, though all the concept's elements need not be effective at once for it to be relevant. In other words, the concept of decent work, as a strategy in training for sustainability, has yet to find a place in the main objectives and aims of organisations involved in training relevant to the informal sector.

(iv) As in the case of decent work, the concept of gender sensitivity appears to be more directly relevant at the level of NGOs and other organisations. Income generation and employment opportunities take precedence over gender issues and decent work elements in the orientation of workers in the informal sector explored. The intervention of

NGOs and intermediary organisations play an important in popularising the values of gender equality and decent work.

(v) Micro-credit institutions are seen as important actors in the development of the informal sector. The formal institutional mechanisms and sources for micro-credit and micro-finance are inadequate and underdeveloped in the informal sectors.

(vi) Much of the training given in the informal sector explored is related to generating and sustaining the traditional patterns and types of employment (leather processing, flaying, cooking, etc.), which characteristically generate low levels of income. Since the bulk of workers in the informal sectors in the rural and urban areas are illiterate and unskilled, the absence such limited training opportunities will further threaten their very survival. Herein lies the importance of providing training in various skills, knowledge and social competencies, which will contribute to workers' economic and social viability.

ROLE OF NGOs AND IMPACT OF TRAINING

It is beyond the scope of the present report to make any comprehensive assessment of the role of NGOs (including other related community-based organisations) and their impact on the larger Indian social and economic context. Remarks here will be therefore limited to the experiences based on the foregoing case studies and some secondary sources of information.

NGOs have come to occupy a significant role in the rural and poor areas of Indian society. NGOs have an edge over other formal institutions because of their ability to understand the problems of the informal sector, and their commitment to doing so. In large measure, NGOs have this advantage because of the methodology they adopt in their day-to-day operations, based on participatory research, in order to understand the rural problems. Since one of the basic features of participatory research adopted by the NGOs (amply revealed in the case studies selected in this study) so as to gain an understanding of social action and the significance of individual actors and communities, the NGOs hold a much better position compared to formal institutions when it comes to designing training programmes for skill development and support services. Moreover, when we look into the nature of the operation of NGOs in our study (i.e. the Barefoot College, AMM and STD) and the key actors, they are not only physically located in the areas of action and the workplace but are able to reorient and redesign their training programmes and methodologies as needed based on the feedback they get from the field. In large measure such involvement with the communities and the field also contributes to what is known as the 'participatory decision-making process'. This is certainly not possible for the government and other formal institutions.

While there are very few or a negligible number of training programmes and providers in the formal sector for the informal sector, the scale and skill of technologies that are being developed in formal science and technology institutions and universities do not fulfil the requirements of the informal sector. In a range of technologies—for instance, food processing, leather, textile and other manufacturing sectors—found in these formal institutions needs to be scaled down in order to suit the micro-enterprises and low scales of economy in the informal sector. This important element which is linked to employment generation and the social development of communities and individuals involves extension-based training, small incremental innovations and a great deal of co-operation with formal institutions. It is here that the NGOs are playing a significant intermediary role in the effort to bring about social and economic change in the rural communities as exemplified particularly by the Barefoot College, CTD/STD and PRADAN. For example, without the intermediary role of CTD/STD in leather, food processing and other fields, the relevance of CSIR technologies for employment generation and social change would have remained minimal or peripheral for the poor communities in several states in which such NGOs are operating.

NGOs such as the AMM, which is operating as an intermediary between the formal banks and financial institutions and poor communities (particularly with women), seem to be better placed to fulfil the social role in micro-credit financing. It is generally impossible for formal financial institutions to deal with the strata of the poor communities which these NGOs reach. Moreover, the excessive bureaucratic paperwork and counter-security systems used in formal institutions and banks are largely dispensed with in the case of NGOs or community-based organisations such as AMM. Most of the NGOs operating in micro-credit are simultaneously involved in empowering people by educating them in legal matters and by raising awareness about 'social entitlements' and welfare-oriented programmes of the government. Further, they are also undertaking various other social and economic programmes aimed at improving the livelihoods of poor people. Hence, they have an advantage over other formal institutions.

Many NGOs and rural community-based organisations, such as the Barefoot College, CTD, AMM and PRADAN, have articulated 'alternative' developmental processes at the grassroots level. This places in question the 'models of planning' and 'large organisational structures' of formal institutions with limited impact at the local level. The indirect impact of many NGOs has been to question the elitist policies of the government on developmental issues. In many cases NGOs and the rural community-based organisations stand to check and audit multinational and big corporations with regard to environmental sustainability and the exploitation of poor communities. This is evident from the activities of NGOs involved in combating bio-piracy and issues relating to bio-diversity. At the same time, there are several NGOs which have played an important role in fighting the exploitative, old 'traditions' of child labour.

Since many NGOs are largely dependent on government and private finances for their activities, there is a natural accountability system built into their system or structure of operations. Their work is not only aimed at achieving results but it must also demonstrate its credibility—which drives and governs the speed, motivation, commitment and efficiency of NGO actors. NGOs are more flexible when it comes to network with a multitude of organisations in the formal and informal sectors, financial institutions and political actors.

As for the impact of training by formal institutions on the informal sector, some views are expressed elsewhere in the report. However, it may be reiterated that much of the impact of formal institutions on the informal sector is indirect, that is to say, it is mediated by NGOs. The fact is that the main actors who have founded NGOs and are playing a leading role have been trained in formal institutions and hence that there will always be this indirect connection. Thus to assess the impact of training interventions by NGOs, it is necessary to understand both the objective and the subjective dimensions. The former relate to the absence of any accepted analysis or framework on the 'impact indicators' beyond counting the number of trainees or people being trained by the training programmes (e.g. the number of children coming out of night schools run by the Barefoot College). Secondly, it is the enhancement of the economic or income level of people who are trained that is the best objective measure or indicator of the success of training. This is evident in the case of poor people and communities being dealt with by the AMM (women entrepreneurs) and PRADAN (flayer co-operatives). Thirdly, when NGOs which are focused on training and technology dissemination such as PRADAN and CTD/STDs replicate their pilot projects and make them self-sustainable without too much financial dependency on the government or other sources, this development can be considered another good objective indicator of the success not only of training programmes offered by an NGO but also of the organisation itself.

The subjective dimensions include social mobility, the ability to communicate, the feeling of empowerment, an increase in awareness of various legal and social matters indicated by the members of the Barefoot College and the AMM. There are also other features—for example, the training and employment of the children of members of the flayers network organised by CTD/STD in the tailoring of leather goods. Similar is the example of children being trained and employed as entrepreneurs in the Annapurna Mahila Mandal Kitchen Centre in Navi Mumbai. The centre also houses 60–70 women who are involved in the supply of midday meals. Other examples are the political education and development of leadership qualities in children through the Children's Parliament programme, which is organised by the Barefoot College, Tilonia, and the education and training of domestic workers by SETU project members in Mumbai.

There are two important aspects to which Mencher (1999) draws our attention which should be underlined with respect to the role of NGOs. The first is that the micro-finance and micro-enterprise projects have a positive multiplier effect for poor people, but they also have a tendency to stabilise people at low socio-economic levels. Hence, in the interest of achieving broader, longer-term socio-economic processes of development and improvements in people's living conditions, the role of NGOs in such endeavours in the informal sector should be viewed as a 'temporary' or 'intermediary' relative to long-term strategies.

Second is that NGOs in India are becoming increasingly dependent on the public or the government, as well as private funds, and consequently are often tied to the donors' programs. Given the paucity of adequate funds and the need to pay fulltime volunteers and staff, there is definitely a tendency to compromise on what they consider to be the 'right approach' and to carry out policies and projects favoured by their donors.

BUSINESS OPPORTUNITIES THROUGH MARKETING AND BRANDING

From a business perspective, two major problems which confront the NGO-supported manufacturing and marketing units in the informal sector are the branding and marketing of products, which determine business opportunities to some extent. While advertising through commercial and private channels increases awareness about and brings some measure of popularity to products, this mode of information dissemination is generally untenable and economically unfeasible for the informal sector. Similarly, the operation of big companies in the formal business sector through a network of dealerships and franchises is also generally not feasible for the informal sector. But this does not mean that the concepts of marketing and branding are irrelevant to the informal sector. On the contrary, the significance of marketing strategies and the process of establishing brand names is becoming increasingly evident. However, the scale, method and strategies will vary from those used in the formal sector. Without making any precise prescriptions, we attempt here to document some initiatives and experiences from the case studies presented above.

CTD/STD operating in leather, fruit and vegetable processing, manufacturing and marketing with a base in the Mandi and Kullu regions in the Himachal Pradesh have already branded their products. Leather products are registered for trade under the name 'ARTISAN'S' and fruit and vegetable products are registered under the name 'FARMER'S'. CTD/STD also obtained clearance from the Fruit Products Order (FPO), which governs processed fruit, so as to conform to industry standards and government regulations to ensure minimum quality. By deciding to market products under the aforementioned brand names, NGOS have helped to ensure a certain standard of quality and taste in processed fruits and vegetables. For example, in fruit juices, jams and ketchups, the standard of quality is maintained by not adding any artificial colours, flavours or preservatives. The naturalness of the products is seen as the main factor which has aided the marketing and the establishment of the brand so far. The bulk of leather, fruit and vegetable processed items are marketed in the local Mandi and neighbouring town. For the past year an effort has been made to use CAPART and other government promotional schemes to promote the products at exhibitions in New Delhi and at international fairs. Thus use of informal channels, for example, 'word of mouth' from colleagues and friends, is also seen as an important medium for the dissemination of information about the products. Maintaining a standard in quality is seen as the key to establishing the brand name.

The Annapurna Mahila Mandal (AMM) which markets its products under a brand name which has a women as its logo, has operated for the past 25 years in the food catering business and has already established a name for itself in Maharastra, and particularly the Mumbai region. The credibility established through its credit society, which has 200,000 members, and its food supply business, which caters to an equal number or more each year, act as 'advertisement carriers' for the products marketed by the organisation. Moreover, Padma Purao, the founder and head of the AMM, has won more than 15 national and international awards, including the most prestigious 'Dr Durgabai Deshmukh Award' in 2000. News of these awards in the mass media has already given the AMM a certain renown and has a multiplier effect regarding the dissemination of information about the organisation and its services. Over the last two decades, the SWRC's handicraft products have become quite popular in Northern India and the Delhi region as Tilonia products. The SWRC has put on various exhibitions and participated in national and international fairs. As in the case of the AMM, Bunker Roy's popularity has also positively affected the branding image of the SWRC's products as Tilonia products. It should be noted that while Tilonia is not a registered brand name, it has nevertheless become popular in recent years.

Given the limited resources at the disposal of firms and enterprises in the informal sector, they have a difficulties in establishing their brands and trade names in the marketplace. Since the establishment of brands is linked to quality, taste and costly advertisement, government departments and relevant institutions, such as trade and product-based councils and export promotion councils, need to intervene.

SOME PRINCIPLES FROM SUCCESSFUL EXPERIENCES FOR REPLICATION

When we begin to explore the principles and factors behind the replication of successful experiences, it appears that the saying 'success breeds success' has some meaning in the projects covered in this study. However, it is necessary to understand various other factors. From institutions such as the Barefoot College, the AMM and PRADAN, which are more than 20 years old, it has become clear that the will, leadership and entrepreneurial ability of key actors in an organisation contributes greatly not only to the success of the organisation but also to the replicability of that success. Good examples of this are found in the likes of Bunker Roy and Padma Purao in our case studies, as well as Ela Bhatt of SEWA.

The second factor of importance here is credibility. The principal actors in the Barefoot College and the AMM have generated tremendous good will and confidence among people over the years due to their good work, commitment and ability to understand problems from other people's point of view, and this has contributed immensely to their credibility. Closely associated with this is the method of participatory research adopted in projects covered in this study. Not only have they established their credibility with society; they have also won a good deal of respect from the donors and formal organisations which have sponsored various projects over the years.

Thirdly, it has been found that scaling down technology to fit the rural situation plays an important role; and this is intimately connected with leadership and entrepreneurship. Taken together, what is crucial is the 'management of rural innovation'. This is evident from the experiences of the Barefoot College in the area of solar energy and CTD/STD's leather projects in replicating their models in other areas. The assumption that projects in the informal sector can be executed without professional input, skill, technology or managerial abilities is simply false. Even in the case of diffusing solar energy devices in the hilly regions and in training barefoot solar engineers, in the initial stages the Barefoot College received very high professional input on the relevant technologies. That the Barefoot College was able to replicate this project successfully points to their ability to demystify the maintenance of technology and to popularise it among laypersons. As for the scaling down of technology-related projects (e.g. CTD/STD cases in replicating leather and food processing units), the economics of project implementation was an important factor.

Fourthly, what is common to all the aforementioned case studies and projects, which have had a fair degree of success in replication, is the quality of training given to workers in informal sector projects and the leadership qualities learned from the leading actors of the chief organisations. Our interviews with some of the key individuals indicate that, more than the internalisation of leadership qualities, there are role models who govern and motivate their actions.

Lastly, support from the relevant formal departments and institutions of the government (CAPART, Ministry of Rural Development, DST and CSIR) is one of the most crucial factors in the chain of events responsible for ability of NGOs such as the Barefoot College, PRADAN and CTD/STD to replicate their successful experiences. No less important is the networking carried out by the NGOs, particularly their leading actors.

CONCLUDING REMARKS: LESSONS, CONCEPTS AND POLICY IMPLICATIONS

When we examine the educational and training needs of workers in the informal sector and the access they have to these sources of skill development, the picture is rather gloomy. An overview of major constraints and recommendations is given in Table 6.

Table 6. Constraints and Recommendations

	Constraints	Recommendations
i	Handicaps and lack of provisions in formal institutions for training workers in the informal sector.	Identify NGOs to be charged with the task of training using public funds but give relative autonomy. NGOs can play a vital role here. Identify educational institutions to be used for training workers during evenings and out of office hours. Need replication of 'barefoot colleges' and centres in rural and urban centres.
ii	Lack of technology upgrading in the informal sector and lack of impact of technology from formal institutions due to scale.	The links between NGOs and institutions like CAPART needs to be strengthened in order to make technology more relevant for employment generation. Promote S&T-based NGOs to bridge 'gaps' between formal and informal sectors along the lines of CTD/STD.
iii	Lack of branding and marketing systems for products in the informal sector.	Form associations with state government support to deal with marketing and use state-run mass media to advertise products from the informal sector.
iv	Insufficient avenues for micro-credit and constraints by bureaucracy.	Established NGOs should be mobilised to expand their operations. Reorient rules in formal financial institutions to suit the workers in the informal sector. Urgently need to promote women and micro-credit NGOs along the lines of AMM/SEWA.
v	Low level of skills in traditional apprenticeships in the informal sector.	Evolve programmes to train 'master' craftsmen/women to enhance their own skill levels in order to transmit their skills to other workers.
vi	Lack of awareness of legal norms and government programmes for workers.	Need to evolve methodologies for the dissemination of relevant information and for the education of workers.
vii	Weak role of universities and S&T institutions.	One-tenth of the efforts of these institutions needs to be devoted to informal sector programmes to enhance their 'neighbourhood effect'. Adult education programmes need to incorporate training in technical skills relevant to new technologies..

People in the informal sector have little or no access to education and training or to training programmes run by public institutions. Consequently, the groups which are most active in skill development and educational and training programmes for workers in the informal sector are the NGOs. However, since most of the NGOs involved in such training and skill development are dependent on governmental agencies such as DST, CAPART and the Ministry of Rural Development for funds, the role of the latter needs to be expanded significantly. There are good reasons to believe that government should develop appropriate policies for identifying NGOs to be charged with the 'task' of education, training and skill development in non-formal institutional ways for the informal sector.

Much of the training in technical and social competencies undertaken by NGOs is given in on-the-job training and apprenticeships where 'learning by doing' and 'learning by interaction' play an important role. The 'new role of NGOs' for imparting outside-job training and skill development programmes should make use of the existing formal schools and institutions in the evening or 'out of office hours'. Not only is the Barefoot College's night schools programme the most appropriate example along these lines, but the Barefoot College itself is the most relevant model for evolving policies directed at institutional innovations in adult and non-formal education in the informal sector. There is no shortcut to aiding and developing the informal sector; the only way to succeed is to provide training and skill development by non-formal means.

Another important lesson taught by the experiences of the Barefoot College is the way in which the college has been able to 'demystify technology' for ordinary people in rural areas and train barefoot solar engineers, hand-pump mechanics, communicators, construction engineers, etc. The college has successfully 'demystified' the conventional assumption that 'technical competencies' and 'technical learning' can be transmitted only through professional and formal institutional mechanisms and means. Here one thinks of a whole range of technical and installation procedures involved in the technologies and devices used in the rural context of industrialisation. By training barefoot engineers and skilled personnel in a range of trades, the college has established a new institutional and conceptual basis for understanding how 'learning by doing' and 'learning by interaction' work in the case of technology dissemination in rural contexts. Together with the Barefoot College and CTD, the important work of Honey Bee Network and GIAN (on these NGOs, see the author's article in Section 1 above) in documenting grassroots innovations and creating viable channels for their transformation into micro- and small enterprises by imparting skills and training also provides an important institutional context for linking formal and informal sectors in the rural knowledge economy for the benefit of those rural communities.

By the same token, the experiences of the AMM also holds many lessons concerning areas of micro-credit and the development of women entrepreneurs for micro-enterprises (in the meals and Tiffin supply networks). The AMM has facilitated women in getting micro-credit for the past 25 years. In a very innovative manner, this NGO has shown how the objectives of training in 'social' and 'collective' competencies (including leadership) can be combined with micro-financing in the informal sector by designing appropriate methods of loan disbursement to groups of women from a particular local area. These methods also give new insights into the recovery of loans by means of an intra-group accountability system orchestrated by the group's leader and other group members. Recurring loans of higher amounts to group members are tied to the repayment obligations of members in the group. This is said to have reinforced the accountability system. The experiences of the AMM and a well-documented case of SEWA, Ahmedabad, have demonstrated the sustainable role of NGOs in micro-credit finance for the informal sector, which formal financial institutions have yet to penetrate due to several bureaucratic problems with guarantee mechanisms. These NGOs have, each in its own way, evolved appropriate methods for the disbursement and recovery of loans at much lower rates of interest than formal financial institutions. These provide relevant examples in micro-credit finance for the development of policies and their promotion in the much larger context of the informal sector, where it is particularly pressing that women workers be trained in entrepreneurship.

One of the major problems in diffusing relevant technologies (e.g. in leather, food processing, building and manufacturing) available or developed in the formal science and technology institutions to enterprises in the informal sector concerns a whole range of extension services, including scaling down the technology to suit micro-level enterprise, upgrading traditional skills to manage technical processes, training in suitable alternative technical processes to traditional processes and networking with formal technology support institutions for 'venture capital' and 'risk aversion' funding. CTD/STD and PRADAN have demonstrated that NGOs are better placed in accomplishing the task of technology diffusion to the informal sector since these organisations have developed certain 'organisational core competencies' which are not generally possible for formal institutions. For example, in the case of diffusing improved vegetable tanning processes for leather, which replaced the traditional and more cumbersome process, the aforementioned organisations helped to establish flayer co-operatives and networks so as to eliminate 'middlemen' in Uttar Pradesh and Himachal Pradesh. In the case of CTD/STD, it combined the training in developing social and technical competencies in the artisans and created nodal tanning centre at Mandi which served as a model to replicate self-sustaining tanning centres in more than 20 towns and villages in India. Without the intervention of CTD/STD, the impact of CLRI technology to improve and sustain the social and economic conditions of flayers and tanners in Himachal and other states would not have been possible. The case of CTD/STD in leather and food processing clearly demonstrates the new role of NGOs in 'consultancy for technology diffusion to the informal sector' and in bridging the 'communication and structural gaps' between the formal and the informal sectors.

Another important problem confronted by the informal sector units is the lack of adequate support for business opportunities through branding of products and marketing channels. In our case studies, CTD/STD as a nodal NGO, which is co-ordinating the activities of several independent small NGO enterprises in leather and food processing had taken upon itself the responsibility to register common brands (ARTISAN'S for leather products; and FARMER'S for fruit and vegetable processed products). But discussions held with various actors involved in the informal sector, reveals the need for co-operative marketing channels promoted by local or state governments and a certain quota of assured procurement of products. The individual state governments and central agencies also need to provide a space in the state controlled mass media for advertising the products from the informal sector till such time the industry is able to absorb the advertisement rents. Rather, training, 'de-scaling' technology to suit small enterprises or upgrading traditional technology, co-operative marketing operations including quality control measures need to be organised in the mode of clusters at the regional level. So far, the support of government agencies is only limited to promotion of products from the small and cottage sector at exhibitions in India and abroad.

Urbanisation and relative economic prosperity of Indian middle class in the recent years created a 'new' demand for domestic workers. The increasing use of mechanical and electronic gadgets, changing food habits and increasing need for child care at home for working mothers in cities has created a demand for training domestic workers in various skill based operations and safety regulations dealing with electric appliances and other objects of daily use. Similarly, new skill based sectors in automobile, construction, electrical, chemical, manufacturing etc in urban centres threaten the migrant workers whose skill base is either very low or absent. There is a need for formal and relevant institutions to urgently look into this new demand pattern.

The ongoing processes of globalisation and opening up of the economy as a result of liberalisation policies is likely to have a serious impact on the developing countries like India. The comparative advantages enjoyed by countries like India due to labour costs is seriously threatened under globalisation. Small sector units which in-turn are dependent on micro level informal sector units are already facing tough competition from imported Chinese goods in a range of manufactured items. In other words, the advantage of cheap labour, natural and local resource endowments for small production units, on which a significant proportion of the informal sector sustains, is not going to last very long. The relevance of new technologies particularly in information and communication technologies, biotechnologies and micro electronics to workers and units in informal sector will depend on the level of skills and their ability to adapt them. There is already a discourse emerging on the question of inequalities and new technologies in the Indian context. In the long run, it is value addition through technical change, skills, organisational and entrepreneurial abilities will increasingly determine business and economic prospects and hence the sustainability factor. It is here that the role of education and training strategies will determine the future prospects of India's informal sector.

REFERENCES

Arunachalam, J., & Azad, N. (1985). Role of women and children in the informal sector. *Productivity*, *26*, 273–76.

Banerjee, B.(1982). The weakest link. In H. I. Safa (ed.), *Towards a political economy of urbanisation in third world countries* (pp. 175–87). New Delhi: Oxford University Press.

Bhattacharya, K. P., & Dey, P. (1991). Problems of hawkers in Calcutta: A case study. *The Indian Journal of Social Science*, *4:2*, 307–19.

Breman, J. (1996). *Footloose labour: Working in India's informal economy*. Cambridge: Cambridge University Press.

Burckhardt, G. (1997), The acquisition of competencies by women in the urban informal sector in Rwanda. *Education*, *55–56*, 113–130.

Chadha, G. K. (1997). Informal sector in the Indian economy: A study of Khadi textiles. Paper presented at National Workshop on the 'Strategic Approach to Job Creation in the Urban Informal Sector in India', Organised by ILO, New Delhi, February 17–19, Surajkund, Haryana.

Corvalan, O. V. (1997). Education and training for the informal sector: Comments on the Focus Reader of the series. *Education, 55–56*, 9–21.

Das, B. (1994). Socio-economic study of slums in Surat City. Surat: Centre for Social Studies (Mimeograph).

Damodaran, S. (2000). The urban informal sector in India: A case study of the leather and leather products industry. Paper presented at National Workshop on the 'Strategic Approach to Job Creation in the Urban Informal Sector in India', Organised by ILO, New Delhi, February 17–19, Surajkund, Haryana.

Dewan, R. (2000). Organised production and unorganised producers in the informal food processing industry. Paper presented at National Workshop on the 'Strategic Approach to Job Creation in the Urban Informal Sector in India', Organised by ILO, New Delhi, February 17–19, Surajkund, Haryana.

ILO. (2000). National workshop on the strategic approach to job creation in the urban informal sector in the urban informal sector in India. 17–19 February, Surajkund, Haryana, India. New Delhi: ILO.

ILO. (1999). *Decent work*. Report of the Director-General, International Labour Conference, 87th Session. Geneva: ILO.

ILO. (1998). *World Employment Report 1998–99. Employability in the global economy: How training matters*. Geneva: ILO.

Kundu, A. (1993). *In the name of urban poor: Access to basic amenities*. New Delhi: Sage Publications.

Kundu, A. (1999). Urban informal sector in India: Macro-trends and policy perspectives. *Issues in development discussion paper, 25*. Geneva: ILO.

Kumar, N. (2000). New technology-based small service enterprises and employment: The case of software and related services industry. Paper presented at National Workshop on the 'Strategic Approach to Job Creation in the Urban Informal Sector in India', Organised by ILO, New Delhi, February 17–19, Surajkund, Haryana.

Lenhart, V. (1997). Vocational training for the informal sector: A typology. *Education, 55–56*, 25–34.

Mencher, J. (1997). NGOs: Are they a force for change? *Economic and Political Weekly, 34:30*, 2081–86.

Nagraj, R. (1984). Sub-contracting in Indian manufacturing industries. Analysis, evidence and issues. *Economic and Political Weekly*, 21:31-33, 1435-53.

National Council of Educational Research and Training (NCERT). (1990). *Vocationalisation of education: Achievements in the seventh five-year plan*. New Delhi: NCERT.

PRADHAN. (1997–98). *Annual Report, PRADAN, 1997–98*. New Delhi: PRADHAN.

Raghunandan, D. (2000). Best practices in technology dissemination for rural industries: National scenario in India. Paper presented at APCTT Workshop on Best Practice for Technology Delivery aimed at Promoting Rural and Small Industries, Bogor, Indonesia, December 1–2.

Roy, S. (1996). De-mystification of SPVs to provide lighting: An example of community-supported on-site initiate in Ladakh in the Indian Himalayas. *Energy for sustainable development, 2:5*, 45–52.

Singhania, S. S. (1997). The dynamism of the informal sector. Paper presented at seminar organised at New Delhi by Institute of Applied Manpower Research (IAMR) and Institute for Human Development (IHD), New Delhi.

Singh, S. (2000). Informal tourism sector in India: A case of Jaipur and Agra. Paper presented at National Workshop on the 'Strategic Approach to Job Creation in the Urban Informal Sector in India', Organised by ILO, New Delhi, February 17–19, Surajkund, Haryana.

Singh, M. (1997). Processes of education and training in the context of local self-help organisations in the informal sector. *Education, 55–56*, 56–69.

Singh, M. (ed.). (1999). *Adult learning and the future of work*. Hamburg: Unesco Institute for Education.

Singh, M. (2001). Reflections on colonial legacy and dependency in Indian vocational education and training (VET): A societal and cultural perspective. *Journal of Education and Work, 14:2*, 209–25.

EDUCATIONAL REFORM FOR LINKING SKILLS DEVELOPMENT WITH EMPLOYMENT IN NEPAL

Poorna K. Adhikary

DEVELOPMENT OF THE EDUCATIONAL SYSTEM

In ancient Nepal the educational system was based on Hindu and Buddhist philosophy. Education was not vocational in character. Within the Hindu *Varna* system, vocations such as metal-works, leather crafts and tailoring were considered the work of low caste people. Sanskrit education was based on the *Veda* and Hindu classics for proficiency in Sanskrit grammar, literature, astronomy, while Buddhist monastery schools (*Gombas*) placed emphasis on the practice of rituals, meditation and a high proficiency in mathematics. Sanskrit schools (*Pathasala*) were opened for the higher caste Hindus, whereas Buddhist *Gombas* were more liberal and open to all (Vir, 1988). Even today this is evident in Buddhist societies in Asia. For instance, Japan, China, Thailand and Sri Lanka have a much higher literacy rate and education level than Hindu and Muslim societies. In ancient Nepal, *gurus* in *Gurukul* (schools in which education is based on the teaching of Hindu classics) provided Sanskrit education, whereas *lamas* in *Gombas* provided Buddhist education.

A systematic Western type of formal education started in the 1940s (Aryal, 1970; NEPC, 1956; Vir, 1988), but for the general masses it began only after 1951, when people took the initiative to build schools in their communities. Formal education was institutionalised chronologically from the pre-primary to tertiary level through structured educational systems.

The Higher Secondary Education Board (HSEB) was established for the purpose of preparing students for the world of work, especially for meeting middle-level manpower requirements in different fields, and of preparing students for a general higher education in various professional disciplines (MOE, 2000). Most of such schools have been established as private ventures and are often very expensive for the general public. Financial support from the government to higher secondary education, support which is to provide assistance to poor students, is minimal or non-existent.

FAILURE OF THE FORMAL EDUCATIONAL SYSTEM TO PREPARE A SKILLED WORKFORCE

Knowledge, skills and attitudes make up the fundamental capabilities which enable individuals to learn, re-learn, re-assess and react to change for an improved lifestyle. As is evident from the foregoing, a considerable degree of effort has been exerted in

Madhu Singh, (ed.), Meeting Basic Learning Needs in the informal Sector, 215-228.

this direction in the field of educational development in Nepal. However, the results of the efforts made so far are not as encouraging as expected.

The National Planning Commission (NPC) and United Nation's Children's Fund (UNICEF) report (UNICEF & NPC, 1996) estimated that only three-quarters of Nepali children aged 6–10 years were enrolled in primary schools. Almost one million children of that age group are still outside of primary education. Of the total enrolment in the primary level, 47 percent are dropouts (MOE, 2000). Only 26 percent of the secondary-school-aged pupils were enrolled at the lower secondary level, and 16 percent were enrolled at the secondary level (UNDP, 1998). These data show that a large number of children either do not join school or are unable to get through even the primary level of education. They are simply pushed out by the school system.

According to the High Level Education Commission Report of 1998, the causes of low quality of the education provided in the entire public educational system are: the high rate of wastage made visible by grade repetition and dropouts, the low quality of physical facilities in the schools, poor academic and pedagogical activities; an excessive number of untrained teachers, teacher absenteeism and ineffective supervision.

The National Education System Plan (NESP, 1971–76) made an effort to set up an integrated system with many attractive methodologies, such as building schools in rural communities. However, the biggest mistake made in this effort was the centralisation of school management, whereby the government took control by nationalising all schools and colleges, even though they were initially built and managed by the local communities. The schools were simply taken away from the community.

The centralised administration could not manage the educational system effectively. Local participation, cost sharing and local controlling mechanisms disappeared completely. The teachers who were previously highly respected by communities as social leaders for change simply became civil servants. Their loyalty to their communities became loyal to government bureaucrats. The student revolt of the late 1970s caused the government to loose its grip on the teacher and student population. As a result the whole public school system was overtly politicised. Since then, the accountability of teachers has come into question and many of them have been found involved in party politics rather than in teaching.

A huge amount of resources invested in the educational system has resulted in waste from the primary to tertiary levels. As a result the quality of public education declined seriously, which generated enormous anxiety among parents. This forced them to turn to private schools.

Due to the failure of the public educational system, the private school system, which initially was confined to a few elite in urban areas, spread all over the country, and this gave rise to the trap of two extremes: extremely inefficient public schools and extremely commercialised private schools. The question now is: Where should people go, since the public system has become non-functional and the private system is so expensive?

Although university education has been expanding over the last decade, only 0.83 percent of the total population has obtained a Bachelor's Degree (0.44%

women and 1.29% men) (UNDP, 1998). Apart from gender and socio-economic status, ethnic and geographical inequalities are even more serious.

The situation is further aggravated by the fact that teaching places more emphasis on textbooks than on skill development. This applies to the whole educational spectrum, from the primary level to university education. As a consequence, thousands of people who ultimately graduate from the formal educational system are unskilled. They lack specific skills which could help them secure gainful employment.

Such a training mainly targets the white-collar jobs in the formal market or public sector, which is already too small to offer opportunities to all those who aspire to work in it. The situation becomes worse for socially and economically disadvantaged segments of the population, which are prevalent not only in Nepal but also in many developing countries. Receiving a full basic education does not guarantee that one will obtain the basic skills necessary for making a living. In Nepal only 16 percent of the age-specific group is enrolled in the secondary education. For the others, the vast majority of whom are pushed or thrown out of the school system, there is hardly any programme worth mentioning. This represents an enormous challenge for those involved in organising the productive incorporation of the vast majority of the disadvantaged population in the workforce.

As such, formal education is not providing the needed skills and competencies to prepare school graduates for their incorporation within the world of work. Educated unemployed youth, particularly those from socially and economically disadvantaged communities, have become a grave problem in Nepal. Being the most vulnerable, they also pose serious security problems. Thus far adult education has focused on literacy only, which does not provide employable or self-employable skills. Many of the training programmes end up in 'target traps', training for the sake of training just to fulfil the targets set up by training providers. Most of the skills development programmes result in training courses which have no strategic relationship to developmental programmes or market demands. The consequence has been a big gap between the world of education and the world of work. Bridging this gap in a meaningful way is the greatest challenge facing Nepal today.

FLOATING POPULATION IN SEARCH OF EMPLOYMENT

Since accessibility is limited to a small fraction of the population, in Nepal, as in so many places in the Third World, too many teenaged or younger boys and girls are employed in household jobs, as domestic servants in restaurants and lodges, as well as in the transport sector and in carpet factories. They have generally dropped out or been pushed out of school and have socio-economic hardships at home.

Limited employment opportunities in the formal sector and the absence of employable skills means that most young educated people must go abroad to search for gainful employment. There is also a great deal of migration of such youths to India and recently to the Middle East, Japan, Southeast Asia, Korea, Europe and America. Many of them lack appropriate skills, which forces them to take up cheap and difficult jobs (Pradhan et al., 2001).

They are generally absorbed in the informal and domestic sectors, where the terms and conditions of work are very poor and where they are employed as shepherds, construction workers, agricultural labourers and household servants. They often end up in situations worse than the ones they leave. Hence, people faced with such hardships feel cheated by the education system.

There is also a serious problem with Kamaiyas, who until recently were bonded labourers. Thousands of Kamaiyas families were freed in 2000 by the government. Although they were traditionally engaged as agricultural labourers, they have no access to land of their own in order to continue to engage in such work. Since they have no other marketable skills, and in the absence of alternate employment opportunities, the former Kamaiyas have great difficulties in finding livelihood. This underscores the necessity of providing rural people with employable skills.

BRIDGING FORMAL, NON-FORMAL AND INFORMAL EDUCATION

In light of the aforementioned problems, it is imperative that education, both in content and form, correspond to the needs of the workplace. The educational system should prepare a man to be productive and useful. There must be correspondence between the organisation of the workplace and the organisation of schools. This calls for a more dynamic educational structure, one capable of addressing the needs of the job market.

The National Education Commission Report of 1992 recommended a diversified structure in the overall educational system. The proposed structure tries to promote possibilities for flexible co-lateral entry with open-entry and open-exit (with bridge lines and courses), from one educational stream to another, incorporating formal, non-formal and informal education, including technical education and vocational training. However, the government still has a long way to go in order to effectively implement this structure. Although the bridge-course concept exists in the policy of engineering education, it has yet to benefit most of the technical and vocational learners.

Technical schools and skill training centres run by various government departments, international non-governmental organisations and private organisations provide long-term and short-term training programmes. Long-term training programmes are generally formal in nature and last one to three years, while short-term training programmes in informal and non-formal settings last from one week to three months. These courses cover skill training in the areas of agriculture, rural construction, carpentry, stone carving, electronics, mechanical maintenance, water supply, sanitation, plumbing, tailoring and tourism, including trekking, lodge management, rafting, resort management, entertainment and wildlife observation (Kafle, 1989; Pradhan et al., 2000). All these training programmes are believed to have had a positive impact on the informal economic sector as trained people are mostly employed or self-employed in the related enterprises.

However, to make formal, non-formal and informal education complementary to one another, it is necessary to establish bridges between them by opening co-lateral entry options. A brief analysis of this is presented below. Through meaningful intervention, reforms can open opportunities to a wider cross-section of the population.

TECHNICAL EDUCATION AND VOCATIONAL TRAINING

It was with the recommendation of the National Education Planning Commission (1956) that institutionalised vocational education come into effect. With the support of the United States Government, multipurpose high schools were established in various parts of the country and vocational teachers were trained in the National Vocational Training Centre (NVTC) in the fields of home economics, industry, business and agriculture. The objectives of NVTC as cited by Belbase (1981) were: to provide facilities for training vocational teachers for the multipurpose school system; to serve as the national centre for in-service training for vocational teachers; to train students in basic skilled-worker courses; to co-operate with the model multipurpose secondary school for the purpose of practice teaching opportunities; to provide skill improvement courses for workers in the industry; to train students for supervisory and junior executive positions; and to train students in various courses for industry, agriculture, business and home economics. But these centres were limited to only a few schools. In addition, the focus was on non-vocational areas as opposed to vocational trades. The system was short-lived.

In an endeavour to revive an effective educational system, a higher level Education Commission was formed in 1998. The 1998 Commission Report states that a policy will be adopted for the preparation of a nation-wide network of technical education and vocational training centres, schools and polytechnics by launching basic level training nation-wide which culminates in lower- to higher-level diplomas (HEC Report, 1998) for the illiterate, as well as for those who have completed the tenth class of basic education. However, the efforts and commitments made so far have not made the contribution to educational reform envisaged by the Report.

The only prominent agency involved in implementing this endeavour is the Council for Technical Education and Vocational Training (CTEVT), which offers a full-fledged long-term technical training programme leading to a diploma for 2,500 regular students and 4,000 short-term trainees annually. Similarly, more than 150 CTEVT-affiliated private technical schools are scattered throughout Nepal and provide vocational training opportunities for about 12,000 students annually (Adhikary, Belbase & Pradhan, 2000). In addition to this, the CTEVT also provides training opportunities through Vocational Training and Community Development (VTCD) centres. Unlike other long-term training programmes, the VTCD centres provides short-term training opportunities ranging from one week to a few months.

Only about 3,000 technicians receive post-secondary education in health, agriculture, education, law, engineering, business management and forestry from 22 colleges of Tribhuvan University, the largest academic establishment in the country. Under the Ministry of Education (MOE), 14 percent of the vocational subjects are provided by 2,309 secondary schools for 290,143 students. Kathmandu University, at its own campus and affiliated ones, provides courses in engineering, education, business management and medicine.

Recognising the fact that training alone cannot create employment, the government often places emphasis on providing training to the poor. Often its targets have been unrealistic, however. There has been an absence of co-ordination among the training institutions (Adhikary, Belbase & Pradhan, 2000) combined with unplanned training programmes. This has been already shown by the investment made through Employment Promotion Committee (EPC).

Recently the EPC has sought to provide training in the information technology sector by linking it with certain market segments. A question often raised is whether their major role is to provide training or to develop the favourable policy framework for the effective participation of other training providers, both in the public and the private sectors.

All the data and information indicate that a large number of organisations in the country are involved in training activities which provide training and skill upgrading opportunities. Considerable investments of time, money and energy have been made by the public and the private sectors to develop technical education and vocational training (TEVT) in Nepal. In the absence of data, it is difficult to say how much is annually invested by the private sector in the TEVT sub-sector. His Majesty's Government (HMG) invests more than one billion Nepalese Rupees for training programmes of various kinds (Pradhan et al., 2000). Unfortunately, these training programmes are not co-ordinated. These are piecemeal investments. On the other hand, from 1991 to 1999 the MOE's budget for the TEVT programme has ranged from 1 to 1.4 percent of the total education budget. This indicates that the education sector has been overly biased in favour of formal education, which receives 97.5 percent of the total education budget (Adhikary, Belbase & Pradhan, 2000). At the same time, this shows insignificant government commitment to the diversification of education in order to meet the country's needs.

Another important challenge for the TEVT system is to control the quality of training provided by public and private TEVT institutions. Because of the diversity of rapidly growing institutions, standardisation and control of programme quality has become a difficult task. Most of these training programmes are available for urban areas or people in district headquarters and in their vicinity, whereas people in the rural areas—who make up the majority of the Nepali population—still lack access to appropriate training programmes. On the other hand, although curriculum has been introduced in the newly founded trades, the curriculum of CTEVT-managed training schools and many other training institutions has not been modified since their interception. This gives rise to doubt over its efficiency in meeting market needs.

Additionally, there has yet to be a study of the exact market needs in the country, and this has meant a gross mismatch between training provided and demands in the world of work. The result has been a wasteful use of resources. For trainees, it has been a source of frustration during the training course since they build expectations of better livelihood that are ultimately not met.

The problems in the TEVT sub-sector can be summarised as follows: The training system is unable to co-ordinate the various training providers. There are weak linkages between training providers and employers. In addition, there is an inefficient use of resources, making the training programmes too costly. Finally, a lack of reliable and up-to-date labour market information places in doubt the sustainability of the training programmes.

NON-FORMAL EDUCATION

Non-formal education is any organised, systematic educational activity carried on outside the framework of the formal system and which aims to provide selected types of learning to particular subgroups in the population, adults as well as children. The objectives of non-formal education, as practised in Nepal, are to provide educational opportunities to out-of-school children and youth aged 8–14 years and functional literacy classes to adults aged 15–45. To make the efforts more effective, a series of reading materials and a number of associated learning activities have been designed for neo-literates so that they can apply their functional knowledge and skills. Local NGO support has also been mobilised to carry out different non-formal educational programmes in various parts of Nepal.

However, as in many other developing countries, it has been difficult to measure the dimension of social awareness, community development and increased agricultural productivity influenced by non-formal education (McGrath et al., 1995). The Nepal study showed that farmers were able to supplement their income through non-agricultural work (UNESCO, 1997). For example, 12.8 percent were found to have opened teashops and other retail business after non-formal training, and 4.2 percent found jobs upon attaining functional literacy training. Another positive impact of adult education programmes was a decrease in the rate of infant mortality.

Non-formal education learners have a significant impact on the informal sector by encouraging their partners, family members and community members in the utilisation of micro-credits for gainful economic activities. This makes non-formal education effective even for those who are unable to access formal education.

INFORMAL EDUCATION, TRAINING AND SKILLS TESTING

Informal education is a lifelong process by which every person acquires and accumulates knowledge, skills, attitudes and insights from daily experiences and exposure to the environment. Such experience and learning may take place at any time, in any setting, at the learner's and the trainer's convenience.

For centuries the tradition of learning employable and occupational skills from parents, senior professionals, and peers has existed in Nepal. Informal learning has been an integral part of life and remains a source of skills in many crafts, trades, agriculture and modern industries. In many cases learners can acquire various skills at their own convenience, through practical work, even with a minimum of theoretical knowledge. Such learning takes place in traditional settings, such as in families and communities of peasants, on farm, in artisans', artists', craftsmen's and tradesmen's workshops (Kafle, 1989).

Accreditation of Skills Acquired through Informal Learning

The National Skill Testing Committee (formerly the National Skill Testing Board) has developed and implemented skill-testing activities at various levels, especially in the sectors of agriculture, health, general maintenance, crafts and industry. The primary objective of this committee is to identify, recognise, and certify the youths who have acquired the skills through informal learning, on-the-job training, informal apprenticeship training or in-plant learning. Such tests are conducted regularly. This facilitates obtaining paid employment and/or self-employment. Certificates are recognised by the Public Service Commission of the government, semi- and non-governmental organisations, as well as private industries. The development of job specification, standardisation and accreditation has enabled employers to recruit qualified skilled workers. Similarly, it has enabled newly certified youths to start a new job, be promoted or be transferred to a more rewarding one. According to CTEVT, a skill test is a test of equivalency based on a skill standard which must be met in order to obtain a national certificate. It indicates that the certificate holder meets the requirement of a trade/occupation. Such tests are open to all workers. Workers do not need a formal education to take the test. The advantages of the skill test are many: Traditional skills and crafts can be nationally recognised. Demands of labour market can be met without formal training. The levels of the technician occupation can be certified in keeping with the demands of the domestic and international markets, thereby increasing productivity.

The eligibility criteria for the national skill test are specified. A minimum of one year's experience in a related occupation is required to be eligible for Level 1. Like wise, the applicants for Level 2 are required to be literate, able to read and write, have knowledge and skill in the relevant occupation and a minimum of three year's work experience in a related occupation. Finally, to be eligible for Level 3 the candidate should be literate, have knowledge and skill in the relevant occupation and a minimum of five year's work experience in a related occupation. As reported by Skill Testing Division (STD) of CTEVT, thus far 106 occupational standards have been developed and 7,423 people have passed various tests. More than 99 percent are employed in paid jobs or self-employed micro-enterprises (Adhikary, 2001).

The creation of the National Skill Testing Committee has been an innovative effort to encourage informal learners to gain certification and be recognised for employment at various levels in both the private and the public sectors. This system has made an important link between formal, non-formal and informal education by providing a nationally certified, recognised and accredited system for certain jobs up to Level 3 in crafts, industries, agriculture and the health sector (Pradhan et al., 2000).

REFORM OF THE EDUCATIONAL SYSTEM

As a signatory of the Jomtiem Declaration for Education for All (UNESCO, 1990), His Majesty's Government of Nepal (HMG/N) set a target of achieving a 67 percent literacy rate by 2000 through the universalisation of basic and primary education. Despite the attempts made thus far, progress has been quite slow. Barely 50 percent of the population labelled literate is able to sign their name.

Although the government has placed strong emphasis on formal education, with 97.5 percent of the education budget (MOE Budget, 1999–2000) being devoted to this sector, it has not sufficiently prepared graduates for employment in the job market. Nearly 30 percent of children (i.e. nearly one million) do not even have access to school (UNICEF, 1996). Of those who enter the first grade, only 20 percent complete the primary education through the fifth grade. It is estimated that barely 16 percent complete tenth grade level education (MOE, 1998).

The formal educational system currently caters to about 25 percent of the population. For the remaining 75 percent, the Ministry of Education has only 2.5 percent (1.4% for TEVT and 1.1% for non-formal education) of the budget left. Unfortunately, this population is dependent on the employment market (Adhikary, Belbase & Pradhan, 2000). Obviously this limited budget is insufficient for meeting the learning needs of those who enter the employment market as unskilled workers.

Thus a huge gap, in terms of budgetary provision, exists between the world of work and the world of formal education, which hardly provides any skill training. At the same time, the formal economy is expanding slowly, making the country heavily dependent upon the informal sector.

Reconciliation of Formal and Informal Educational Systems

In view of the urgent need for poverty eradication and economic development in the country, the TEVT sub-sector is important as a bridge between formal education and the job market. Non-formal education could act as a bridge between formal education and TEVT, as demonstrated in the following figure. However, this restructuring of the educational system would need corresponding investments in these sub-sectors. Such a scheme would not only orient those who leave school at various levels to the job market but also allow individuals to make use of training and education opportunities vertically through collateral entry possibilities. Non-formal education can provide bridge courses to facilitate an individual's collateral entry. In this way education can allow the growth of individuals both horizontally and vertically.

Figure 1. Inter-relations among Formal Education (FE), Non-Formal Education (NFE), Technical Education and Vocational Training (TEVT) and the Job Market/Workplace

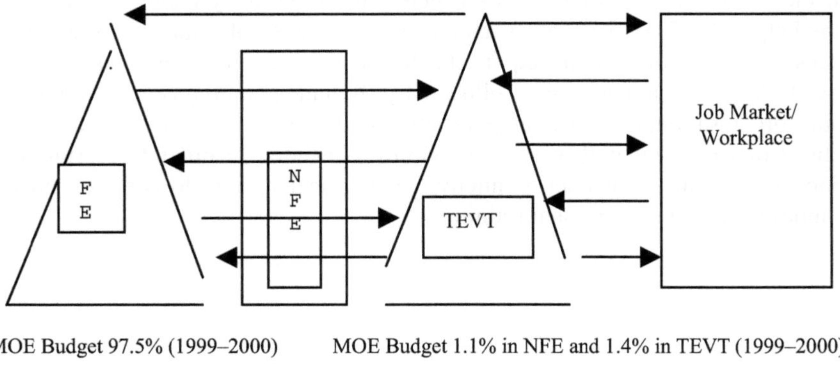

Incorporation of Traditional Skills in the Curriculum

Within both academic and non-academic educational systems, curriculum should compulsorily incorporate information about traditional skills. The CTEVT should design curriculum in such a way that the trainees in trades like construction and carpentry receive traditional skills. Due to the relatively high costs of implementing vocational training programmes, it has not been possible for many private parties to offer them. There is limited availability of government training opportunities. This means that they have been unable to reach many people. Therefore, to open opportunities to many areas, dovetailing should be tried on an experimental basis.

Integration of the VTCD Model in the TEVT System

The vast majority of the Nepalese population is outside the formal educational system. The MOE's concerns are overwhelmingly focused on formal education. There are no signs that this focus will change soon. This present paper argues that there is a need for the MOE to clarify its position on addressing the educational needs of the population outside the formal educational system. If it wants to meet the needs of these people, there should be a significant shift in educational investment such that there is a significant increase in investment in the non-formal and TEVT educational systems. If this is not implemented, then the MOE should dispense with its role in dealing with people outside the formal educational structure. HMG/N should look into the issue of education for all, to which it is a signatory, so as to address the basic educational and livelihood needs of the majority of population, which works in the informal sector.

From the foregoing, it is clear that skills training and upgrading is needed for a large proportion of the population engaged in the informal economic sector. This could be one means of providing formal and non-formal education to the vast majority of the population in rural and remote areas. The tested VTCD model could be integrated into the CTEVT structure and linked to local-level development institutions such as District Development Committees (DDCs), Village Development Committees (VDCs) and municipalities, as shown in Figure 2.

Since the DDCs and VDCs know more about the local market needs, they should design the skills training programmes which could effectively address such needs with the help of VTCDs. Such an arrangement could save both financial and human resources. However, this would require the political will and commitment to reduce poverty. A clear government policy followed by strategic planning is needed in order to ensure organisational change for both horizontal and vertical co-ordination. Decentralised management with greater autonomy is needed in order to recruit staff with increased equity in gender, ethnicity and regionalism and to contract out for social mobilisation and vocational training.

Figure 2. Appropriate Structure for VTCD

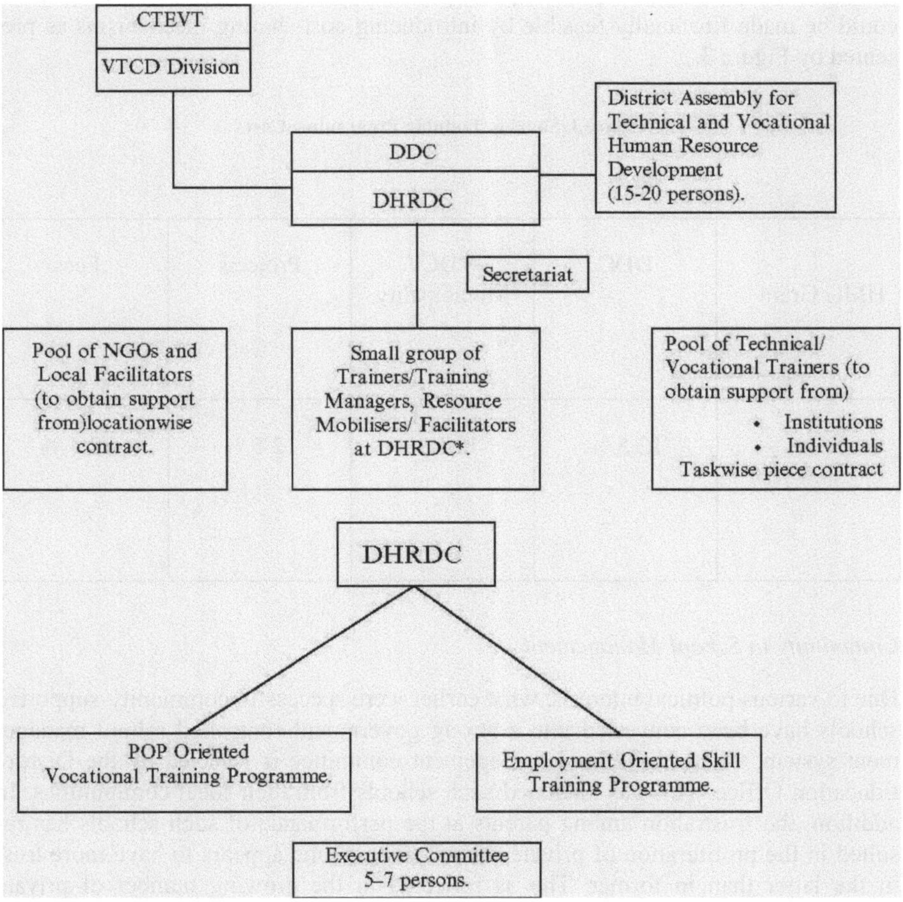

District Human Resource Development Committees (DHRDC) should be an integral part of DDCs, which should co-ordinate all skill development programmes in the district. These programmes should have a two-pronged approach: a special programme oriented towards the poorest of the poor and a general market-based programme oriented towards out-of-school youth and adults, who after acquiring certain skills can either get employment or engage in self-employment. The CTEVT could provide needed technical support by organising skill development courses and/or linking them to other governmental, non-governmental and/or private institutions. It could be made financially feasible by introducing cost-sharing mechanisms as presented by Figure 3.

Figure 3. Sharing Training Programme Cost

HMG Grant	DDC	VDC / Municipality	Projects	Fees
50.0 %	12.5 %	12.5 %	12.5 %	12.5 %

Community in School Management

Due to various political interests, what earlier were successful community-supported schools have been converted into a strong government-controlled school management system, where the school management committee is selected by the District Education Office. This has alienated such schools from their local communities. In addition, the frustration among parents at the performance of such schools has resulted in the proliferation of private schools. The public appears to have more trust in the latter than in former. This is reflected in the growing number of private schools in the country, regardless of the location where such schools are established.

Despite this scenario, there is large gap between what the poor can afford and school tuition fees. There is the need to overcome this gap by setting up community-managed schools whose growth will be dependent on their ability to provide education with sufficient employable skills. Learning from the past experience of other countries, it is important to involve the community in school management. The impact of schools on the community depends very much on how a school system is organised and the extent to which it is integrated with community. In other words, it is important how and to what extent the community is involved in the school management. The recent educational bill passed by the parliament already endorses the idea of community-managed schools.

CONCLUSION

This paper has examined the gap between formal education and the world of work in Nepal. Further, it has pointed out that globalisation does not necessarily support the interests of the poor and indigenous trades of persons working in Nepal's informal economy. The paper suggests that skills development and TVET could provide a bridge between basic education and the world of work. To do so, basic education would need to incorporate a strategy of skills development. The following policy changes are suggested: (1) TVET needs to be decentralised, and a participatory approach should be adopted. There should be better co-ordination between public and private sectors and between NGOs and communities. A decentralised skills development strategy needs to promote training that cuts across various sectors, such as agriculture, forestry, health, industry and civil construction. (2) Appropriate policy needs to be put in place to protect indigenous industries and to promote the marketing of indigenous products at the national and international levels. (3) To reach the poorest of the poor, an appropriate mix of socially oriented skills development programmes and training is needed. It is necessary to mobilise Community Learning Centres to cater to the training needs of the poor, the marginalised and the excluded, women, minority castes, the unemployed and the special needs population. (4) Vocational skills should be adapted to the needs of the local market. (5) Skills training should be financed in a participatory and shared manner. For efficient use of the available resources and for better co-ordination among providers, funds should be pooled in a National Training Fund. (6) It is necessary to recognise and accredit specific skills possessed by different communities in Nepal. (7) Technical education and skill training policy should be revised to focus on rural needs.

REFERENCES

Adhikary, P. K. (2001). *Final evaluation of VTCD.* Kathmandu: CTEVT.

Adhikary, P. K., Belbase, L. N. & Pradhan, H. (2000). *Report on TEVT sub-sector development.* Kathmandu: COMAT.

Aryal, K. R. (1970). Education for the development of Nepal. Kathmandu: Shanti Prakashan.

Higher Education Commission (HEC). (1998). *Higher education commission report.* Kathmandu: Ministry of Education.

Kafle, A. P. (1989). Operations manual for the National Skill Testing Board and Skill Testing Division, Nepal. Kathmandu: CTEVT.

McGrath, S., King, K. & Carr-Hill, R. with Ocansey, O. B., D'Souza, K., Messina, G. & Oketch, H. (1995). *Education and training for the informal sector*, Overseas Development Administrtion. Education Research 1, Occasional Papers on Education 11. London: Overseas Education Administration.

Ministry of Education (MOE). (2000). *Education information on Nepal.* Kathmandu: MOE.

Ministry of Education (MOE). (1998). *High Level Education Commission Report.* Kathmandu: Ministry of Education.

National Planning Commission. (1998). *National planning commission report.* Kathmandu: Nepal National Planning Commission.

National Education Planning Commission (NEPC). (1956). *National Education Planning Commission Report*. Kathmandu: Ministry of Education.

National Education Commission (NEC). (1992). *Report of the National Education Commission* (English version). Kathmandu: Ministry of Education.

Pradhan, H. et al. (2000). *Profile of training providers in Nepal*. Kathmandu: CTEVT.

Pradhan, H. et al. (2001). *Survey report on human resource market analysis*. Kathmandu: CTEVT.

UNDP. (1998). *Nepal human development report*. Kathmandu: UNDP.

UNICEF and National Planning Commission (NPC). (1996). *Primary education*. Kathmandu: National Planning Commission-UNICEF.

UNDP/UNOPS. (1999). *South Asia Poverty Alleviation Program (SAPAP), Annual Progress Report 1999*: Social Mobilisation Learning Centre, Pokhara, Nepal. Kathmandu: UNDP.

UNDP/UNOPS. (2000). *South Asia Poverty Alleviation Program (SAPAP), Draft Regional Report 2000*. Kathmandu: UNDP.

UNESCO. (1997). *Impact of non-formal education*. Bangkok: UNESCO Principal Regional Office for Asia and the Pacific.

Vir, D. (1988). *Education and politics in Nepal: An Asian experiment*. New Delhi: Northern Book Centre.

TRAINING IN MODEST HOUSING CONSTRUCTION FOR THOSE WHO NEED IT MOST: AN EXAMPLE FROM NICARAGUA

Peter Gerasch and Arturo Durán

The paper deals with the dire housing and training situation existing in Nicaragua and the government's attempt to improve the situation by promoting programmes that combine the acquisition of skills in the construction trade with the practical experience of house building. It describes a training scheme for the construction of social housing which began in 1998 but became even more important after thousands of mostly modest homes were destroyed by Hurricane Mitch, which hit Nicaragua at the end of 1998.

The double purpose of the programme regarding education and training is highlighted. The training scheme provides not only an opportunity for training but also meets a basic need of low income people. It especially demonstrates just how much this programme has been able to increase the motivation of young people and adults to improve their living conditions by acquiring new skills.

In the present paper we analyse the social profile of the participants, the selection process, the organisation of training and teaching practices and comes to the conclusion that, despite many obstacles and serious limitations, an informal training programme can contribute to the improvement in the quality of life of people from low income segments of society.

We conclude by making some proposals for strengthening the programme and enlarging the positive effect—for instance, by aligning it more closely to the local labour markets as part of a labour access facilitation policy.

MEETING BASIC NEEDS IN NICARAGUA: THE EDUCATIONAL SYSTEM AND HOUSING

Nicaragua is a country of young people (Incer, 2002). Official figures for 2000 show that half of its total population of 5,126,860 is under 18 years of age, and 1.5 million of these are under 10 years of age. The official data indicate that, of the 2.2 million children and young people aged 3–18 years, 1.4 million participate in the educational system; 821,900 or 36,7 percent of that total do not attend school. The current composition of the educational system is 62 percent enrolment in the primary school, 23 percent in secondary school, 1 percent in technical education and 5 percent in university. The country's population growth rate is 3 percent.

Madhu Singh, (ed.), Meeting Basic Learning Needs in the informal Sector, 229-238.

Over the last two decades, the average year of education of the adult population aged 25 and older in Latin America and the Caribbean has gone up by 1.7 years: from 4.1 to 5.8 years (Ferranto et al., 2003, pp. 35–41). A slow pace by any means of calculation. Hence the relevance of all the programmes in the region which aim to improve the basic skills of the population, its educational levelling, and the labour market access of those who may have the chance to participate in training initiatives.

Training and formal technical education are part of the country's educational system. The Instituto Nacional de Tecnología (INATEC) provides and regulates the services. Access to technical training and formal technical education has a variety of modalities. For rural school pupils, access to the technical system is an option after the third year of primary school. Such informal training (*capacitación*) offers several options to the training candidate, provided that he or she meets the educational requirements. This informal education includes training in basic techniques (*habilitación*), apprenticeship, complementary and specialisation courses. A parallel option to primary school is a three-year adult basic education programme, which enables entry into the training system. Programme graduates obtain a state certificate from the INATEC which enables him or her to work in construction, normally as a mason master assistant.

Labour market indicators show that, out of an economically active population of 1,954,000, the formal rate of unemployment for 2002 was 12 percent. Estimates for 2003 predicted that the unemployed labour force would increase by 40 thousand people, underemployment would be 27 percent and 564,000 people would not have generated income.

The scope of informal labour activities has increased, particularly among males; unofficial estimates show that at least three quarters of the labour force engages in informal activities, mainly in rural areas and trade.

The construction sector has shown a yearly growth of approximately 7 percent. While it has a formal workforce of 9,865 (2002) people registered with the national social insurance system, its estimated real active workforce is at least 50,000 workers. Private housing construction companies concentrate on the housing demand of a small middle class sector, each year building 2,000 to 2,500 housing units with a value of over US$ 15,000 each. By contrast, social housing construction does not seem to be an attractive market for private investment. Other sectors that show positive growth rates are financial, energy and water, livestock and industry.

Nicaragua has a shortage of approximately half a million housing units, with a yearly shortage increment of 20,000 units. Traditionally, people have had to construct their own houses mainly in rural areas; this is done by families with the help of local masons. At least 80 percent of housing construction is this kind of self-construction, which typically is of poor quality and which, consequently, endangers the lives of families, particularly in the many emergency situations the country has gone through in recent years.

In Nicaragua, especially in rural areas, simple housing construction is mainly an informal activity. In its traditional modality, construction does not meet technical standards, nor is there any quality control. Since Hurricane Mitch (October 1998), local authorities have sought, with the aid of the international organisations, to promote an increase in the social housing construction in Nicaragua. A training programme in self-construction began in 1992, in the aftermath of a previous catastrophe (Cerro Negro), when INATEC and the German Agency for Technical Assistance (GTZ) agreed to promote the programme. During the first period (1992–1997), the programme targeted different sectors of the local populations in need of assistance, since social needs had diverse sources: poverty, extreme housing shortages, etc.

The second period of the programme, which began in 1998 and continues today, also is also being supported by the GTZ, and occasionally by other international agencies. Graduates of the training programme in the self-construction of housing receive a certificate in *basic techniques* of construction. Requirements of previous education for entry are low. During this second period, at least 565 apprentices have mastered the basic techniques of construction from one of 23 training and construction projects the programme has carried out in different districts (*departments*) of the country. Since 1998, 1,280 families have been beneficiaries of housing. Given the large size of Nicaraguan families, it is reasonable to estimate that at least 6,000–7,000 individuals have benefited from the initiative so far. Both components of the programme have a relevant, direct social impact.

Regarding the indirect social impact, the decongestion of households has been an important effect; it has led to the improvement in the quality of life in those households. Data on trainees' households (Gerasch & Durán, 2003, p. 28) show that most of the trainees are housed in small houses with an average of $36m^2$, with a household size of five or more persons.

SOCIAL PROFILE OF APPRENTICES

The training programme in the self-construction of social housing has taken the form of informal basic technical education. The social profile of current trainees indicates that the programme has not discriminated according to age or educational background. This informal feature of the training programme derives mainly from the focus on self-construction since the trainee candidates have been proposed mainly by the beneficiary families, the trainee being in most cases a relative of the beneficiaries (70% in Posoltega, 75% in Pueblo Nuevo). In more than 50 percent of the cases, the trainee moves into the settlement as part of the household (48% in Posoltega, 59% in Pueblo Nuevo). This has been the social strength of the programme and has assured a social impact in the localities where the training projects have been carried out. It also means that the programme has helped young and adult populations to accumulate training experience. Another positive social impact is that the training programme offers the trainees who have dropped out of primary and secondary education and belong to low income families a second chance to obtain a relevant education. The impact is greater in low income and impoverished families than in households with higher incomes.

Table 1. Social Profiles of the Trainees and Graduate Trainees (MuyMuy). (Programme Sites: Posoltega, Pueblo Neuvo and MuyMuy)

	Posoltega	Pueblo Nuevo	MuyMuy II
Number of apprentices at each programme site	30	32	12
Average age of trainees	22,9	25,8	22,5
Range of ages (difference between youngest / oldest)	23 (14-37)	33 (17-50)	17 (15-32)
50% of the apprentices ≤ x (years old)	20	23	21
Education, years of school attended (6 years = completed primary)	7,4	5	7,2
% of apprentices living at parents' house (with both parents or their mother)	54 %	60 %	75 %
Total number of persons dwelling at apprentice home	168	178	78
Total number of persons who work	45	49	28
Total number of children ≤ 10 years old.	24	49	24
% of apprentices living in homes with >5 persons	33 %	50 %	58 %
% of apprentices living at homes with one person working to sustain it.	57 %	41 %	33 %
% apprentices living at homes where no one works	7 %	13 %	0
% Married apprentices	40 %	18,8 %	25 %
Number of sons and daughters of apprentices	29	35	12
% of apprentices living in homes where the parents (one or both) work	43 %	44 %	16 %
% of apprentices whose father works	50 %	60 %	58 %
% of cases where the apprentice is the main provider	13 %	3 %	33 %
Average housing surface of the apprentices' homes	46	52	49
Apprentices living in concrete-block housing	16/30	5/32	5/12

% of apprentices who have worked in local cultivation*	53 %	41 %	67 %
Average amount of economic aid granted to apprentices by beneficiary families	C$ 152	C$ 74	Salary
% of apprentices who declare kinship ties to beneficiary family	70 %	75 %	25 %
% of apprentices who declare that they will live in one of the houses under construction at the site	48 %	59 %	0

In September 2003 a social profile description of the apprentices (Gerasch & Durán, 2003, pp. 30–44) was drawn up based on field data collection, and interviews of apprentices were carried out (Gerasch & Durán, 2003, pp. 45–52). The main results of the social profile study are as follows:

The Posoltega training site has 30 trainees and the Pueblo Nuevo site has 32; 12 graduate trainees from MuyMuy I (March 2001) are currently working at the social housing construction site MuyMuy II.

The average age of trainees is 22.9 (Posoltega), 25.7 (Pueblo Nuevo) and 22.5 (MuyMuy II) years. However, Posoltega has three main age groups: the group of the youngest, who are 20 years old or younger; a second group of trainees aged 21–30 years; and a third group in their mid-thirties. Pueblo Nuevo has the same age distribution over three age groups, but the older trainees range in age from 40 to 50 years.

The educational background is diverse, too. Trainees in Posoltega have an average educational level of 7.4 years; in Pueblo Nuevo the average is 5 years of school; and in MuyMuy II the average is 7.17 years. In Posoltega and MuyMuy, a greater part of the trainees have reached secondary school; in Pueblo Nuevo, a mere 35 percent of the apprentices has reached secondary school.

More than half of the trainees said that they live with their parents. This is the case for 54 percent (16/30) in the district of Posoltega, 60 percent (19/32) in Pueblo Nuevo and 75 percent (9/12) in MuyMuy. The fact that most of the latter live with their parents is most probably because many of them were very young during their training and because they had difficulties finding work after the training year (2000).

Forty percent (12/30) of the trainees in the district of Posoltega are married, whereas 19 percent (6/32) in Pueblo Nuevo and 25 percent (3/12) in MuyMuy are married. The total number of children of the trainees is 29 for Posoltega, 35 for Pueblo Nuevo and 12 for MuyMuy respectively.

Twenty-four of the 74 trainees (current and former) live in $36m^2$ housing units. Altogether, these 24 households include 140 household members with an average of 5.83 people per $36m^2$ housing unit: that is the case for 33% of the trainees of Posoltega, 41% at Pueblo Nuevo and 17 at MuyMuy (Gerasch & Durán, 2003, p. 29).

A high proportion of the trainees have worked in local cultivation during 2002: 53.3% of those in Posoltega, 40.6% of those in Pueblo Nuevo and 50% of those in

MuyMuy. The cultivation work is done either on family cultivation property or on local cultivation estates as day workers.

The weekly average economic aid granted by the beneficiary households to the trainees amounts to C$ 152 (US$ 10) in Posoltega and C$ 74 (US$ 5) in Pueblo Nuevo. The weekly aid amounts rannge from C$ 40 to C$ 450 in Posoltega and from C$ 30 to C$ 200 in Pueblo Nuevo.

At Posoltega the main source of aid is the trainees' beneficiary families (39%), where the trainee is a son, brother, or father of the beneficiary; in 17 percent of the cases the aid source is a spouse or partner and in 26 percent of the cases the trainees have no family ties to the beneficiary. Pueblo Nuevo has a different distribution: the largest group comprises those who do not receive any aid (37% or 10/29); then there are the trainees who obtain aid from beneficiaries who have no family ties to them (27%); other trainees obtain the aid from a spouse, a partner or beneficiary relatives.

Seventeen percent (5/30) of the trainees in Posoltega and 37 percent of those in Pueblo Nuevo do not receive any economic aid. Most of these trainees belong to the beneficiary families and/or will later dwell in one of the settlement houses. Seventy percent of the trainees in Posoltega, as compared to 75 percent in Pueblo Nuevo, belong directly to the beneficiary families or to the extended families (relatives).

TRAINING ORGANISATION AND TEACHING PRACTICES

To date the normal length of the training projects has been one year with about seven hundred hours of teaching. The programme has implemented a system of learning-by-doing, adapted to the specific subject of housing construction and to the educational background of the apprentices. The curriculum is closely connected to the various steps involved in housing construction (Gerasch & Durán, 2003, pp. 11–12). A site master, an engineer, and the training instructors (mason masters) are in charge of the training. They teach the theoretical and practical subjects while also co-ordinating trainee group activities. Each group is composed of five trainees who are charged with the construction of five houses. Each group has a monitor who has been chosen from among the trainees by the instructors; this selection is made two or three weeks after the training has started (Gerasch & Durán, 2003, pp. 11–12). Monitors are responsible for co-ordination and operation. There are two handbooks, one for the apprentices and one for the trainees. Ten subjects are taught, including an introduction to basic subjects, earth movement, concrete structures, masonry, roof, floor, and doors and windows. For each step of housing construction, the trainees proceed in a reiterative manner: for instance, for the foundation task, they start with house 1 and end with house 5; once this step has been completed, they begin the next step, from house 1 to house 5 (Gerasch & Durán, 2003, pp. 11–12).

THE NEW HOUSING POLICY AND THE LINK TO THE LOCAL LABOUR MARKET SITUATION

The primary impetus for initiating training projects has been the local shortage of housing. The result has been the initiation of projects without consideration of the state of the local labour market. The data collected for Posoltega and Pueblo Nuevo on the previous work experience of apprentices and the information obtained through interviews concerning their current views on the local labour market give clear indications that, although they have mixed opinions about the local construction labour market, they generally agree that the labour market is difficult to access. Data collected in MuyMuy II shows that the access to the local construction labour market is stabilised partially three years after graduation, the first year after graduation being the most difficult. A previous INATEC sample (2002) from six project sites showed that 83 (72.8%) were working in construction (Niggebrügge, 2002). Only 114 graduates from a total of 178 graduates were working in construction.

A policy which more aggressive facilitates the link to local labour activities would help to keep the new trainee labour force in their localities. The availability of information on public investments at the district *(department)* and municipality level could provide valuable on this issue (SNIP, 2004).

The creation of the Instituto de la Vivienda Urbana y Rural (INVUR) has been a step in this direction. This new governmental agency, which is in charge of housing policy and the formulation of a housing subsidy policy aimed at lower-income households, has created a new situation in the social housing market. With the support of the Inter-American Development Bank (IADB), INVUR has planned the execution of US$ 25.3 million for the first phase of the Direct Subsidy Program 2003–2006, with the financial support of the IADB and the non-refundable co-financial support of the Austrian Mitch Fund of US$ 0.3 million and local matching funds of US$ 2.5 millions (SECEP, 2003, pp. 62–64).

The future housing policy envisages a new self-construction strategy in which the apprentice candidates will be chosen mainly with help of INVUR and the program team. Beneficiaries will have a reduced role in selection. This means a dissociation of the kinship ties which have been a part of the current apprentice selection system. The social profile of the apprentices will probably change as a result of the new selection criteria: they will have a better educational background and a younger age range. A selective policy could mean the end of policy criteria for the broad social access to training which was in force until recently. The programme will become less informal. It may have a social cost, since the most disadvantaged people may not be able to access the programme as trainee candidates

THE NEW PROGRAMME FORMULATION

The programme for 2004–2008 has recently been revised. It will start in 2004 with four pilot training projects in the municipalities of Moyogalpa (Rivas), San José de los Remates (Boaco), Chichigalpa (Chinandega) and Granada (Granada). Each project aims to train 50 apprentices and to construct 50 housing units, keeping the programme rule of one apprentice per house. Each project is designed to be carried out in four months time; 200 families will benefit from access to housing through a housing subsidy (Gerasch & Durán, 2003, p. 19); and probably over 60 percent of the trainees will obtain the programme certificate. New entry requirements are being formulated; among others, candidates will have to have completed primary school and priority will been given to people younger than 28 years old. External resources have been approved for 2004 (Gerasch & Durán, 2003, pp. 7–8);[1] for 2005–2008 it remains to be seen which international institution will support the programme (Gerasch & Durán, 2003, p. 8).

The social function and general social impact of the programme are beyond question. The programme has contributed to the improvement of the housing situation for the population that most needs housing. And it has contributed to the creation of a qualified construction-technical workforce in the localities where the projects are carried out. The programme has the capacity to be proactive regarding new situations and challenges.

CONCLUSIONS

The social housing self-construction training programme meets the basic social needs of the people. It improves the quality of life of the beneficiary families in at least two ways: it provides housing and training for low income families.

By the end of 2003, 50–60 percent of the trainees in Posoltega and Pueblo Nuevo will have obtained a state certificate in basic construction techniques, which will enable them to work as qualified construction workers. Sixty-two families will move into the new housing units, and the Pueblo Nuevo and Posoltega settlements will become alive. Some 300 people will have improved their living conditions in a fundamental way.

An important indirect impact is the decongestion of the households. Most of family houses are initially overcrowded, as data on housing conditions of the trainees show.

Data from MuyMuy shows that access to the labour market in the three years following graduation is gradual and that many graduates access it on an occasional basis. This may be an indicator of a weak local construction activity. The greatest difficulties in accessing work are encountered during the first year after graduation. Integration into the labour market and consolidation takes place only during the third year after graduation. Half of the 12 graduate masons worked six months or more, whereas the other six masons worked five months or less. During the first year after graduation (2001) four of the 12 masons did not work at all in construction. The reason is that the local labour market demand is not considered in the selection of the location of projects. Rather, the social housing requirements, the availability of land and the housing shortage faced by low income families are the key criteria for deciding on the location of the training projects of the programme. This means that the programme is carried out independently of the local construction labour market situation. A work access facilitation policy would mark an important improvement in this situation, as well as in the programme itself.

The programme appears to be more concerned with the management of housing construction than with the educational activities of the trainees. This is probably due to the bias resulting from the complexity of administrating the construction work carried out in local areas. Another reason could be the time pressure during the evaluation—the programme is due to end in December 2003.

The trainees' identity is not well defined. Some consider themselves as trainees rather than as workers, which is probably a result of the fact that greater emphasis is place on the construction rather than on education.

RECOMMENDATIONS

To strengthen the educational and training component of the programme and promote a better articulation with the local labour market, it is necessary to establish a better equilibrium between education and training on the one hand and the management of housing construction on the other. To improve the apprentices' technical education, it has been proposed to conduct a pilot training programme in 2004 as an opportunity to carry out the organisational changes this may require.

It has also been proposed that greater autonomy be given to the central programme regarding its educational training function and that its authority be increased in matters relating to educational training in order to strengthen the theoretical and practical curriculum at the project sites. A reinforcement of monitoring and evaluation activities is also regarded as a complementary and central aspect.

Another proposal is that curricular activities be revised and updated. An incentive for this curricular reformulation could be given through workshops organised and carried out by independent training experts.

To standardise the curricular activities linked to the training component, it would be worthwhile to extend the training to the instructors working at the project sites. Also during the training period a complementary curricular unit should be implemented which gives the trainees the basic formal skills needed to perform as independent masons.

Depending on budget constraints, an improvement of the didactic material with the help of interactive technology would also be desirable.

It is also necessary to carry out a preliminary assessment of the local labour market construction activities in each project area so as to avoid an oversupply of masons in localities that already have unemployment problems in the construction sector.

The results of the training programme thus far point up the need for a policy that will facilitate labour market access by building bridges between project training and access to local work markets once a project has been completed.

Finally the programme team should consider innovative environmental solutions to basic services, such as energy, water and latrines, related to housing. These could include implementing cost-reducing solutions in the form of, say, solar energy, promoting low-cost complementary water reservoir facilities and advocating alternative latrine technology which each family can build in their backyards. All these innovations, when linked with housing settlement and educational projects, would mean a long-term improvement in the health and living conditions of residents.

NOTE

[1] See Gerasch & Durán (2003), 7–8: The funding of the programme. For the programme in 2004, an investment of US$ 641,600 was calculated, of which 40 percent (US$ 260,000) will be financed by the bonus contribution of INVUR, with the financial support of the IADB.

REFERENCES

Incer, J. (2002). *Geografía Básica de Nicaragua*. Managua: Hispamer S.A.

Ferranto, D. de, et al. (2003). *Closing the gap in education and technology*. Washington, DC: World Bank Latin American and Caribbean Studies.

Instituto Nacional de Tecnología (INATEC). (2003). Webpage URL: http://www.inatec.edu.ni.

Gerasch, P., & Durán, A. (2003). *Capacitación en el Sector Informal. Capacitación en la Construcción de Viviendas Modestas para los Más Necesitados: Un Ejemplo de Nicaragua. El Programa de Autoconstrucción de Viviendas Sociales*. Managua: INATEC-GTZ.

Niggebrügge, J. (2002). *Estudio sobre un programa de capacitación en el ámbito de la autoconstrucción de viviendas diseñado e implementado en una iniciativa conjunta entre la GTZ y el Gobierno de Nicaragua*. Managua: GTZ.

Sistema Nacional de Inversiones Publicas (SNIP). (2004). Webpage URL: http://www.snip.gob.ni. (Information on public investment in Nicaragua.)

Secretaria de Coordinación y Estrategia de la Presidencia (SECEP). (2003). *Informe 2002, Política Social y Económica*. Managua: SECEP.

INDEX OF NAMES

INDEX OF SUBJECTS

CONTRIBUTORS

POORNA K. ADHIKARY is Programme Co-ordinator at the Communications and Management Training Institute in Kathmandu, Nepal.

ARTURO DÚRAN has worked as a consultant for various government agencies in Chile, and is currently teaching Sociology and conducting a research programme on culutral heritage at the University of Valparaíso, Chile.

PETER GERASCH was formerly Co-ordinator of the Programme on Integrated Promotion of Micro- and Small Enterprises, German Agency for International Development (GTZ), Nicaragua.

LAILA RASHED ISKANDAR is Managing Director, Community and Institutional Development (CID) in Cairo, Egypt.

V. V. KRISHNA is Professor at the Centre for Studies in Science Policy at the School of Social Sciences, Jawaharlal Nehru University New Delhi, India.

ANACLARA MATOSAS is Consultant on Gender, Training and Employment with Cinterfor/ILO in Montevideo, Uruguay.

AMIT MITRA is an independent researcher and was formerly Associate Director, Centre for Science and Environment, New Delhi, India.

CHRISTINE NATHAN is Education Project Officer at the Institute for Occupational Health and Safety in Bangkok, Thailand.

BERND OVERWIEN is Professor in the Unit for Global Learning and International Co-operation of the Technical University Berlin, Germany.

ENRIQUE PIECK is Researcher at the Unidad de Investigaciones Interdisciplinares en Educación, Universidad Iberoamericana Mexico City, Mexico.

SARA SILVEIRA is Consultant on Gender, Training and Employment with Cinterfor/ILO in Montevideo, Uruguay.

MADHU SINGH is Senior Programme Specialist at the UNESCO Institute for Education in Hamburg, Germany.

RASHED AL MAHMUD TITUMIR is Assistant Professor in the Department of Development Studies, University of Dhaka, Bangladesh.

MIX
Papier aus verantwortungsvollen Quellen
Paper from responsible sources
FSC® C105338

If you have any concerns about our products,
you can contact us on
ProductSafety@springernature.com

In case Publisher is established outside the EU,
the EU authorized representative is:
Springer Nature Customer Service Center GmbH
Europaplatz 3, 69115 Heidelberg, Germany

Printed by Libri Plureos GmbH
in Hamburg, Germany